A Queer Mother for the Nation

A Queer Mother for the Nation

The State and Gabriela Mistral

Licia Fiol-Matta

University of Minnesota Press

Minneapolis

London

All photographs in this book are reprinted courtesy of the National Library, Santiago, Chile.

Chapter 1 previously appeared as "Race Woman: Reproducing the Nation in Gabriela Mistral," *GLQ* 6, no. 4 (winter 2000): 491–527; copyright 2000 Duke University Press, reprinted with permission from Duke University Press. Parts of chapter 3 appeared in "The 'Schoolteacher of America': Gender, Sexuality, and Nation in Gabriela Mistral," in *¿Entiendes? Queer Readings, Hispanic Writings*, edited by Emilie L. Bergmann and Paul Julian Smith (Durham, N.C.: Duke University Press, 1995), 221–29; copyright 1995 Duke University Press, reprinted with permission from Duke University Press.

Letters from Inés Mendoza de Muñoz Marín to Gabriela Mistral are reprinted by permission from the Luis Muñoz Marín Foundation, Trujillo Alto, Puerto Rico.

Published by the University of Minnesota Press
111 Third Avenue South, Suite 290
Minneapolis, MN 55401-2520
http://www.upress.umn.edu

Library of Congress Cataloging-in-Publication Data
Fiol-Matta, Licia, 1964–
    A queer mother for the nation : the state and Gabriela Mistral / Licia Fiol-Matta.
        p.   cm.
    Includes bibliographical references and index.
    ISBN 0-8166-3963-9 (HC : alk. paper) — ISBN 0-8166-3964-7 (PB : alk. paper)
        1. Mistral, Gabriela, 1889–1957—Political and social views.
    2. Mistral, Gabriela, 1889–1957—Sexual behavior.   3. Feminism and literature—Latin America—History—20th century.   4. Women and literature—Latin America—History—20th century.   5. Feminism and literature—Chile—History—20th century.   6. Women and literature—Chile—History—20th century.   I. Title.
    PQ8097.G6 Z556   2002
    861'.62—dc21   2001005554

Printed in the United States of America on acid-free paper

The University of Minnesota is an equal-opportunity educator and employer.

12 11 10 09 08 07 06 05 04 03 02   10 9 8 7 6 5 4 3 2 1

A mi hermana, Lynn Fiol Matta
A mi madre, Emma Matta Méndez
A mi padre, Juan Fiol Bigas

Contents

Acknowledgments

Because I have researched Gabriela Mistral for more than ten years now, this book spans years of both my personal and professional lives. As a result, there are numerous people and institutions to thank. First, I need to acknowledge two early sources of financial support: a postdoctoral grant from the Ford Foundation and a Special Assistant Professor Leave from Barnard College, which enabled me to complete the research for *A Queer Mother for the Nation* in 1996–97. Indeed, the Ford Foundation provided, and Barnard College matched, an institutional grant that underwrote many of the expenses of the first phase of my writing. With this support, I was able to travel to Chile in 1997.

I must thank my good friend Diamela Eltit, not only for her hospitality and illuminating conversations but also for arranging interviews and contacts that otherwise would have been virtually impossible to obtain. Thanks also to the Chilean friends who exchanged ideas and gave me their unqualified support as I embarked on this project, most especially and warmly Nadia Prado, Malú Urriola, and Nelly Richard.

After 1997, I faced two difficult years before I was able to secure a contract for publication. However, during this time I was fortunate enough to meet scholars affiliated with New York University's Faculty Working Group for Queer Studies, who greatly helped to publicize and disseminate my work. In particular, I thank Ann Cvetkovich, David Eng, Elizabeth Freeman, Gayatri Gopinath, Janet Jakobsen, José Muñoz, and Ann Pellegrini for their critical support at various times during 1998–2000 and, most of all, for truly engaging my work. Special thanks are in order to my buddy, Judith Halberstam. Thanks also to the audiences who listened to sections of this work as it was in progress and contributed their suggestions.

I owe a world of gratitude to Lisa Duggan, who always went out of her way to provide concrete intellectual support for this project and who, I was delighted to learn afterward, was one of the book's readers on behalf of the University of Minnesota Press. Similarly, Jean Franco, whom I regard as a mentor, has given me her unconditional support for years without ever chiding me about the book's completion. Thanks to Jean for sharing her fantastically brilliant insights with me and for reading the book manuscript.

Aside from many an enjoyable and thought-provoking conversation over many years now, Luis Avilés and Ivette Hernández provided an incisive critique of the initial draft of chapter 6, from which I greatly benefited. Oscar Montero kindly read the draft of the final chapter, making invaluable suggestions. Assorted thanks go to individuals who made suggestions that found their way into these pages, or with whom I've had helpful conversations that influenced me: Cathy Cohen, Unique Fraser, Arnaldo Cruz-Malavé, Lawrence La Fountain-Stokes, Irma Llorens, Agnes Lugo-Ortiz, Francine Masiello, Robert McKee Irwin, Rita Molinero, Sylvia Molloy, Carlos Pabón, Juan Carlos Quintero, Julio Ramos, Doris Sommer, Diana Taylor, Judith Weisenfeld, Ken Wissoker, and George Yúdice. Thanks to the anonymous readers who reviewed "Race Woman" in its first incarnation; even if they rejected the draft, I greatly profited through their critique. Thanks to Richard Morrison, my editor at the University of Minnesota Press, for not only his efficiency but also his genuine enthusiasm for my project. Thanks also to Tammy Zambo for her excellent copyediting.

In Puerto Rico, I am profoundly indebted to the Luis Muñoz Marín Foundation for permission to use the letters of Inés Mendoza de Muñoz Marín. My interpretation of these letters is, of course, solely my own and does not in any way reflect the foundation's endorsement. Although efforts to gain access to Mendoza's personal archives proved unsuccessful, as they are sealed until 2007, I thank Luis Agrait, of the University of Puerto Rico, for his attempts to secure permission.

A second trip to Chile in 2000 was made possible by a Faculty Research Grant from Barnard College. During this visit, I was fortunate to receive the attentive help of Pedro Pablo Zegers, an expert on Gabriela

Mistral and director of the Archivo del Escritor of the Biblioteca Nacional de Chile. I am especially indebted to Pedro Pablo and the National Library for permission to reproduce the photographs of Gabriela Mistral, which form part of their iconographic archive. Many thanks also to Luis Vargas Saavedra for his kind replies to last-minute clarifications, and to Ilonka Csillag Pimstein, director of the Patrimonio Iconográfico Nacional, for answering my questions about the photographs' context.

I cannot overstate the importance of financial support from the Spencer Foundation during the last year of work on the book, after I had completed my initial draft. This grant allowed me, most importantly, to enlist the help of professional editors; it also relieved me of costs for indexing, permissions, computer and clerical services, and final fact-checking research. Thanks to Amy Reading for her first-rate editorial feedback. I thank most of all Gayatri Patnaik, who read the book twice—some sections more than that—with her unmatched, talented editor's eye.

My family and friends have shared many good times and some hard moments with me, and I thank Sheenah Hankin and Wanda López for helping me take care of my well-being through the 1990s. Thanks also to my brother Juan Fiol-Matta and my sister Lía Fiol-Matta for their company in New York. I hope to convince them that I did, in fact, do something productive all these years! And thanks to my other siblings in Puerto Rico, Liana, Antonio, and Carlos Fiol-Matta, for their love and solidarity.

Four individuals sustain me especially. I turn to Louise Murray and Liza Fiol-Matta to sort out personal affairs, professional quandaries, and finer intellectual points; I depend on them also for giggles and bellyaching laughs. Their love, support, and humor kept me going through my research and writing, and I thank them for always being there for me. José Quiroga, one of the most insightful and kindest people I know, has been my soul mate since we first met at the Yale Graduate School. Thanks to him for reading the manuscript in its entirety, for helping me with last-minute chores, and for taking care of me generally. I have been blessed to find my partner, Gayatri Patnaik. She came on board during the final stages of my writing *A Queer Mother for the Nation,* and her input took the book to another level. Thanks to her for bringing me the joy I sought, and for being my source of hope in moments of severe pain and anxiety.

It may sound corny, but I believe that after submitting her figure and work to such close scrutiny, it is fitting to reach into the past and thank

Gabriela Mistral. My positions and feelings do not coincide with my subject's views of, and role in, the world she inhabited. Still, the long-standing passion I have felt for this research and this book stems from my belief in Mistral's extraordinary importance, which I want to acknowledge from the very beginning.

A Queer Mother for the Nation took shape after the loss of my mother, Emma Matta-Méndez, the person I loved the most. More recently, my book has seen me through the loss of two other immediate family members: my dear father, Juan Fiol-Bigas, and my beloved sister Lynn Fiol-Matta. This book is dedicated to the three of them in loving, faithful memory. It was my dream that they would share its publication with me. Mom, Dad, and Lynn were avid readers and rigorous thinkers, and to them I owe any measure of these qualities that I may possess. I can only hope their presence and spirit are reflected in these pages.

INTRODUCTION

The Schoolteacher of America

From the beginning, Gabriela Mistral defied the odds. Born Lucila Godoy Alcayaga in 1889, she grew up in the Elqui Valley of northern Chile, renowned for its view of the magnificent Andes. Although geographically stunning, the Elqui Valley was remote and sparsely populated, and many of its inhabitants, like Mistral's family, were impoverished. Mistral's father, Jerónimo Godoy, deserted the family in 1892, and Mistral, her mother, Petronila, and her older sister, Emelina, lived in a two-room shack while Petronila worked as a seamstress to support them. Though Mistral received some formal education at the primary level, it was erratic at best and she was essentially self-taught.

Who could have imagined that Lucila Godoy Alcayaga would become one of the central architects of Latin American nationalism in the twentieth century—or would be the first Latin American to win the Nobel Prize for literature in 1945—or would be known as "Gabriela Mistral" and become an international celebrity? Called "a walking educational mission" by the Chilean critic Fernando Alegría[1] and "a uterus birthing children for the motherland" by the contemporary Chilean author Diamela Eltit,[2] Mistral possessed fame and personal charisma as striking and affecting in public as they were in private.

Although Mistral became the living embodiment of the race/sex/gender politics at the heart of Latin Americanism, after her death in 1957 her stature and work were neglected, obscured, and virtually forgotten. This can be credited to the national narrative that elevated her as the "Schoolteacher of America" [la Maestra de América], an epithet indicating Mistral's consecration as a celibate, saintly, and suffering het-erosexual national icon.[3] For years, Gabriela Mistral's place in the Latin American literary canon was justified only by her status as national schoolteacher-mother. Her work was not only barely read but sneered at, because it was "sentimental" and supposedly solely concerned with and aimed at mothers and children. As this book documents, Mistral's audi-ence was much wider. Furthermore, sentimentality, far from being a minor, incidental genre, was critical to the articulation of the national-ist state project. Sentimentality still permeates a Latin American hagio-graphic narrative best conceived as a national sob story, sensationalistic at every turn, that plays up the emotionalism of national belonging through a bizarrely distorted account of Mistral's life and desires.[4]

As Mistral was a closet lesbian, one wonders if homophobia played a critical role in the oversight of her figure and work after her death and until recent feminist reevaluations. But homophobia doesn't begin to name the complexities of Mistral's decisions and her reception. The ho-mophobic subject believes itself cleanly separated from its object of ha-tred, but Mistral inspired affection as well—a type of national child-likeness. She was both repudiated and loved, a revealing contradiction.

Mistral's life often veered from the sublime to the tragic. Her moment of greatest national apotheosis occurred in Chile but only when she was dead, after long years of illness and a great, accumulated bitterness toward her homeland. Thousands lined the streets of Santiago to pay their last respects, a striking event considering the level of vilification Mistral endured while living in Chile prior to her exile in 1922. In life, she received the Nobel Prize from the hands of the king of Sweden, be-coming the first Latin American to be graced with the honor; but Mis-tral appeared alone, while the other women in attendance held on to the arm of a man. Dressed in a long black velvet gown, she wore neither makeup nor jewelry, in stark contrast to the ladies of the elite society in attendance, with their white gowns and accessorized, feminine bodies.

Mistral's personal life was in shambles. Her adopted son, Juan Miguel Godoy, had died only two years before. Apparently exhausted by an overly emotional existence, Juan Miguel committed suicide in a most sentimental way. Like the nineteenth-century heroine Emma Bovary, he ingested a lethal dose of arsenic, dying a slow and painful death. Why he decided to commit suicide in this particular manner remains a mystery. Did he understand its impact on his mother and the world? Without realizing it, in real life Juan Miguel supplied the last missing item in the national fantasy life—the enormous tragedy entailed in the loss of a child—thus sealing the myth of the childless sufferer in Mistral's iconography forever.

Mistral buried Juan Miguel in a cemetery in Petrópolis, Brazil, where they were living at the time. Why she didn't take his body to the beloved valley where she herself wanted to be buried (and was), or why she chose not to transport him to Spain, where his birth mother reportedly was from, seems peculiar. Perhaps it was an expense she couldn't afford at the time, but the fact remains: Juan Miguel's grave continues to rest in Petrópolis, Brazil—receiving neither visitors nor prayers—whereas Mistral is buried splendidly, and alone, in her native Montegrande, surrounded by fresh flowers and tourists.

What an irony that Mistral's maternal persona, the one that birthed the nation and upheld the importance of blood ties, collided tragically with her chosen nonreproductive experience of motherhood. The sentimentality that she certainly deployed as a norm for mass affect eerily coincided with the circumstances of her son's death. One can only speculate whether the child's uncertainty about his biological origin or the status of his national belonging played any part in his death.

Like the Cuban José Martí, Mistral has been claimed as being both radical and conservative. But I suspect that, although exceptional, she was truly neither radical nor especially conservative. Mistral is not the perfect female exemplar of the state—as her official discourse would indicate—nor is she a subversive lesbian writer whose feminist politics can be recuperated by queer readings, waiting to be discovered by contemporary scholarship. What is indisputable is that she is the first female transnational figure of Latin America, with major influence across the hemisphere.

Mistral created a public discourse that supported a conservative role for women within the state, but her private life deviated significantly from the state prescription. There are, of course, numerous ways to interpret this bifurcation. In *A Queer Mother for the Nation*, I posit that Mistral's decision to anchor the state's nationalist project was exactly that: a decision, and not an accident of fate. As with all decisions, it occurred within a historical context, and this book reconstructs part of that period, along with key aspects of Mistral's life.

Close attention to Mistral's corpus of prose works, which includes dizzying amounts of correspondence, speeches, newspaper articles, and consular reports, reveals an ambitious and brilliant woman who sought international fame and political power. She actualized all three of her ambitions—literary renown, international recognition, and a revered place in politics—in an extraordinary life.

Disciplined and motivated, she worked from the age of thirteen in various posts around her immediate region in Chile. From her earliest years, Mistral worked diligently on two fronts: contributing to local educational publications, and sending poems to local and regional literary journals. Eventually she worked her way up through a series of school postings in different regions of Chile away from her native town, which took her to the capital city of Santiago only in 1921, a year before the start of her lifelong exile.[5] By then, Mistral had invested approximately twenty years in creating the successful persona of the schoolteacher.[6]

After this assiduous and draining process of self-promotion, the state took notice of the steel schoolmarm. Certainly, Mistral's public persona was expected to affirm traditional women's roles, and she advertised herself accordingly as a champion of the home and the family, even though she had neither a stable home nor a heterosexual family. The state had a considerable investment in promoting women's advancement while simultaneously restricting their participation to primarily the service sector within the rising industrial economy, and Mistral aligned herself to this project. Aside from the demand for women's labor, the state needed to recruit women as teachers, for reasons that include those discussed in accounts of nationalist education and the role of women in nationalism.[7] But, following in the footsteps of critical revisions of nationalist thought, this book advances hypotheses that depend on a close attention to the state's relationship to queerness and, in particular, to the queerness of women. Mistral's role was pivotal in this regard.

Mistral's process of self-invention began early in life, and it included some hesitancy as to how she should present herself publicly. Mistral went through several versions of her pen name initially, from a mere capital "Y" in her very first writings as a girl, to gender-ambiguous pseudonyms like "Alguien" [Someone] and the more feminine names "Soledad" [Loneliness] and "Alma" [Soul] while she was an adolescent. She used "Alma" often between 1904 and 1908, when she was a frequent contributor to regional newspapers. In 1911, Mistral published a short story, "The Rival," and signed it with the pen name "Gabriela Mistraly." The story features an amusingly transparent double for Mistral in the protagonist, Gabriel, who provides a melodramatic first-person account of his tragic losses, in terms of female lovers. Lucila Godoy assumed her mature pen name, "Gabriela Mistral," in 1913. Even her mature pseudonym can be read as a sign of masculine identification; though feminized, it appears that she took the names of two men, Gabriele d'Annunzio and Fréderic Mistral.[8]

Before leaving Chile, she still used her real name, mostly for official correspondence and journal articles relating directly to education. Most anything related to her career as a writer, however, including correspondence, she signed "Gabriela Mistral." After 1922, Mistral stopped using her real name altogether, and the pseudonym became her name, the sole exception being in her writing of consular reports and other official paperwork.

Mistral's first major triumph as a poet came in 1914, when she won the prestigious national prize of the Juegos Florales, organized by the Society of Writers of Chile, for her famous poetic cycle "Sonetos de la muerte" [Sonnets of death]. Undoubtedly this prize enhanced her value as a national poet and as the "teacher-poet," a persona she cultivated during these early years in Chile. "Sonetos de la muerte" also became fodder for the morbid story of unrequited love, culminating in the male lover's suicide:

Del nicho helado en que los hombres te pusieron,
te bajaré a la tierra humilde y soleada.
Que he de dormirme en ella los hombres no supieron,
y que hemos de soñar sobre la misma almohada.

Te acostaré en la tierra soleada con una
dulcedumbre de madre para el hijo dormido,
y la tierra ha de hacerse suavidades de cuna
al recibir tu cuerpo de niño dolorido.

[From the freezing niche in which men laid you to rest, I will lower you to the wet and sunny earth. Men will never know I will put myself to sleep there too, and that we will dream while lying on the same pillow.

I will lay you down in the sunny earth, with a mother's sweetness toward the sleeping child, and the earth will turn into a soft cradle, once it receives your body, like a child in pain.][9]

Mistral herself stated plainly (years later, to be sure) that she had not written these verses in connection with any existing relationship with Romelio Ureta, a Chilean rail worker and family friend who allegedly was in love with Mistral; and that Ureta had not committed suicide because of any lover's despair. But, clearly, Mistral did not refute the story during her early period of increasing notoriety.

The young Mistral was apparently already a master publicist, aware of the extent to which withdrawal and aloofness could spark national curiosity. In fact, she didn't accept the Juegos Florales prize in person but, it seems, attended the ceremony incognito, delighting in the awarding of the prize while underscoring her absence from the ceremony. It might be noted that she didn't fit the image of the feminine woman, even though she had authored verses of the most intense maternal despair. Perhaps Mistral intuited that in the elite society of the big city, her figure would strike an undesirable masculine note.

Mistral's pose as national mother initially served a number of practical purposes, although maternal discourse would become central to her writings for more complex reasons. One of the more obvious benefits of the pose concerned Mistral's sources of financial support: the Republic of Chile always remained her main employer, first as a schoolteacher, then as a lifelong consul. The stance of national schoolmarm enabled Mistral to leave Chile in 1922, where she was trapped in a consuming bureaucratic existence that afforded her limited possibilities for intellectual growth and literary recognition. José Vasconcelos, Mexico's minister of education in the first years of the Mexican Revolution, met her while on a trip to Chile immediately after the revolution. Clearly intrigued by Mistral's presence, he invited her to visit Mexico to assist in the creation of rural schools to be founded by the government in the wake of the revolution.[10] Gabriela Mistral arrived in Mexico on 30 July 1922; she was thirty-four years old.

Mistral's trip to Mexico, undertaken as a state representative, proved crucial to her career as a writer, because it provided an international profile. The Mexican Revolution occupied center stage in world media at that time, complete with photographs and newsreel images. In fact, it was one of the first world events to be experienced visually through the mass media. Additionally, modern Mexico itself was erected as a nation largely through visual spectacle, evident not only in the work of the three famous muralists Diego Rivera, David Siqueiros, and José Clemente

Orozco but also in public-works constructions such as the Mexico City Stadium and the Jalapa Stadium in Veracruz.[11] Because of this trip, and her identification with the newly founded Mexican state, Mistral achieved quite a coup in the publication of the 1922 volume *Lecturas para mujeres* [Readings for women], commissioned by the Mexican government as a textbook for use in girls' schools. Mistral astutely included her own writings in the volume; they account for nearly a third of the total entries. Significantly, she deployed "sentimental" discourse and placed the female subject squarely in the project of Latin American nationalism much more successfully than any of her predecessors.[12]

Mistral was courted by other countries as well, most notably Argentina. Had she traveled to Argentina instead of Mexico, her international profile would have been markedly different. For instance, she could not have assumed populist and racialized politics with such ease. She probably would have embodied Argentina's national and racist goal of European whiteness—the opposite of the image of racial harmony advocated by the Mexican government.

Mistral returned to Chile three times after 1922: in 1925, 1938, and 1954. She became a world traveler, moving frequently on account of state business and responding to engagements that resulted from her ascending fame as the schoolteacher-mother-poet-model for all Latin American women. Once named *cónsul particular de libre elección* [consul of Chile with the liberty of choosing post of residence], Mistral was able to choose residence anywhere in Europe, Latin America, or the United States.[13] She was consul in Madrid, Spain (1933); Lisbon and Porto, Portugal (1935); Nice, France (1938); Niterói, Brazil (1940); Petrópolis, Brazil (1941); Los Angeles, California (1945); Santa Barbara, California (1947); Veracruz, Mexico (1949); and Rapallo and Naples, Italy (1950–1952), in addition to short-term postings in other locations.[14] In 1953, she decided to set up house with her companion, the American Doris Dana, who lived in Long Island, New York, and requested a posting as commissioner in the United Nations.

After she left Chile, as a means of supporting herself, and responding to the publicity needs of the government in many instances, Mistral contributed to major Latin American newspapers, a practice she continued throughout her life. She became a consummate essayist, writing about a variety of subjects—geography, customs, pedagogical issues, social issues, celebrities, and religion among them. The challenge in assessing the Mistralian corpus for major themes or consistent opinions is that she herself rarely followed clear-cut lines. Her positions shifted strategically, making it difficult to gauge how she really felt about a number of issues—feminism, for example. Moreover, the fact that she was perpetually ambivalent on issues regarding gender, race, and pedagogy makes it even more challenging to provide a clear trajectory of her social thought. Generally speaking, she is regarded as a defender of the disenfranchised, especially of the mestizos and the indigenous peoples. She is also celebrated as a pacifist; her work toward international peace and human rights is often cited in this category. Finally, she is, above all, the transnational champion of motherhood and child rearing.

Mistral's career is closely linked to the League of Nations, with which she was affiliated from 1926. After the League's demise, Mistral joined the United Nations in various official capacities. She may have been one of the authors of the Universal Declaration of Human Rights. Her friendships and acquaintances with world personalities included Dag Hammarskjöld, Thomas Mann, Henri Bergson, and almost certainly Eleanor Roosevelt, among many others. Many of these contacts began with her work in the Institute for Intellectual Cooperation of the League of Nations, the precursor to UNESCO, between 1926 and 1934.

Mistral's poetry, by contrast, is resolutely hermetic and often has a nightmarish quality. Even her nominally straightforward verses—those having to do with elements of nationalism, such as national symbology and national landscapes—contain a surreal quality. Mistral surrounded herself with and was surrounded by metaphors of silence, shame, and secrecy. Much of her poetic oeuvre revolves around a private world difficult to decipher, a world of loss and despair, of fantasy escapes into other realities. Many of her poems are bathed in what Walter Benjamin would describe as aura—a trace of a world that no longer existed as industrial society developed in Chile, but that redoubled its symbolic intensity in the face of uprooting, deformation, and loss of former ways of life.

The disconcerting nature of Mistral's poetry is probably best demonstrated by the fact that Patricia Rubio, Mistral's foremost bibliographer, estimates that of the nearly four thousand bibliographic entries she collected for her book, astonishingly, most focus on Mistral's first book of poetry, *Desolación* [Desolation].[15] It is no coincidence, of course, because this first book can be most easily encased in the narrative of the barren, frustrated mother, bereft of her only male love at an early age and forever pining for him.

Mistral's oeuvre consists of six poetry books and several volumes of prose and correspondence. During her life, she published four volumes of poetry. Her first book, *Desolación,* was published in 1922 in New York City, under the auspices of Federico de Onís, professor of Spanish at Columbia University. The book attracted immediate attention. Mistral's second book of poems, *Ternura* [Tenderness], soon followed, in 1924, and was published in Spain, with Calleja Press. Three editions were printed before *Ternura* underwent a transformation and was reissued in 1945. For its final form, Mistral removed all the lullabies and "children's poems" that were originally part of *Desolación* and the later *Tala,* and put all the children's poems in the definitive edition of *Ternura.* She also added poems written independently, some of which were markedly different from earlier, pedagogical celebrations of childhood. *Ternura* became Mistral's most popular and best-selling book. Her third, and perhaps most important, book is *Tala* [Felling] (1938). Dedicated to the Basque children orphaned during the Spanish civil war, the book was published by Victoria Ocampo's prestigious publishing house Sur in Argentina, a major cultural clearinghouse of the day. *Tala* was reissued in 1947. For this edition, Mistral took out all of the children's poems and, as mentioned, placed them in a single volume, the 1945 edition of *Ternura.* This second edition is the definitive version we know today. Mistral's final book, *Lagar* [Wine press], was published in Chile in 1954. Two posthumous volumes of poetry also exist: *Poema de Chile* [Poem of Chile] (Santiago, 1967) and *Lagar II* [Wine press II] (Santiago, 1991).

Mistral never compiled her hundreds of prose pieces for publication; they are still, in fact, in the process of being collected. There are many compilations; I will briefly highlight the ones most important for this study. Roque Esteban Scarpa, a noted Mistralian, was responsible for compiling much of Mistral's prose during the 1970s: among other volumes, *La desterrada en su patria* [Exiled in her homeland] (1977), *Magisterio y niño* [Teaching and the child] (1979), and *Gabriela anda por el mundo* [Gabriela wanders around the world] (1978) feature some of her key writings on education and culture in Latin America. Luis Vargas Saavedra is responsible for an important volume, *El otro suicida de*

Gabriela Mistral [The suicidal other of Gabriela Mistral] (1985), and for compiling most of her published correspondence. Mistral wrote thousands of letters during her lifetime, spending several hours each day reading and writing letters, and dispatching them internationally. Interestingly, much of the correspondence is still not available to scholars but exists in the private hands of collectors or with acquaintances and friends. It is tragic yet, it seems, certain that some extremely significant letters were destroyed, either intentionally or through neglect. A specialist will immediately notice gaps in Mistral's published correspondence: there is very little available, for example, that relates to close female friends.

Being awarded the Nobel Prize in 1945 only increased Mistral's already frenzied pace of activity due to her by-then-well-established international fame. Aside from her consular work, Mistral held several visiting professorships in Latin America and the United States. She was a prestigious guest speaker, delighting audiences with her brilliant and deceivingly simple conversational style. Mistral reveled in the art of conversation, and apparently whisky and cigarette smoking too, making her a favorite in bohemian circles.

Mistral's extraordinary success, only outlined here, is all the more remarkable when her significant deviations from accepted "feminine" appearance and conduct are taken into consideration. Although the state offered Mistral as the transnational model for proper feminine conduct, it is curious that she was often described as being more masculine than feminine—or as ambiguous or simply "queer."

Although hard documentation of her sexuality simply does not exist, it's quite possible that Mistral's exile was in part sexual. Certainly, the assumption of the schoolteacher's image resonated with her need for self-protection while she was in Chile, as did the heterosexual "love" correspondence she shared with Manuel Magallanes Moure, a Chilean writer who was married at the time. Some specialists argue that she saw Magallanes in person twice, at social gatherings. Others claim they had an affair. Whatever the truth is, neither outcome disqualifies the issues I will examine throughout this book.

To date, there are no known love letters to women or diaries to construe as a personal sexual confession by Mistral. None of her associates have ever talked openly for the record in order to provide the apparently necessary "proof" of her "different" sexuality. As Elizabeth Horan writes,

"Latin Americanists familiar with the extraordinary range of her work claim to be ready to reject Mistral's kitschy canonization as 'spiritual mother,' but it seems that until some literary detective appears with documentary 'smoking-vibrator proof' of the subject's lesbianism, few will posit in print what virtually all concede in private."[16] References to gossip and murmurs about Mistral's unmarried status appear in correspondence with her friend and fellow Chilean Isauro Santelices, and in the memoirs of Pablo Neruda. Mistral regularly mentions anonymous letters of insult that followed her to all corners of Latin America, the United States, and Europe. The content of these letters has not been verified. Some Mistralian specialists have debated whether the letters were part of Mistral's narcissistic and paranoid musings. I believe that she probably did receive insults, and they probably had to do with her gender difference.

It's true that Mistral's tone in her known correspondence suggests that she had clear tendencies toward paranoia. Additionally, her letters indicate that she was an acute observer and analyzer of the boundaries of discourse, with a particular interest in discourse about herself. Despite the volumes of praise bestowed upon her as "the mother of America," her letters reveal an insecure and sometimes resentful woman. Mistral considered her success hard-won, regarding it as fraught with all kinds of unspecified dangers.

Mistral was not a frustrated mother and wife; she did find plenty of loves to match her early affair; and she was not the unconditional defender of children and racial minorities. These were, however, many of her self-figurations. The riddle is that there is something personal in Mistralian discourse, but not in the way that has been canonically assumed. Thus, *A Queer Mother for the Nation* unfolds contrapuntally along public/private lines, demonstrating how Mistral's initial manipulation of the boundaries between the two realms became, in fact, a confounded and confusing blurring—with personal and social consequences.

The personal consequences affecting Mistral remain obscured by the near hagiography of Mistral criticism; and the social consequences affecting Latin Americans persist as problems to the present. The chapters of this book are organized along knots of private/public concern that are most taken for granted and least understood when it comes to a discussion of Mistral and of women in the first half of the twentieth century: the love of mothers and children; the love of racial minorities, especially indigenous peoples; the love of the schoolteacher and of education; the love of country; and, finally, personal love.

Because the Mistralian corpus is enormous, I had to engage in a process of selection, one that conformed to the needs of the book's central arguments. Instead of providing a sequential, monographic analysis, the book is focused on the areas that are most contradictory in Mistralian discourse. The primary method employed throughout the book is Foucauldian discourse analysis. Some sections rely on psychoanalytic concepts, as reformulated in queer and postcolonial theory and, I hope, without reproducing the tendency of psychoanalysis to dehistoricize the subject.

Because *A Queer Mother for the Nation* focuses on Mistral's intervention in state politics, its main focus is on political, social, and educational essays of Mistral that are, for the most part, unknown to readers of English and little discussed in the Spanish-speaking world. Most of these essays come from two compilations, *Magisterio y niño* [Teaching and the child] and *Gabriela anda por el mundo* [Gabriela wanders around the world]. The book also engages Mistral's best-known but least-understood poetic work—her lullabies and ditties for children, collected in the 1945 volume *Ternura* [Tenderness].

A Queer Mother draws throughout upon the published correspondence of Mistral and examines letters that were written to her by friends and colleagues and are housed in an archive in the Library of Congress. In addition, I analyze a selection of Mistral's photographs, which document the wide circulation of her image. The chapter on the photographic archive should give readers an inkling of her visibility and influence as a national and international celebrity.

A born wanderer, Mistral traveled to more places of the world than it is possible to reflect on here. *A Queer Mother* considers her paradigmatic relationships to Chile, Mexico, Brazil, and Puerto Rico, with some mention of Cuba and Argentina. It also engages Mistral's relationships to a selection of major Latin American figures: the Mexicans José Vasconcelos and Salvador Novo; the Cuban Lydia Cabrera; the Venezuelan Teresa de la Parra; and the Puerto Ricans Inés Mendoza de Muñoz and Jaime Benítez. Naturally, her vexed relationship to Chile runs as an underlying and not always apparent thread throughout her life, and the book takes notice of and interprets that fact.

A Queer Mother privileges those available materials that enable an unforeseen and unpredictable angle both into Mistral's writings and politics and into key Latin Americanist debates and issues. Because the book is about Mistral's relationship to state politics and the state's gendered, raced, and sexualized deployments of "national culture," the reader should know in advance that there are areas of Mistral's existence and work that are not covered here; however, this does not mean I consider them secondary.

The book's unflinching look at Mistral's less flattering aspects may strike some readers as perhaps occasionally harsh. My attempt is to do justice to Mistral's stature as cultural iconoclast, even as I deconstruct her involvement in the state project. Conceived as a work of scholarship pertinent to the fields of feminist analysis, queer theory, and critical race theory, the book certainly keeps its focus on Mistral's own writings.

The intention is not to bury Mistral; on the contrary, the book places Mistral squarely on the map of both Latin American studies and hemispheric queer studies. My belief is that Mistral's actions and words weren't always commendable, but her life was certainly an exceptional and fascinating one.

"Race Woman," chapter 1, is a gritty portrayal of Mistral's racial politics, and its main concern is to perform a Foucauldian genealogy of the concept of *mestizaje* in Latin America. It demonstrates how the championing of the indigenous peoples—a defense of their continued "life" within the nation—occurred at the expense of the depredation of Latin Americans of African descent—a rationalization of their "death" within the nation. Some readers may be surprised to find that Mistral's racial pronouncements were far from benign, raising the specter of her violent racial mothering of the state. Certainly, Mistral's "personal" feelings regarding race and sexuality were at a disjuncture with her public discourse on the Latin American "race."

"Schooling and Sexuality," chapter 2, analyzes the figure of the schoolteacher in depth. Mistral became the singular image of the national schoolteacher, a figure related to the mother but significantly differentiated from her. Additionally, chapter 2 argues for a psychoanalytic understanding of the child's relationship to the modern Latin American schoolteacher, proposing this relationship as a double of national belonging. The state capitalizes on the citizen's desire to fulfill his or her anaclitic needs, postponed indefinitely by the process of national schooling. Mistral's queer figure, described as such by her contemporaries, was part of this deployment.

"Citizen Mother," the third chapter, closely examines and contextualizes two central essays in Mistral's career, "Palabras de la extranjera" [Remarks of the foreigner] and "Colofón con cara de excusa" [Colophon to offer an apology]. The former is the introduction to the book *Lecturas para mujeres* [Readings for women]. The latter is the afterword to the second edition of *Ternura* [Tenderness]. The chapter acknowledges the fact that Mistral practiced "separate spheres" thinking in some key ways (thus separating women from men in some instances) but questions whether this was a uniform discourse to be accepted at face value, or whether this female discourse was an instance of a far more complex and troubling self- and state enunciation. By historicizing Mistral's woman-centered essays, the reader will discover that maternal discourse is neither uniform nor uniformly benign.

"Intimate Nationalism," chapter 4, examines Mistral's vexed relationship with her own child, Juan Miguel Godoy, or "Yin Yin," tying personal circumstance to the literary production of sexually ambiguous "children's literature." "Intimate Nationalism" relates Mistral's own narcissism to the kind of narcissistic nationalism that was influential in the emergence of the Latin American liberal states of the twentieth century. The miniaturization of the state's cultural politics is evident in Mistral's ditties for children. One particular version of the "queer family" is presented, not to denigrate the idea of lesbians who have children but rather to perversely interrogate the bases of the national family. The national family inhabited a closed, anguished, and claustrophobic world. Two closeted women attempted to recreate its parameters, and they closed in on the object of their and the state's affection: the white child. Ironically, Juan Miguel Godoy suffered the fate projected for the racially marked child. He was asphyxiated by mother- and father-love and did not survive—or so goes the narrative of the letters between Mistral and her former secretary, the Mexican woman Palma Guillén.

"Image Is Everything," chapter 5, focuses on the photographic image of Mistral. It analyzes the progression of her image from demure and feminine writer-teacher to masculine "Mother of America." Some people consider Mistral's image as being asexual or repressed. Others have compared her physicality to that of the nun. I don't agree with either assessment; for me, Mistral was masculine and was seen in her own time as being mannish. "Image Is Everything" interprets the circulation of her sexual indeterminacy and speculates as to its possible ends. Mistral was not conventionally feminine, nor was she passing as a man—but she was not androgynous or asexual either. She was a prime example of what Judith Halberstam has usefully conceptualized as "female masculinity."[17]

"Pedagogy, Humanities, Social Unrest," chapter 6, discusses some of Mistral's key pedagogical writings, tracing first the contradictory emergence of the visual within the basic materials needed to teach literacy to children. Enamored of the visual image, Mistral came to express an almost fascistic belief in the image's powers. At the same time, she foresaw the printed word's changing relationship to an ascending cultural industry interested in quick, repetitive consumption rather than critical thinking. Mistral lamented the "death" of ideas, even as she enthusiastically aligned herself to the rise of the image.

After this exposition, chapter 6 moves on to the first of two historical examples in the field of education, to test the importance of such "image making" for the state. The first is a student strike; the second, colonial education. Puerto Rico, my native country, is the axis of these examples, but not because of my national origin. The reason for the inclusion is twofold. First, materials in Puerto Rico have not been as heavily censored as elsewhere, because Puerto Rico is often forgotten in Americanist narratives. Second, Puerto Rico is certainly "queer" with respect to the rest of Latin America, especially in its colonial relationship to the United States. As such, it is ideal for this analysis. Because Puerto Rico has existed as a colony of the United States since 1898, was a primary target of U.S. capital investment, and became the showcase for U.S. intervention in Latin American economic life, Mistral's attachment to Puerto Rico is especially paradigmatic of a larger Latin Americanist projection. (It's worth remembering that during the cold war, Puerto Rico was regarded as a model for U.S. policy in Latin America.) The two examples taken from Puerto Rican politics act as historical studies.

The second part of chapter 6 offers an examination of the cultural politics of the public university, especially through the example of the colonial government in the wake of a student strike at the University of Puerto Rico in 1948, one of many such strikes across Latin America. Mistral was the commencement speaker. Her internationally acclaimed image was critical to the successful crushing of the strikers and the dissident views they espoused. My intention is not to suggest that the state had a singular agency that dictated flawlessly the existence of social and individual subjects. As the student strikers demonstrated, although the state had fantasies of social control, its subjects in many instances acted independently of the state's imposition. The confrontation is both chilling and fascinating; it included visible and brutal state violence, but it also provided Mistral with an occasion to promote her views on how to manage social conflict through educational practices.

Melancholia became not only a strategy—perhaps a failed one—but also the defining affect of the pedagogical state. Chapter 7, "Education and Loss," demonstrates the blurring of the truly private and the carefully crafted private discourse disseminated by the state, especially through the nation's women. The manufactured "personal" discourse becomes that which is used to communicate the truly personal, threatening to efface the space where the supposed "truth" of (queer) sexuality resides. To illustrate this point, the chapter examines the correspondence between Mistral and a schoolteacher–turned–first lady of Puerto Rico, Inés Mendoza de Muñoz. This correspondence shows not only how these women communicated their affections but also how the affect represented by their truncated interactions got translated into state policy regarding education and, in effect, penetrated the arena of social policy.

At one level, *A Queer Mother for the Nation* is about refuting, or at least complicating, the dominant interpretations of the life and work of a very famous and influential twentieth-century figure: Gabriela Mistral. At another level, this book is about aspects of Latin American nationalism that illuminate the state's investment in that writer's nationally projected queerness. Broadly speaking, the first part of the book considers the possibility of constructing a "gay hagiography" for Mistral, in David Halperin's words.[18] The second part moves on to the vexed question of "queering the state."[19]

The word *queer* is used as adjective, verb, and noun throughout this book. As an adjective, *queer* is much more than a translation of *rara,* an appellation contemporaries used to describe Mistral. I use *queer* to center issues about sexuality, race, and gender that may, upon first glance, appear "off-center" but are, in fact, critical to nationalism.[20] Thus, *queer* does not signify certainty about Mistral's sexual identity; neither is it dependent on Mistral's having had any clear-cut identity as a lesbian, although it does not discount this possibility either. As a noun, the "queers" in this project may be Mistral herself; some of her employers and associates, who may or may not have been conscious of their attraction to this icon; schoolteachers made "strange" and isolated intellectually, socially, and economically by educational policies; or a culturally "unmoored" country like Puerto Rico, appearing in the transnational narratives of Latin America as simultaneously "lost" to U.S. imperialism, culturally dead, and privileged because of its residents' U.S. citizenship—but queerness is, above all things, a shifting and unstable position, not an identity to be applied across the board to any off-center situation. Finally, "to queer," as a verb, indicates my active deployment of critical methodologies designed to circumvent at least partially the limitations of earlier gay/lesbian studies approaches, which could lapse into nostalgic or recuperative projects even where "hard" evidence of sexuality could not be found. Thus, "queering" gives the researcher more agency to critique sexuality's uses and to make much broader the spectrum of people and practices accountable for homophobia, racism, and sexism. This means that an individual or circumscribed group will not bear the burden of being at fault for reproducing the status quo nor, conversely, become a heroic "precursor" for resisting. It's important to stress that such projects may be viable in certain instances, but they can't be the end point of queer scholars.

The term *queer* might at times be too elastic; yet it works in this particular study because the period was characterized both by intense activity around the normalization of subjects, particularly around sexuality, and by the centralizing potential of a strong state. This book in particular belongs with recent scholarship that takes queerness to task for its normalizing actions. This is to say not that all queerness has a normalizing effect, but merely that queerness is as susceptible to normalization as any other sexual or gender experience and that queerness can abet certain forms of heteronormativity.

Part I
A Gay Hagiography?

I belong to those whose entrails, face and expression are *irregular and perturbed,* due to a grafting; I count myself as one of the children of that twisted thing that is called racial experience, or better put, *racial violence.*
                    —Gabriela Mistral, "Colofón con cara de excusa"
                              [Colophon to offer an apology]

CHAPTER ONE

Race Woman

By examining Mistral's status as "race woman"—a public position that she fiercely claimed, as opposed to any public nonnormative sexual stance—it's immediately clear that Mistral was instrumental in instituting sexual and racial normativity through nationalist discourse.[1] Within the Latin American public, Mistral upheld the heterosexual matrix. But was her queerness completely out of public view? Certainly, Mistral alluded to reproductive sexuality every time she spoke of race. She consistently portrayed herself as the spokesperson of Latin America—which she referred to as "our race" [nuestra raza]—posing as the mixed-race mother of the nation. Mistral devoted many prose pieces to the subject of a Latin American unified culture achieved through individual and social reproduction. Well known for her defense of the indigenous peoples of Latin America, she frequently and vigorously alluded to the process of *mestizaje*.

Through the stance of race woman, Mistral aided the state in managing Latin America's racially heterogeneous populations, regarded as a problem since the wars of independence. Both publicly and privately she addressed topics ranging from the classification and hierarchical ordering of racial "mixings" to the status of black Latin Americans in nationalist discourse, from desirable *mestizaje* in the Latin American territory to dangerous *mestizaje* beyond the watchful purview of the state.

It is tempting to separate Mistral's sexual and racial identities, envisioning one as private and the other as public, one secret and the other on strident display. Typically, the quandary of a subject such as Mistral is addressed by analyzing one identity at a time. The story of her romantic life is separated from the story of her public career, even as her public figure unfolds in accordance with the narrative of republican motherhood. Salacious attention to the invented details of her private existence meshes happily with a hagiographic view of her role in world affairs. But to understand Mistral's complexity more fully, it is useful to view her private and public identities less as discrete chunks of self and more as spliced and interdependent.

Examining the intersection of race and sexuality in Mistral is vital in more senses than one. Dispelling myths about her is important, but understanding a mythology put at the service of the state is critical. Both racial mixing (collective sexuality) and Mistral's ambiguous sexuality (seen as a private affair) involve the *social* demarcation of acceptable and unacceptable sex; in both instances, sex is coded as reproduction. In the state project that Mistral helped articulate, reproduction meant not only maximizing women's bodies to produce fit laborers and to manage productive, patriarchal, heterosexual families but also establishing and enforcing the parameters of who belonged, racially speaking, in the nation. This was true of the restricted sense of the emerging nation-state (*What* is a Chilean? *Who* can be considered a Mexican?) and of the expansive, indeed massive, sense of Americanism *[latinoamericanismo]*. Enforcing the stricture of belonging entailed a submerged but no less potent role for Mistral's "silent" sexuality. As I have discussed elsewhere, the language of reproduction and child care functions as a kind of closet that paradoxically has made public what was to remain private.[2] In the more far-reaching context of public or collective sexuality, Mistral deployed the same language to draw a firm, frequently onerous line of national belonging. Elucidating the connection between her queerness and the racial discourse she successfully deployed is my goal in this chapter.

An intersectional analysis reveals that Mistral's symbolic heterosexuality was meant to guarantee or benefit not heterosexuality per se (i.e., not all heterosexuals equally) but a particular heterosexuality, one tailored to the state's project. Mistral offered her own body as the representation of an entire race, a race created from an invented tradition.[3] But how could a woman who bore no biological children for the race, who was always coupled with women, become the lasting symbol of the national mother? Her lived sexuality did not coincide with the national prescription, but was her queerness the linchpin of her national pose?

In "The Politics of Posing," Sylvia Molloy classifies queer Latin American posing as perverse posing, that is, posing as effeminate or as a sodomite, for example, in the face of prescriptive masculinities. Expanding the concept of posing to include poses such as Mistral's, I articulate a notion of display more closely linked to deployment. Molloy discusses the pose of the queer [raro] as a type of gender and sexual resistance to a prescriptive nationalist ideology: "I want to think about *posing* in Latin America differently, not as the vapid posturing of some ghostly *fête galante,* a set of bodily or textual affectations at odds with national and continental discourses and concerns from which Latin America ultimately recovers, but as an oppositional practice and a decisive cultural statement whose political import and destabilizing energy I will try to recuperate and assess."[4] Mistral made use of a straightforward posing, as mother, as mestiza, but her posing abetted (instead of destabilizing) the national discourse. Indeed, posing is part of nationalism's effectiveness, for it engages the complicated question of identification. Conservative Latin Americans may have felt that their identity as national subjects suffered no threat from the elevation of a queer like Mistral, but there is more. As Foucault established, power is at its weakest when it does no more than negate.[5] Mistral's figure enabled citizens to take part in the productive nature of power, specifically in the pleasures of identification—pleasures that underwrote both liberationist and repressive actions, to be sure. It was not simply a posing *pro patria* of the kind Molloy observes in José Enrique Rodó's *Ariel*—a posing meant to hide homoerotic desire, visible only at the moment when Prospero caresses the bronze statue of Ariel and "finds Rodó out";[6] Mistral's example provides a model for the incorporation of queerness into the state's project and makes the case that Latin American queerness was not as invisible as one may have thought.

It is paradoxical and extraordinary, at the very least, that Mistral attained the status of symbolic guardian of the national family. Had she chosen to emphasize her variance publicly—her masculinity, her choice of intimate arrangements, her failure to marry and have children—without engaging the play of identification on a national and transnational scale, the state, with its ample resources, would have crushed her ambitions. The state, however, was attracted to her queerness, to what she and only she could accomplish in a biopolitical realm of power. So the union was consummated: Mistral would perform in the public sphere as the state's star attraction, posing as so married to the national cause that she had sacrificed her most personal fulfillment for the good of her and the state's "national children," the citizens.

Mistral most definitely planned and executed her participation in the state agenda. Consider her avowal of her own potential, as well as her intense self-focus, in a 1923 letter to Pedro Aguirre Cerda: "Of all the South American nations, Chile does the least for its propaganda in the exterior. It doesn't care about its image, or it believes that only the ministers and consuls can generate this propaganda; but they only live the good life and don't divulge things Chilean. I believe I can do what they have not yet done, and that I can do it with the only tools of effective propaganda: the *schools* and the *press*."[7] Undoubtedly, Mistral's almost mercenary assumption of culture entailed a measure of self-protection. However, could it have exceeded the demands of self-protection? Additionally, did it signify beyond naked self-advancement? Did Mistral identify with the national project?

In 1918 Mistral was sent to the southernmost province of Chile, Magallanes, with a specific mission, "to Chileanize" [chilenizar]: "I had to Chileanize your [Roque Esteban Scarpa's] homeland, on orders of my minister and friend."[8] Such a statement, in conjunction with a knowledge of the period's significant acts of protest against the state,[9] reveals much about the state's racial project: to assimilate or annihilate indigenous peoples in the province, to promote immigration from northern Europe to Chile to "whiten" the race (Mistral mentions Yugoslavs and Germans in the same text), and to symbolically implant the idea of citizen allegiance to a Chilean nation, targeting most specifically the working classes. Mistral spoke rancorously about her stay in Magallanes, yet the same national prerogatives that she occasionally decried governed her public and private discourse until her death. Though Mistral evinced perplexity at her role in this endeavor, she internalized and enacted it thoroughly, to the point that her own feelings meshed with the state's racial project.[10]

Mistral's preoccupation with national boundaries became obsessive in her racial discourses and practices. In this sense, she (and the state) practiced a kind of social prophylaxis. But they married the individual and social practices of prophylaxis to such a degree that these practices were experienced as one and the same. When read through the lens of race, Mistralian discourse is not "personal" in the way that the much touted, but not very convincing, biographical fable would have us believe. Mistral emerges as someone different from the frustrated mother and wife, who never found another love to match her early romance—and, more crucially, from the unconditional defender of all children, all mothers, and all racial "minorities."

Mistral was, arguably, fueled by a desire to erect herself as a pillar in discourses of mass appeal and as a player in the transformations that ensued partly through the deployment of these discourses. Her difficult experiences of gender and sexuality, while very real, did not counteract the maturing of an early racial identification with the nation-state. Indeed, her "open secret" interacted with her identification with the Chilean racial project and her overwhelming ambition to anchor the racial state. It is essential to note that Mistral's racial identification was not a reflection of her unique personality; her treatment of racial others and of *mestizaje* may seem idiosyncratic at times, yet she was shaped by the racial project as much as she shaped it when she became its active enunciator. Collective racial identifications in flux, experienced by the majority of Latin American citizens during a period of uneven modernization, were refracted uniquely through Mistral, hardening into a common national identification tailored to the state's desire.

Mestizaje

Mistral is commonly heralded as the champion of the indigenous peoples of Latin America, particularly of the mestizo. *Mestizaje*, as it appears in her essays, is not a spontaneous racial mixing dictated by movements and contacts between peoples but a state-sponsored and -managed phenomenon. Racial mixing was an entire arena of social policy and discursive practice, requiring classification, expertise, and policing.[11] Michel Foucault's 1976 lectures at the Collège de France on the genealogy of racism, specifically his notion of violence in biopower, are singularly suited to this discussion. According to Foucault, violence in biopower has less to do with overt acts of killing than with institutionalized exclusions and hierarchies designed to guarantee that only some have "the capacity to live" in a society of normalization.[12] A Foucauldian genealogy of *mestizaje* in Mistral's work—an attempt to define the conditions for, and to locate, its precise emergence—indicates that she took this concept directly from José Vasconcelos and the great project of nation building after the Mexican Revolution. Moreover, it strongly suggests that, for Mistral, *mestizaje* essentially meant marshaling a cultural notion of "unity" in the service of an integrationist agenda.

Mestizaje implies a binary that marginalizes Latin Americans of African descent. At best, they are folklorized as an "exotic" minority; at worst, they are literally eliminated. But before exploring the treatment of the black (Latin American) subject more fully, it is instructive to revisit a critical issue in Mistral's racial discourse: the status of her "defense" of the indigenous peoples.

As shocking as it may seem today, the young Mistral was attracted to white-supremacist beliefs. Ana Pizarro reports that very early in her career, Mistral spoke of "saving the white man" [la salvación del blanco] and "the purity of the race" [la pureza de la raza] on, of all holidays, Columbus Day [el Día de la Raza].[13] Interestingly, she abandoned this virulent discourse and began speaking on behalf of the indigenous peoples only after her first visit to Mexico, in 1922, when Vasconcelos invited her as part of his educational reforms. But was this change heartfelt and humanitarian, or was it a strategic adoption of a discourse of normalization? Pizarro believes that it was the former.[14] At the very least, Mistral's change of heart was impeccably timed.

As modern Mexico's first minister of education, Vasconcelos was Mistral's first international employer. His invitation substantially increased her sense of personal power in the cultural politics of the day, and it is conceivable that she viewed her championing of the indigenous peoples as an opportunity. Jaime Quezada believes that Mistral's change of heart occurred while she was stationed in Magallanes, prior to leaving Chile, but there are no pedagogical texts from the period that exalt the indigenous or mestizo person in Chile. Quezada bases his opinion on texts that Mistral wrote in 1932 and 1948, which may, in fact, show her finessing her Chilean past and her role in Chileanizing the country. Chile's model of racial management was most surely Argentina, its Southern Cone neighbor, not populist Mexico.[15] Aguirre sent Mistral to Punta Arenas to direct a girls' school. Girls' schools were intended for the privileged daughters of the nascent bourgeoisie, not for the children of workers and certainly not for indigenous children. Sent to the most indigenous- and immigrant-populated sector of Chile to run a school of "true" female nationals, Mistral, presumably, would have avoided any danger of incorrect sexual proclivity. Yet, as Jorge Salessi notes, in Argentina a

well-developed criminological-pedagogical literature discoursed on the
"dangers" of lesbianism (called "fetishism" and "uranism") in the homosocial world of the girls' school.[16] Was Mistral's assignment merely a historical irony?

Mistral's awareness of her heightened prestige after her visit to Mexico accounts for her authoritative tone in the letter to Aguirre quoted in
the preceding section. Her visit to Mexico hinged also on an interesting
detail. Vasconcelos was attracted to her because she was queer *[rara]*,
rejecting many other models of femininity that he might have imported
from the Southern Cone. Gleefully confiding in her friend Radomiro
Tomic, Mistral comments on the impression that her image made on
Vasconcelos in Mexico:

> It would suffice, I tell you, for me to be on an equal footing with the
> other consuls, in spite of being a woman. That would be enough, I
> repeat. I will go back in time to clarify the facts for you. [President
> Arturo] Alessandri told Vasconcelos, when I was in Mexico, what a
> mistake he had made, bringing Gabriela Mistral to Mexico, instead of
> [Amanda Labarca Hubner]. And at the banquet afterward Alessandri
> introduced her to Vasconcelos and made her sit next to him. When
> Alessandri got up to leave, Vasconcelos told him: "Of *these* [meaning
> women like Hubner], we have lots in Mexico; in fact, too many. But the
> one I took with me [meaning Mistral] is different and queer [strange,
> odd]." He laughed as he told me about it.[17]

As Mistral recounts the episode, she and Vasconcelos are sharing a private joke. Her confidence to her "friend," Tomic, places this account
squarely in the realm of personal discourse, yet Mistral is clear about
the consequences of her "queerness" for her chances of a public life in a
world of men. The comparison with Amanda Labarca Hubner, perhaps
the most important Chilean feminist of that time, points unequivocally
toward Mistral's, and possibly Vasconcelos's, disdain for the prevailing
public image of woman. Such feminists would not fit the bill of transnational image and spokesperson. They would never elicit the endless fascination that Mistral evidently considered herself capable of. The testimony of many of her contemporaries confirms that this impression
was not delusional and attests to the fact that her "masculinity" largely
accounted for the attraction.

Vasconcelos was searching for an unusual icon, an off-center woman.
What Mistral represented to him was not "a great cultural relief, similar

to the 'we don't have that here' of certain anxious constructions of nationality," but exactly the opposite.[18] Vasconcelos had finally found the embodiment of femininity he wanted. "Queerness" is what Mexico did not have and presumably needed. Evidently, Vasconcelos thought that queerness had to be enlisted to make his nationalist educational endeavor work. His perverse brilliance rests on this fact: although a homophobe of the first order, he hired prominent gay and lesbian intellectuals and writers to assist in his educational reform.[19] The usefulness of this tactic had dawned on Aguirre, too, but Vasconcelos appears to have had a much more developed vision. He saw that there was something in the despised queer that could be linked to the despised racial other, something about the queer's inclusion as a solitary and inaccessible being that could further the symbolic inclusion of the indigenous in the same terms.

Naturally, Mistral exploited the regional lesson of Mexico. With the international visibility that the Mexican Revolution had achieved firmly in mind, she created a veritable transnational pedagogy. Mistral's call for greater "propaganda" in favor of the Chilean government reflects a remarkable change from the attitude she expressed in her letters to Aguirre while an unknown schoolteacher in the provinces of Chile. In those letters Mistral entirely deferred to him as "the man in charge": "You will always be for me minister, the intellectual and spiritual authority whose pedagogical credo I aspire to realize, the source of the most satisfying approval and the most saddening censure."[20] She realized that she needed a male protector acting on her behalf to ensure what Juan Villegas Morales labels the state's role as "patron" [mecenas].[21] What the young Mistral did not fully realize before 1922 was the potential of her queerness. Although aware that her sizable literary talent would rescue her from Chile's stifling environment, she wanted more. She identified with and was attracted to power. Despite her championing of the indigenous peoples, Mistral was white and white-identified, which is partly why her mixed-race pose was regarded as queer. Her racial discourse avowed and disavowed her queerness at the same time.

Mistral's self-appraised ugliness, her pose of self-hatred and premature aging,[22] takes on an entirely different character when juxtaposed to her universally recognized, excessive identification with the "Indian." The two poses bear striking similarities. Perhaps Mistral did feel deeply for the Indian and the mestizo. Certainly, she took her cross-identification with them to heart. More important, this identification—a queer one—

had a social and political dimension of inestimable historical value. Mistral embodied the pedagogical image of the Indian and the mestizo. Thanks to her, this image entered schools around Latin America. The widely anthologized essays "El tipo del indio americano" [The type of the Indian of the Americas] and "A la mujer mexicana" [To the Mexican woman], examined shortly, are but two examples of its pervasiveness.

Mistral offered an attractive morality tale: a beautiful object mistaken for an ugly one, a millenarian and singular icon fatally detached from social life, an oddity deserving a curious admixture of pity and admiration. This narrative showed how it was possible both to love and despise the other and to love and despise oneself. Mistral encouraged the Latin American citizen's identification with this image of the indigenous person and encouraged national subjects to lock, through her queer figure, into a psychic play with the nation-state. Identification, cross-identification, and counteridentification became the primary exercises of citizenship.[23]

As her self-estimation as ugly coincided with her exaltation of the indigenous person as beautiful, Mistral in the 1920s and 1930s concentrated on the classification of the indigenous body. Though she had taught since 1914 and had written precepts of conduct for schoolteachers and eulogies of the public-school system, Mistral undertook her most powerful writings on education a decade later. They reveal her preoccupation with "our race"; to borrow a phrase from Michael Omi and Howard Winant, "racial common sense" permeated her work until her death.[24] Consider an excerpt from "El tipo del indio americano" [The type of the Indian of the Americas] (1932):

> One of the reasons for the native repugnance to confess the Indian in our blood, one of the origins of our fear of telling the world that we are loyal mestizos, is the so-called ugliness of the Indian. We hold this as an irrefutable truth; we have accepted it without question. It goes hand in hand with such phrases as "The Indian is lazy" and "The Indian is evil.". . . We should have taught our children about the differentiated and opposed beauty of the races. A long and slender eye is beautiful in the Mongolian, while in the Caucasian it debases the face. A yellowish color, ranging in shade from straw to sheepskin, accentuates the delicate nature of the Chinese face. In the European it suggests sanguine misery. Curly hair is a glorious crown on the head of the Caucasian; in the mestizo it hints at *mulataje,* and we prefer the flat locks of the Indian.[25]

Apart from interpreting beauty racially in this essay, Mistral analyzes racial mixings for their advantages and disadvantages through binaries.

The binary of beauty/ugliness and the Vasconcelian idea of "aesthetic selection" inform all of her writings after 1922 and could well be interpreted as the subtext of her subsequent, increasingly frequent, and deeply problematic self-description as "india" or mestiza. So profound was her discursively produced racial transformation that it became commonplace in the public record to refer to Mistral as mestiza. Her biographers and critics took this identification to be a biographical fact, and it persists to this day.

Mistral's negation of "the so-called ugliness of the Indian" [la llamada fealdad del indio] is generally regarded as a defense of the "indigenous element" in the racial configuration of the universal Latin American subject. In an insightful essay about Mistral and Victoria Ocampo, Amy Kaminsky recognizes Mistral's problematic use of racial stereotypes as she fashioned a symbolically beautiful Indian; Mistral's well-known essay "Silueta de la India mexicana" [Silhouette of the Mexican Indian woman] (1923), for example, "does little more than bring the Indian woman into the field of vision and make of her an object of beauty."[26] Kaminsky believes, however, that essentially Mistral cared for the indigenous peoples and that championing their cause made her a social "outsider." But might this not be a superficial reading? It is vital to contextualize Mistral's "defense" and to unearth where the idea of ugliness emerged. To uncover what the defense enabled—or at least glossed over—it is fruitful first to ponder Vasconcelos's considerable influence.[27]

In his treatise La raza cósmica [The cosmic race] (1925), Vasconcelos presents a true exceptionalist narrative, placing Latin America squarely at the center of world affairs through a racial construction or, in Omi and Winant's terminology, a "racial project."[28] Mestizaje, Vasconcelos argues, constitutes Latin America's racial specificity and claim to centrality. This region alone contains the four races of the world, which means that the next (and, according to him, last) leading race—the fifth, or cosmic, race—will originate in Latin America. Notably, the process of mixing is not haphazard; it is meticulously selective. In a highly questionable but fascinating passage, Vasconcelos predicts that "uglier races" will voluntarily "phase themselves out" through the principle of "aesthetic eugenics," or the criterion of "taste":

> The lower types of the species will be absorbed by the superior type. In this way, for example, the Negro will be able to redeem himself, and, little by little, through voluntary extinction, the uglier races will pave the way

for the most beautiful. The inferior races, through education, will become less prolific, and the best specimens will ascend on the scale of ethnic improvement. On this scale, the uppermost type is not the white man but a new race, to which the white man will also have to aspire for the synthesis to be achieved. The Indian, by being grafted onto a race with which he has affinities, will take the leap over the million-year gap that separates Atlantis from our time. In a few decades of *aesthetic eugenics* the Negro will disappear, along with the types that the free instinct of beauty signals as fundamentally recessive and, for that reason, unworthy of survival. In this way a process of *selection by taste* will take place. It will be much more efficient than the brutal Darwinist criterion of selection, which may be relevant, at best, to inferior species but not to man.[29]

This excerpt establishes three clear connections between Vasconcelos and Mistral. First, both writers link sex and the transmission of "culture," whether that of the European or those of the indigenous and black communities of Latin America. Second, both value whiteness and Western culture most highly, even if Vasconcelos symbolically elevates the mestizo. That the fifth race is not identical to the white race underlies the ambivalences of Vasconcelos's text: a sense of racial inferiority in the face of "true" whiteness and a vague but exceedingly important sense of racial panic aroused by an impending and intimate, if unwanted, relationship with the United States. This racial sensibility is transparent in the black/indigenous comparison. Although Vasconcelos acknowledges the black people in Latin America, he happily reports that "they have been transformed almost entirely into mulatto populations" (37). He also uses blackness to demonstrate that Latin America not only has a better strategy than the United States for dealing with its black population (assimilation) but also is better positioned to be successful at racial mixing, because it has a more palatable other (the Indian): "North [i.e., Anglo-] Americans are very firm in their resolution to keep their lineage pure, but of course that is possible because they have the Negro in front of them—the other pole, the exact opposite of the element that they could elect to mix with. In the Ibero-American world, the problem is not as crude. We have very few blacks, and the majority have been transformed into mulatto populations. The Indian is a good bridge to *mestizaje*" (37). Superficially, the indigenous peoples fare better than blacks in this scheme, but it is important to note that they too are destined to disappear in the process of *mestizaje*. It is precisely in this context that Mistral's championing of indigenous peoples emerges. The comparison between these two groups as poor and good bridges to *mestizaje* constitutes the back-drop against which to consider both the aesthetic criteria that are primary in Mistral's first descriptions of the "indigenous element" and her recourse to the idea of "ugly/not ugly." While these categories undoubtedly have something to do with the commonsensical racism of the time, Mistral's crafting of an entire racial discourse at the public and official levels exemplifies a more developed speech genre.

Third, Vasconcelos proposes to replace the "brutal Darwinist criterion of selection" with "aesthetic eugenics": "As soon as education and the common good are disseminated, there will no longer be any danger that the most opposite types will mix. Unions will happen only in accordance with . . . the law of sympathy, refined by the sense of beauty" (23). Vasconcelos singles out education and parameters for the "common good" as the chief means by which "taste" and "aesthetic eugenics" will be cultivated in mass terms. The state, presumably, will manage such practices, though the essay does not say so. Nor does it name children as the telos of this endeavor, as miniature citizens or citizens-to-be. Childhood and education are precisely the arenas in which Mistral shrewdly and aggressively positions herself. Arranging the national strands that Vasconcelos leaves dangling, she insists that correct mixing is the foundation of the pedagogical intervention, because the national child is the desired creation of the public-education system (to emphasize the Foucauldian view of primary education).

The phrase "aesthetic eugenics" was used in an attempt to make an unsavory social action philosophically palatable. The management of social life entailed the elimination of certain social subjects and the eradication of their cultures. This loss of life—the life of people, the life of cultures—had to be masked as the continuation of another life, that is, the life of a nation so gloriously vital. Was Mistral an adherent of eugenics? According to historian Asunción Lavrin, Mistral participated in debates on eugenics programs in Latin America: "Her ideas on social eugenics mirrored those of the *higienistas* and feminist doctors of her generation and no doubt were grounded in her experience in Chile."[30] Lavrin writes that Mistral advocated organized social charity to combat syphilis, tuberculosis, and alcoholism, firmly believing that, in Mistral's words, "the quality of the new generation" was at stake. In an untitled government tract of 1926, she spoke of "biological patriotism" as a more suitable concept for the state than either nationality or race, championing a special role for women as social workers. "Mistral's ideas on women's role in national health schemes would shortly thereafter become a pedagogical and policy reality as Southern Cone nations launched schools of social work and increasingly entrusted their graduates with roles similar to those she suggested" (164).

Mistral clearly retained the concept of nationality and adhered to the idea of Latin America as a "race," contrary to her assertions in 1926. But her championing of "biological patriotism" betrayed the eugenicist understanding of populations as shaped by elements from superior and inferior races. Essays in which she copied the Mexican model of *mestizaje* may not obviously demonstrate this fact, but when her essays on the Argentinean paradigm of white immigration are taken into account, it is impossible to maintain with confidence that Mistral held the indigenous peoples in the same esteem as white people.[31] Even white immigrants were a sore point for her on occasion; in "El folklore argentino" [Argentinean folklore] (1938) she speaks of folklore as "the defense of the race against dangerous immigration," apparently taking a page from U.S. policy: "'Argentina for the Argentineans,' plagiarizing Monroe; conquering the immigrant and the native . . . through folklore."[32]

In her important study of the eugenics projects of early-twentieth-century Latin America, Nancy Leys Stepan summarizes the relationship between race and national belonging as follows:

> The desire to "imagine" the nation in biological terms, to "purify" the reproduction of populations to fit hereditary norms, to regulate the flow of peoples across national boundaries, to define in novel terms who could belong to the nation and who could not—all these aspects of eugenics turned on issues of gender and race, and produced intrusive proposals or prescriptions for new state policies toward individuals. Through eugenics, in short, gender and race were tied to the politics of national identity.[33]

Mistral was attracted to the problem of the national population—the question of who should be part of it—and to the sexual reasoning that authorized this discourse. Her views constituted a subtle, insidious form of eugenics; far from confined to a small circle of specialists with influence only in medicine and health, Mistral's views were naturalized across Latin America. Accessible in mass venues such as the schools and the press, her "race-speak" became synonymous with a national understanding of self and essential to the affective register of national belonging.

Blackness

Critics have held that when Mistral mentions "the race," she means a civilization, not biological characteristics or the separate populations within *mestizaje*.[34] Her references to a mestizo Latin American race, they argue, represent a recognition of four hundred years of *mestizaje* that, presumably, arrived at a final point more or less coinciding with the advent of the modern Latin American state, sealed in a liberal social contract that needed no revision. Nevertheless, it is clear that Mistral's racial worries were not primarily, but only tangentially, about the survival of one civilization under pressure from others, especially the pressure of Latin America's feared northern neighbor. Her worries gravitated around three key issues: whether blacks and immigrants were part of Latin American *mestizaje*, what to do if they were, and how to privilege the indigenous over the black in a binary construction that exalted Latin American heterogeneity while tightly controlling its impact.

Mistral understood the connection, and contrast, between indigenous and black racial constructions in the context of the state project. The condition assigned to the indigenous woman revolves around that connection. In an early pedagogical essay, "A la mujer mexicana" [To the Mexican woman] (1922), she writes: "You have been told that your purity is a religious virtue. It is also a civic virtue: your womb sustains the race; the citizen masses are born out of your breast quietly, with the eternal flowing of the springs of your fatherland."[35] In other words, the indigenous woman is the sealed receptacle in which the race is kept pure, the acceptable vessel of reproduction. Projections about making the Indian woman feel pure resonate instantly with the eugenicist project to improve the quality of the population. The link between the indigenous woman's body and the black woman's body is crucial. Whereas the indigenous woman is a receptacle of the race, a national mother, the black woman is a vehicle through which the national seed and thus national life are lost.

Mistral also saw herself as a receptacle of the race. Patricio Marchant has summarized Mistral's appeal as mother:

> Mistral appears in Chilean mythology, both popular and literary, . . . as the mother par excellence . . . competing with the Virgin Mary for this post. Mother par excellence because she is mother without children. A possibility that fuels desire if the place of the "legitimate child" exists as a vacuum . . . if infantile desire is about being the real child, the only child,

the most loved child. Psychoanalytically, the unconscious knows this is impossible—precisely the reason that makes the mother faithful, pure, virgin, good.[36]

Mistral placed the indigenous woman in a similar position: inaccessible and remote, removed from her children even as she births them. The black woman is the obverse. Too accessible and physical, too likely to betray the race by "intermingling," she becomes the very agent of biological national pollution.

In the widely anthologized "Primer recuerdo de Isadora Duncan" [First recollection of Isadora Duncan] (1927), Mistral compares Duncan's white body to Josephine Baker's black body. She privileges the former as the repository of aesthetic beauty and links the latter to the decline of art. This text documents Mistral's racism against people of African descent, even hinting at a sympathetic attitude toward white supremacy in the United States. The essay opens with an indirect reference to lynching and, wittingly or unwittingly, exploits the lynching narrative by creating subtle but sensationalist undertones. The narrative rests on a racist construction of sexual trespass against the body of a white woman or, more specifically, the body of the white man's wife and the bearer of his children. This time, though, a black woman's body, Baker's, is the agent of transgression. Mistral's narrative is both homoerotic and racist. Duncan is the object of Mistral's desire (as incisively noted by critic Alberto Sandoval Sánchez), but she has been indirectly violated by another woman, a black woman: Baker.[37] "Greek" dance is figuratively transgressed by the Charleston, which in Mistral's opinion is a debased and sexual dance performed by debased and animal people:

> Isadora was also a Yankee. But she was an Irish Yankee, and, at any rate, she belonged to a generation that had not yet fallen into the smelly basement of slave dealers.
>
> What a curious vengeance the Negroes have exacted on the Englishmen of North America. They, who eat, pray, and exist apart; they, who cannot embrace a white woman's body without having the sons of Lynch descend on them and send their only whiteness, their brains, spilling onto the pavement; it is they who have communicated to the enemy (the Super White Man, as some call him) their filthy jiggling of guts. They have created for the white man the bestial rhythms to which New York now awakes, with which it lives and goes to sleep.
>
> Isadora has left the enormous Charleston dance hall that the world has become—not too late, thank God, and with the elegance of a

polished visitor, who opens the door and slips away on seeing that her hosts are drunk.[38]

This passage cynically draws on the relationship that the lynching narrative establishes between race and sexuality or, more concretely, between blackness, sexuality, and crime. Simultaneously, it resonates with the supposed horror of sexual relations between members of opposite races (a horror seen earlier in Vasconcelos's *La raza cósmica*). Mistral actually specifies correct and incorrect couplings in "El tipo del indio americano," written shortly after "Primer recuerdo de Isadora Duncan"; there she speaks warily about *mulataje,* the mixing of white and black. The topic of undesirable couplings later echoes in Mistral's comments on the consequences of marriage between Mexican men and black women. Panic pervades her writings about such couplings, and she is anxious to distance herself from any legacy of blackness. One way to de-emphasize the existence of blacks in Latin America was to displace that blackness toward the United States. In "El folklore argentino," the comparison emerges once more: "I like the tango! I told Lombardi. Some tangos have triumphed for twenty years over the North American 'blues.' Those black rhythms won't do us any good; they are not our own."[39]

Much of Mistral's article about Duncan describes a vilified object, Baker's body, that carries within itself its own degeneration. The aesthetic criterion authorizes this violent description with its main refrain, the idea of ugliness, implicit in such loaded terms as "monkey," "bestiality," and "foul-smelling" (which appear throughout the article), as well as "filthy jiggling of guts" (in the quotation cited earlier). Although Sandoval, the only critic to have examined the text, correctly observes Mistral's "racist gaze" at the black woman's body, he assumes that this gaze contains no desire and that this lack of desire, this hatred, stems from Baker's blackness, conceived as a stand-in for all blackness.[40] Sandoval reads in Mistral's loving recasting of Duncan's veiled body the repression of Mistral's attraction to women and, implicitly, to whiteness. But her queer desire also appears in her treatment of the black subject, and, significantly, it is not as repressed.

Mistral reexamined and reworked the injurious racism of "First Recollection of Isadora Duncan" when she visited the Spanish-speaking countries of the Caribbean and, later, Brazil. After these travels, undertaken in the early 1930s, the person of African descent became an object to know and to incorporate into the discourse of "us," of Americanism. In a 1933 letter to the Mexican writer and intellectual Alfonso Reyes, Mistral writes: "I suffered through both the United States winter and the Spaniards; both are brutal. I got to know a zone of our race that I did not know anything about; the Spanish language of America, softened by their land and virtues; and the mulatto and the Negro, who are different, so very different, from our mestizo and our Indian. (How I missed the Indian, Alfonso!)"[41] The presence of a black Latin American subject complicates the binary of *mestizaje* and the Mexican ideology that "we are all mestizo." Mistral replaced her initial rejection of blackness and her uneasiness with *mulataje* with a Nietzschean "will to know" and "will to power." Once blackness emerged as a fundamental and undeniable presence in Latin America, Mistral searched for ways to reconcile blackness with *mestizaje* while ensuring that the binary of indigenous/white continued to be the motor of contemporary Latin American history and the rationale behind all the state's racial politics and policies.

Latin American ideologies of racial democracy rested on a conceptualization of Latin American slavery that held it as more benign because it was supposedly more affective and erotic.[42] Queers are not exempted from this legacy. Queer desire is not immune to racialized constructions of eroticism or to the lure of achieving national belonging through a collective exercise of racial fetishization. Globally, queer desire has often been associated with private acceptance and public shame. Within a liberal order, racial condescension or hatred often appears uncensored in private venues while it is tempered or silenced in public discourse. Thus, one unspoken citizen prerogative under liberalism is to accede to a private sphere where prohibited queer desires interact with racialized, hierarchical eroticism. Mistral exoticized and sexualized the black subject in this private sphere. Her letters to the Cuban anthropologist and ethnographer Lydia Cabrera offer an example. Before traveling to Brazil, Mistral shared her intentions with Cabrera: "Look, seriously, whenever you want to go there, please, don't hesitate to come to our house. I am consul in Niterói, a beach in Rio, across from the city as you traverse the beautiful bay. It's only half an hour away. It's a sinecure, because I will hardly have any work to do. My state is the most beautiful and has the most inhabitants. People there seem courteous and well mannered. And of course there's the magnificent Negro."[43]

At the time of this correspondence, Mistral was living in France with her secretary and companion, the Puerto Rican Consuelo Saleva, or "Connie," and was working as consul of Chile. It is not known whether the letters collected by Rosario Hiriart in *Cartas a Lydia Cabrera: Correspondencia inédita de Gabriela Mistral y Teresa de la Parra* [Letters to Lydia Cabrera: Unpublished correspondence of Gabriela Mistral and Teresa de la Parra] represent all of the correspondence between Cabrera and Mistral. Given that Mistral kept up a voluminous correspondence with hundreds of people throughout her life, it is likely that there were other letters.

Molloy has demonstrated that the exchange of letters between Mistral, Cabrera, and the Venezuelan novelist Teresa de la Parra is coded as lesbian. Molloy refers to Mistral's participation in some of the two women's "lovers' quarrels" and to her urging them to "patch things up."[44] Mistral's startling racial references and lack of self-censorship invite further reflection, and, because they are directed at a lesbian addressee, they may signify as a common viewpoint about "black people." Mistral assumes that the black man and black woman, or "blackness" in general, are objects of desire for Cabrera and Parra.[45] The fellow lesbian, who shares the bond of secrecy and the fear of societal shame, participates in a discourse forbidden in other quarters. Perhaps Mistral's own fear of retribution in, and her consequent silence on, sexual matters had to do with her uninhibited declarations in racial matters. It is peculiar that Cabrera, a well-known author of seminal books on Afro-Cuban religions and "folklore,"[46] was the recipient of Mistral's racial and racist fantasies, because Cabrera explicitly sought to portray the black people of Cuba in "respectable" terms, as profoundly religious people.

A negative sexualization of the black subject is apparent in "Primer recuerdo de Isadora Duncan," but initially Mistral understood the sexualization of Latin American blackness differently. In the correspondence she repeatedly alludes to Cabrera's collection *Cuentos negros de Cuba* [Black tales of Cuba] (French, 1936; Spanish, 1940), written to entertain Cabrera's lover, Parra, while she was in Switzerland undergoing treatment for tuberculosis, a disease that was ultimately fatal. Certainly, Mistral felt affection for both Cabrera and Parra, but there was even more at stake in this friendship: she may have wanted to experience two circuits of desire vicariously. One was the bond between the two lovers; the second was about Mistral herself, about incorporating Cabrera's folkloric "Afro-Cuban" tales into the master narrative of *América*.

In contrast to Mistral, Cabrera and Parra were well-to-do Latin American femmes. Expatriates living and writing in Paris when they met on a boat off the shores of Cuba, both wore impeccably stylish skirts and dresses, cropped their hair flapper-style, and exuded a carefree attitude. Their relationship with national allegiance was exilic in a different sense from Mistral's. For one thing, they did not need to work, whereas Mistral did. Additionally, Cabrera and Parra's initial involvement with Americanist discourse occurred under the European influence of primitivism, in a bohemian ambience. Neither had to network hard to get her first works published, whereas Mistral, who labored for twenty years as a schoolteacher in Chile, had to court male protectors on bases other than female coquettishness and family money.

The bond between Cabrera and Parra was probably all the more tantalizing to Mistral because of the tragic nature of Parra's sickness. Sickness was a major organizing principle of Mistral's self-representations. Mistral grew ever more resentful that she had had to work uninterruptedly since childhood, even after she had become famous. Ironically and sadly, she eventually did develop a variety of illnesses, including diabetes and arteriosclerosis, before dying of pancreatic cancer. Many critics have assumed that her references to sickness, decay, and age were faithful reflections of her own health, but this self-characterization began long before she was afflicted. It is profitable, then, to separate her empirical experience with disease and decay from her assumption of a subjectivity defined by illness and excessive work. The leisure that enveloped Cabrera and Parra deeply attracted Mistral. It marked them as members of a class to which she never quite belonged. Mistral's psychic need to become the "subject of work"—subjected to and subjectivized by labor, physical or mental—was related to her need to become the subject of illness.

Cabrera and Parra's model of the national writer, an individual freed from the shackles of iconicity, resonated deeply with Mistral's own troubled subjectivity. Mistral, electing to represent a kind of Latin American work ethic, had chosen to emphasize the utilitarian relationship between citizen and state. Furthermore, she had gendered and racialized this relationship of acquiescence to the common good, implanting it in the national psyche by posing as a mixed-race person. Cabrera and Parra, by contrast, remained resolutely white.

Mistral's letters to Cabrera inscribe eroticism as a racialized fantasy directly engaging black people. The first letter opens with a reference to a presumably shared racial discourse: "Dear Lydia: I have not forgotten about you. Connie always thinks of you as well. Believe me, both of us experience a sweet desire: that of knowing that you are a little happy, but not only with the Negroes."[47] Racial discourse functions as erotic teasing between couples who are "in the know" about each other. The connection between "happiness" and an unspecified group of "Negroes" [los negros] is laced with this obvious erotic tone.

In this passage from a letter written in Lisbon or Nice on 17 October 1938 or 1939, Mistral explains the substance of her own desire for a readily available, docile "blackness":

> I love you very much, even though I am mostly silent about it. I've had to move a few times; I've had an enormous amount of correspondence to deal with, as well as sicknesses of my own. And now the conflict of our people stuck in France without any money. I think I will soon leave this place; I know not when, or where I will go. I've had—it's been a few months now—a violent desire to go to the countryside; I think I will do everything possible to go to a place where there are very few people, where a foreign language is spoken, and where I can live with cows, pasture, and guinea hens. I feel ashamed at asking; sometimes I feel like trying out a great adventure and going off without any paid employment to live in a semitropical, American land and be a farmer. Do you know that [the French writer Georges] Bernanos, desperate as he was, has gone to Brazil and lives there, in a beautiful and barbaric land, which cost only two hundred francs per hectare? I feel sorry for you. This time around, you were very much the citizen, the lady of Lyon or Blois, but I increasingly feel that a field with black witch doctors, banana trees, and pineapple groves is my solution as well as yours. I hope I can offer you as much in a short period of time: a place without the European cold, without the decadent white man, and full of the many beasts of your [illegible].
>
> I will tell you as soon as I have it. Connie has undertaken to arrange my consular papers so that I can sleep and offer my happiness to black men, black women, and the grass. Don't think I have gone crazy because of the war; I've thought about it quite a lot. (73–74)[48]

Black people occupy a space parallel to that of women and indigenous people, since all three are deployed in Latin Americanist discourse as representations of archaic times, a period before "modernity." Moreover, for Mistral as well as for the Americanist discourse that she helped consolidate and eventually represented, black people occupied space in a remarkably different way from the indigenous peoples. Certainly, both blacks and indigenous people were part of spectacle. Indigenous people belong in the theater of labor; they are circumspect and detached from social life even as they materially contribute to it and anchor the national subject in an originary time. Blacks, though, exist in an unspecified but clearly ludic—and not precisely childlike—relationship to Mistral. Their interaction with her occurs in dream time, and it is to be played out in a pastoral setting, in "the grass."

Notably, women and indigenous people are always the subjects of work in Mistral's Americanist essays, always utilitarian and productive, whether of labor or of children. Mistral states that she yearns for Brazil, where she can work less and get more for her money, so to speak. What precisely will she get more of? More land, more time to write, and more pleasure— frolicking in the grass—a desire made explicit by reference to black people as fetishes. In the quoted passage, Mistral "couples" herself to this leisure time. This metaphor contrasts sharply with her actual "coupling" to Connie, who is joined to the work of keeping Mistral's affairs in order, as all her "secretaries" do. The lesbian couple emerges as the epitome of social order and utility, divorced from desire. Cabrera and Parra, partly because they traffic in this "entertaining" (private and sexualized) racial discourse, represent a rather different couple.

Mistral's desire, transcending her own fantasies, is projected onto the national screen of fantasies. She exhibits clear interest in the publication of Cabrera's folkloric tales. Offering to have *Cuentos negros de Cuba* published in Chile and to write a prologue for it, Mistral chides Cabrera for not working hard enough on the book. She argues that, since *Cuentos* was originally published in French (as *Contes nègres de Cuba*), it is imperative that it be published in Spanish so that it can find its true audience. Limiting the book to French is literally a crime [*villanía*]:

Why have you not written? When are you going to finish what you started? Do you want your *Black Tales* published in Chile? Make several typewritten copies, and once you know my address send them to me. Do you hear me? The Spaniard is a born suicide case, but I hope that you still have three drops of Indian blood and that they will save you. (74; Lisbon or Nice, 17 October 1938 or 1939)

I want you to publish the Spanish translation of the *Tales* once and for all. It is a crime to keep the book only in French. Do you hear me? I seem to recall offering you a prologue of mine. It's yours. (77; Nice, probably 1938)

In spite of her offer, Mistral never wrote the prologue, and the book was never published in Chile. Instead, Cabrera's well-known brother-in-law, the anthropologist Fernando Ortiz, penned the prologue, and the book was published in Cuba in 1940.

What would Mistral have written in her prologue to *Cuentos*? Surely she would not have included her racial fantasy about black people frolicking in the grass and witch doctors. An inappropriate tone might have seeped into the prologue, however, as it did into other writings of hers about the Caribbean and Brazil. Her essay "Antillas" [Antilles] (1930) was unfavorably received by the Cuban intelligentsia, who took exception to her description of the Caribbean islands as "a gypsy not addicted to bathing."[49] Mistral's representations of black schoolchildren in her pedagogical writings are often offensive. In "Recado de las voces infantiles" [Message about children's voices] (n.d.), for example, she describes them as perpetually dancing, laughing, and singing. Swaying their shoulders and hips "for everything," they are pleasurable little bodies occasionally given to impenetrable introspection, when they become plaintive and sullen. Nowhere in Mistral's known and published correspondence and prose works is there similar derision of or condescension toward indigenous peoples.[50] They are rendered childlike in another way: in the racist imaginary, they require parental intercession to be modernized; the state must supervise their labor. Black people, by contrast, are sexualized, as in Baker and the "witch doctors," or criminalized, a characterization that became personal with the death of Mistral's adopted son.

"Mulataje"

Mistral's writings about her stay in Brazil, where the Chilean government posted her at her own request at the outbreak of the Second World War, are markedly negative. Mistral did not experience her racial fantasy while consul in Petrópolis, and her adopted son, Juan Miguel Godoy, committed suicide in 1943. These two events—the dissolution of her fantasy and the trauma of real-life loss—led Mistral to level strident accusations of xenophobia at a generalized delinquent Brazilian *mulataje*, negating Brazil's inclusion in the rhetoric of *mestizaje*:

[To Reyes, 1947:] In that horrible country that you like so much—
Brazil—three doctors ruined me when they treated me for diabetes,
for tropical amoebas. They are bastards, *like most of the population.*

[To Tomic, 1948:] It has been five years since the murder of Yin Yin (he
did not commit suicide; he was "suicided" by xenophobic mulattoes).
His shadow walks alongside me. It is not horrible at all, but sweet and
faithful.

[To Tomic, 1951:] You may be surprised at this, but, let me tell you, I have
no intention of leaving Italy. I have come to love it much as I would a
person. I hate myself for having left her and having gone off to live out
the xenophobia of the Brazilian *mulataje.* I sacrificed Juan Miguel to
that country. You esteem it so much because you know it so little. There
I became acquainted with the most hateful and tribal xenophobia.

[To Reyes, 1954:] It is so sad not to have any family, my friends! I don't
even have a fourth cousin. Years ago I wrote some verses that went something like this: "Mine shall go with me into the lasting night." And I was
right. If I had somebody, they would kill him, Brazilian-style, and then
they would say he killed himself like Yin supposedly did. (How late I
came to realize this! How I resented him so!) The "gang" came up to my
very table one Christmas evening. They cynically confessed their deed.
After I had offended his memory with this pent-up hate! One never
knows the complete facts of anything. Sometimes not even one drop.[51]

The word *mulataje* first appeared in Mistral's article "El tipo del indio
americano" in 1932, just prior to the Cabrera correspondence. To understand the full implications of Mistral's often-remarked championing of
mestizaje, it is essential first to understand *mulataje*'s conceptual implications. The word *mulataje* does not merely describe a particular racial
mixing—white with black—but also denotes the presence of a racial
threat: the destruction of white children and the white family. Indigenous women may function as receptacles to carry the seed of the white
man, yet their racial mark is rationalized as minor compared with the
degrading and deforming mark attributed to black people. The sexualization of blacks changes to the pathologization of them as murderers.

Central to Mistral's racial narrative of Brazil is her recollection of
the death of her son, affectionately referred to as "Yin Yin." The circumstances of Yin Yin's birth—and death—are unclear. Mistral claimed that
he was her nephew, the son of an illegitimate brother (whom she had
never met) and a Spanish woman. How she located him, or was found
by his parents, has never been determined. Some critics suspect that Yin

Yin was not related to Mistral at all but was a Spanish infant she adopted during her years in Spain. Recently, a Chilean TV broadcast featured an interview with Mistral's last companion, the American Doris Dana. Dana alleged that Mistral had "confessed" the secret of Yin Yin's birth to her before she died: Mistral herself was Yin Yin's biological mother. However, Dana did not substantiate other biographical details nor provide any indication of when the birth had occurred, how and where Mistral had hidden during the final months of her pregnancy, or who the father was.[52]

At sixteen Yin Yin ingested a lethal dose of arsenic, and his death was ruled a suicide. Mistral, who never reconciled herself to this fact, created a narrative around his death by which she exonerated herself for his actions. In the following excerpt of a 1954 letter to Reyes, for instance, Mistral recasts the event as a racially motivated murder by a "gang" of black youngsters:

> Come Christmas, the gang that had tormented him in school came to my house. All four of them. I summoned the courage to ask them why they had killed such a sweet soul, who had been such a good friend to each one of them. This was their reply:
> "We know that Madam is still upset over this matter but *it had to be.*"
> I bolted out of my chair and replied: "Why did it 'have to be'?"
> "He had more than his fair share of things."
> "What did he have 'more than his fair share' of? I had to trick him so that he would go out with me. I had to tell him we would be buying clothes and shoes for me."
> "He had his name, your writer's name, which gave him prestige. He was also too white for his own good."
> "Villains," I said. "His being white and your being black were not his fault."[53]

Mistral believes that her child's death resulted from three factors: jealousy over his material possessions, the privilege of his whiteness, and the prestige of his writer mother. Mistral positions herself at the center of the tale as the reason for the murder and the ultimate source of whiteness. The relationship that matters is the one between her and the "gang." Yin Yin and his death are secondary. Mistral is convinced that his death was due to an excess of black people around him (there are four black children to one white child). In her racist vision, the balance of power favors violent criminals. Significantly, the scene of the crime is the school, its perpetrators are schoolchildren, and its victim is a student.

This excerpt represents the other side of Mistral's racial fantasy of excess. In this scenario the mother-child dyad is broken. *Mulataje*, a derogatory word indicating the racial mixing of white and black, is responsible for the disappearance of the (white) family. In other words, it interrupts the harmonious mix of *mestizaje* and destroys the national family. The black subject becomes excessive once again, but this time it is overtly rendered as violent, criminal, and cynical.

The evil children ("villains") cite Mistral's importance as a writer as one reason for his "murder," establishing the link between whiteness, writing, recognition, and fame. Mistral's own narcissism doubles as a nationalist narcissism in the context of a country well known for instituting prophylactic immigration policies to keep so-called undesirable seed out of Brazil. At that time immigration policies went hand in hand with policies of whitening, not only in Brazil but in all the nations of the Southern Cone.[54] In his 1976 lectures at the Collège de France, Foucault argued that in biopower, the war between "races" is replaced by state racism, which is characterized by a homicidal and suicidal impulse to make the race itself pure by exterminating some of its nationals. Mistral's morality tale eerily recalls Foucault's observation, as it provides a racial reason for the death of the race, rendered allegorically in Yin Yin's "murder."

Reyes was the same correspondent to whom Mistral described her initial reactions to the black Latin American subject; he was the privileged addressee when Mistral writes of her racial concerns. The anecdote of her son's death, however, did not circulate merely among acquaintances and friends. Mistral included it in her consular report for 1947 to the Republic of Chile, where it exists as part of the state record: "My tragic experience of Brazil—the death of my kin, provoked by the fact that 'he was too white for his own good'—persists like an open wound in my memory."[55] Mistral specialists agree that her accusation of murder is false and that Yin Yin committed suicide. They attribute the narrative to Mistral's delirious musings, aroused by grief, illness, and/or old age. However, its racist and violent implications should not be summarily dismissed.

One might wonder whether Mistral's charge of xenophobia against Brazil was confined to a mostly private or unofficial space, namely, her correspondence, but one of her late essays, "Imagen y palabra en la educación" [Image and word in education], delivered as a speech in 1956, shortly before her death, suggests otherwise:

> Sometimes the foreigner goes there [to a certain country] because he has read in the newspaper that the country needs specialists in this branch or the other. Or he comes merely to enjoy a climate that is recommended for his health. One day a corpse appears in an apartment or in a street. The city then knows that a harmless creature, who once celebrated the beautiful land that sustained it, has been eliminated for no reason at all. Only because of a grotesque antipathy toward a white face and blue eyes. The investigation is launched. When the perpetrator or his accomplice is found, he usually declares without any remorse whatsoever, and often with pride at having eliminated the foreigner, that "that man was too white for his own good." I am here relating my own experience, of my own kin. I offer it without mentioning the country, out of respect, because it is a Latin American country. . . . I speak on behalf of those who cannot speak for themselves. I speak because it is absolutely necessary that in those regions of the world we add to the penal code the crime of xenophobia, a crime which is little known but frequent. I shall not give the names of these countries, because the only thing I care about, as a Christian, is that racial crimes disappear once and for all from the face of the earth. I am talking about crimes committed because of light or dark skin, or the simple fact of speaking another language.[56]

This passage exhibits the same ambivalence that surfaced in relation to legalized white supremacy in "Primer recuerdo de Isadora Duncan." Mistral speaks out against racial crimes but refuses to choose as a representative example the obvious victims of racial crime in Latin America: black or indigenous people. Instead, Mistral's example of xenophobia is the invented crime committed against Yin Yin (now a "man"). The guilty party becomes an entire country marked as black, Latin American, non-Spanish-speaking, and criminal. Brazil is portrayed as a dangerous and criminal country. Mistral codes its black identity in official language as xenophobic, and hatred of the foreigner becomes hatred of whiteness. The formerly mestiza Mistral is now white—"too white for [her] own good." And Mistral, the national writer of Latin America, is in danger. She epitomizes Latin America, and Latin America—at least the one that must survive—is white.

Immigration

Mistral saw the indigenous woman as the bearer of mestizo national children. The black woman was the creator of murderous black children.

Both were subordinate, of course, to the white elites. The elites always sought, as a first solution, to keep their whiteness intact, either by preserving themselves as a small landowning group with power, by cordoning off their women from any threat of contagion, or by aggressively promoting policies to whiten and Europeanize the general population. Therefore, queer sexuality in Latin America cannot be divorced from the primacy of whiteness in the national social hierarchy.

Notable Latin American queers, such as Mistral, were just as notably invested in maintaining their status as "white people." Some of the most important queer writers and intellectuals turned their attention to immigration as a solution to the nation's racial problematic. The discursive manipulations of *mestizaje, mulataje,* and immigration happened at one and the same time, conforming the subjectivities and shaping the writing of much of Latin America's queer canon.

Mistral could not fully pursue a literary career in Chile, and she was indirectly expelled from the country even as she was upheld as its national symbol and emissary. As Mistral specialists have indicated, Chile's attitude toward its own icon was always conflicted.[57] The ambivalence was connected to Mistral's equivocal gender status: Chile's most famous international patriot was not a "son" but a "daughter," and this fact was undoubtedly experienced as a psychic dilemma, suggesting a queer origin for the nation. Chile's beloved daughter was also a "mother" of the nation, but this mother resembled, most certainly, a man. Mistral was masculine in both appearance and demeanor and inhabited a public sphere managed by men.[58]

The question of who should be allowed inside Chile and who should remain outside dominates Mistral's writings on immigration. In the article "Sobre la mujer chilena" [About the Chilean woman] (1946), Mistral lists the "better" migrations to Chile, as well as the "unproductive" ones.[59] Her insistence on racial difference and correct versus incorrect racial mixings is striking; it recalls her racial reasoning in "The Type of the Indian of the Americas" and is echoed later in her life as a kind of paranoia, verging at times on fascistic nationalism.

The issue of reproduction is also central to Mistral's articulation of immigration. Interestingly, Mistral's image of the indigenous woman—that is, a woman who transcended being abhorred by becoming beautiful—uncannily mirrored her own experience in Chile. From objects of disdain and even hatred, both images evolved into beautiful and sealed receptacles of nationality that nevertheless remained outside in an important way. Mistral became a revered icon in Chile (through much fabrication) only when she no longer resided there. Her elevation was contingent on her displacement from the national confines. The indigenous woman might have been the receptacle of the race, but she was never hailed as a significant social actor, much less as a leader.

It is a commonplace that Mistral was the first Chilean to defend the mestizo and to call for an improvement in the lives of indigenous peoples. This aspect of *mestizaje*, it is assumed, had been all but absent from mainstream Chilean discourse on nationality and race. However, the entire idea of a Chilean personality, of the authentic Chilean, is a racial project in itself (to return to Omi and Winant's useful formulation). Moreover, Mistral's was not the first instance of the vindication of indigenous peoples in the context of nation building. Major Chilean thinkers had recurred to a biological argument grounded in racial mixing to develop the idea of a Chilean personality and collective destiny.[60] Néstor Palacios, author of *Raza chilena* [Chilean race] (1900), exalts the Chilean *roto* as the genesis of the modern Chilean, the descendant of the equally bellicose Arawak and Teutons. His reference to a "mestizo race" represents a fascistic faith in racial depuration, defined by social and biological civil war. It is also a thoroughly gendered *mestizaje:* indigenous woman paired with white man. Palacios attributes the success of this *mestizaje* to the "good fortune" of the Teutons, who kept their race "pure" until they conquered Chile. Unsurprisingly, he privileges the white race in this construction.[61]

"Sobre la mujer chilena" provides an example of the differential racializations of women and of their stratified link in the common function of reproduction for the good of the nation:

> One has only to see and hear for a brief moment to know that the refuge high in the lairs of vultures is the industry of a single woman. The Andean man does not know any other thing than to go down to the mines ... and dynamite rocks. He does not take care of himself; he does not succeed at forming a nest. ... If he does not have this woman by his side, he slips, day by day, ever closer to the barbarism of the first Indians. The type of pure action, of action no matter the cost that is the imprint of the Chilean male, from Lautaro to Portales, seems to take over his companion, tearing her away from the vicissitudes of sedentarism and turning her into his likeness.[62]

The woman is whitened as the opposite of the Indianized man, whose tendency toward barbarism dominates him. The woman is also masculinized, taking over the male prerogative because the man has become dangerously effeminate as well as barbarous. Consider Palacios's narrative of the conquest: the strong Teuton man arrived in the nick of time to provide his seed to the indigenous woman and thus create the strong Chilean race. But here the woman is white and the man is indigenous. In contrast to the timeless, immobile indigenous woman, this "white or *mestiza* woman" is on the move to compensate for the lack of masculine behavior in "her man":

> They say she is "temperamental." The starting point of her rapture is almost always absolute love, from whose flame the most sensible of actions as well as the most unbridled of fantasies emerge. This white or *mestiza* woman follows her man to the desert of salt, without reproaching him for her exile. This brave woman will raise six children in the Central Valley, stretching a salary that will sustain only two. She will migrate in order not to lose her born wanderer. She will go to the Argentinean provinces or to California, where she will do battle for her bread in the midst of all the foreigners. If she is young and should chance to go to school, there she will also succeed in creative exercises or in the subtle art of forming a household. (62)

More than a sentimentalized notion of motherhood or a cover for Mistral's own lack of children, the issue of reproduction is truly a matter of hierarchies, specifically racial hierarchies. Immigration is not a case of national generosity, tolerance, or practicality; it is a battle in which the strongest will survive. There is here, however, an appeal to psychologistic, gender-based language. The dualism between sensible actions and unbridled fantasies is highly suggestive in the context of national allegiance. Mistral speaks of "absolute love," setting up the white woman as an active exemplar for a populace, a different type of vessel from the indigenous woman. This argument suggests that the state cannot afford merely to appeal to reason and utilitarianism; it must enlist or spark other emotions as well, especially those most closely associated with the queer woman, for, at the end of the passage, there is a somewhat queer turn toward education that does not quite fit into the description.

Thus, Mistral "queers" national racial thinking. Nevertheless, her unspoken alliances with the racially privileged in Chile have a clear genealogy. These alliances are powerful precisely because they are internalized, silent, and unchallenged. Latin American racial discourse resolves competing racial mixtures in binaries: *mestizaje* indicates white/indigenous; *mulataje* indicates white/black. The issue of immigration presents the state with the haunting specter of endless combinations even as it utilizes immigration to whiten the population. This is the context in which Mistral's adherence to the Mexican model of *mestizaje* should be understood.

Mistral regarded true racial heterogeneity as disturbing, and only the binary implied in *mestizaje* was comfortable for her. For Mistral, *mestizaje* was a thoroughly gendered construction, similar to Palacios's argument. She discussed her ideas on immigration regularly with her contemporaries. In a 1948 interview with Salvador Novo, she hoped to address her discomfort with the subject directly to Miguel Alemán, president of Mexico.[63]

Alemán had recruited Mistral through Jaime Torres Bodet, persuading her to return to Mexico. Alemán probably hoped that she would take up permanent residence in Veracruz, for she perpetually sought the perfect place to live and the perfect climate in which to nurse her ever-increasing ailments. Nominally, Mistral's health justified her preference for "tropical" climates. But her attempts to take up permanent residence in Puerto Rico; in Brazil; in Santa Barbara, California; and in Veracruz uncannily coincided with state agendas regarding black populations.

Why Mistral was invited to live in Mexico a second time is uncertain. By 1948, when she arrived in Veracruz, she had long been estranged from Vasconcelos, her original patron. The Mexican scholar Luis Mario Schneider observes that "precise information about the purpose of her second visit to Mexico is lacking. Perhaps the documentation will be found someday in the official archives. The only thing we know for sure is that Jaime Torres Bodet, minister of foreign relations, conveyed the official invitation from President Miguel Alemán."[64] Schneider perceives that there may have been a political reason to invite Mistral, and this would not be surprising, as all official invitations carry a political bent. However, it is highly significant that Mistral was asked to take up residence in Veracruz, historically the state with the largest black population in Mexico. Yet, as Sagrario Cruz and researchers working primarily in anthropology have noted, Mexicans who live in Veracruz and are descended from its black communities rarely identify themselves as black.[65] These historians and anthropologists argue that this lack of self-identification stems from the Mexican state's aggressive promotion of *mestizaje* as the identity of Mexicans. They maintain that Mexican blacks have been eliminated from public discourse so that the indigenous peoples may be upheld as the true subalterns of Mexico. There have been some studies of Mexico's blacks during colonial times, but there has been little research on the government's policy toward them immediately following the Mexican Revolution. It is conceivable, given Mistral's importance in the enterprise of propaganda for the Latin American states and in light of her correspondence and interviews with leading Mexican intellectuals, that the government's invitation to her was tied, at least in part, to an undisclosed policy toward blackness.

One such intellectual, Salvador Novo, offers an interesting point of comparison. Novo wrote about his sexual exploits in his autobiography *La estatua de sal* [The salt statue], unpublished and forgotten until its recent rescue by the noted Mexican writer and public intellectual Carlos Monsiváis.[66] It is clear from the text that Novo's homosexuality was anything but a secret. Today he would be considered an "openly" gay writer. So it is reasonable to ask whether Mistral's sexuality also was not only a known fact but also, perhaps, an ingredient in her attractiveness to the state project of mothering the nation.

In discussing Mistral's stay in Veracruz, Schneider refers to an interview Novo conducted with Mistral for the Mexican press. Schneider excerpts only a few brief lines from the interview. The complete text contains a telling exchange:

> And then I heard a defense from her [Mistral's] lips, which I transcribe here and subscribe to with the greatest fervor:
> "There is one thing that I should like to call to the attention of President Alemán. It is a grave and dangerous situation, and a very painful one, for those Mexicans who cross the border to work in California. It is urgent and necessary that this situation be taken care of immediately."
> Gabriela Mistral lives in Santa Barbara, California, a state of the Union whose laws prohibit the marriage of Mexicans—"colored"—with white women. When they happen, they are annulled and [the participants] fined, but they don't happen too often. The trucks with cattle are loaded with Mexican workers. Single men, destined to live in separate neighborhoods, where they are discriminated against. The only contact they are allowed is with black women, ugly, of the worst species.

As the years go by, the entire region boils with mestizo creatures of black and Mexican blood, [a mixture] that degrades and effaces the fine Mexican race.

"Why in God's name do they not let the Mexicans take their women with them?" [Mistral asked.] . . .

Connie listened to our conversation, and she offered new and painful examples of this tragic situation.[67]

Novo did not exaggerate Mistral's racial animosity in his rendering of the interview. She repeats the incident verbatim in correspondence with Reyes from 1950, referring to the children of Mexicans and blacks as a threat to the national identity: "Soon there boils a *mulataje*, and this, *this* is what they call Mexican!" Reyes replies: "A very serious thing indeed, the condemnation of *mulataje* that you mention to me. I will talk with the appropriate people."[68]

Here Mistral believes that the matter of national reproduction is at risk; she finds that sex between Mexican men and black women, as well as their offspring, is unacceptable and not Latin American. There are other, more subtle and fascinating issues at stake as well. First, Mistral addresses Novo, another prototype of the national writer and, like Mistral, gay and employed by the state (in the Ministry of Education, no less). Second, the anecdote concludes with a reference to "Connie," Mistral's companion. A triangle of queer intellectuals discusses the possible disappearance of the Mexican race, caused by unregulated blackness, specifically by black women. All lay claim to women nationals as "theirs," serving one function, reproduction, which has one end: to produce the best nationals, mestizos. But none of these three queer subjects produced any biological children, much less mestizos. Even Mistral's son was emphatically represented as white. Their conversation raises a question: Why should the offspring of Mexican men and (presumably American) black women not be considered mestizos, too?

This much is clear: Mistral was on a quest to become the sealed receptacle of the race, much like the indigenous woman she exalted. She considered herself a vessel of reproduction and a keeper of the national and racial essence, and in a perverse way her queerness abetted her status as singularly suited to this endeavor. Although publicly she often referred to herself as ugly, privately she may well have thought of herself as special, if not beautiful. In mirroring Novo's perception of black women as "ugly, of the worst species" [feas, de la peor especie],[69] did Mistral not somehow present herself as a vessel of beauty, as the product of the successful "aesthetic eugenics" that Vasconcelos promoted? In cooperating with other queer intellectuals to uphold a heteronormative ideal of respectability, did Mistral not affect the shape of Latin American queerness to come?

The idea of ugly races, expressed by Vasconcelos, survived in Mistral's work to the end. Despite the accolades included in her official discourses, Mistral never abandoned the private belief that Afro-Latin Americans were not Latin Americans and did not meet the aesthetic requirements of "the race." Whereas Vasconcelos believed in the voluntary phasing out of "inferior" races (of which his example is black people), Mistral claimed that Mexican-black couples brought unacceptable children of mixed mestizo and black heritage into the world, children who by definition could not be Latin American, because they failed to meet the aesthetic criterion. Notably, this was not only Mistral's belief; it was shared by Reyes and Novo, two pillars of the ideal of Latin American *mestizaje*. Queer Latin American writing, then, is, at least on some important occasions, imbricated with heteronormative desire.

Queerness?

Three critical operations are at work throughout Mistral's writings on the subject of the Latin American "race." The first is the disavowal of blackness. Simply stated, black populations have existed since colonial times in all the viceroyalties. The fact that the communities did not survive in the Southern Cone after the nineteenth century indicates that the founding of the nation-states therein depended on a process of forgetting and reinvention, not unlike that of repression in psychoanalysis. How should the fact that Mistral praised blacks publicly and despised them privately be addressed? Should scholars simply dismiss this as a minor point, in consideration of Mistral's championing of indigenous peoples and of women and children? It is extraordinary that Mistral acted as if she had never known of the black populations of Latin America prior to her travels to the Caribbean in the 1930s and that she responded to the black subject with stereotypical white responses: anxiety, sexualization, and pathologization. The celebrated Freudian formula of disavowal perfectly describes this operation.[70] Mistral knew that there were Latin Americans who were black, but, for her, Latin Americans were indigenous, period. The discursive operations of Latin

Americanism obliterated the black subject from aesthetic and also political representation.

The second operation in Mistral's writings is the complicity of the language of diversity in the practices of white-supremacist thinking.[71] Some critics have dismissed Mistral's story of Yin Yin's death as mere "madness" or as a "personal" deviation. The genealogy of *mestizaje* in her thinking demonstrates, however, a bifurcation between what Mistral publicly declared and what she privately believed. The confidences shared in less formal venues, such as correspondence and interviews, were not, of course, entirely private; their circulation among a select group of intellectuals and newspaper readers suggests, at the very least, public racial ambivalence. Mistral's cry of racial murder in the death of Yin Yin, though certainly inflected with grief and possibly guilt, cannot be attributed solely to these feelings. That is, one can be either aggrieved or mentally unstable and still be a racist. While critics have discounted the seriousness of Mistral's accusations because of the extreme circumstances that gave rise to them, they have effaced another extreme: Mistral's characterization of black national subjects.

The third operation is the role played by Mistral's queerness in her racialized nationalism. Mistral "queered" the nation, to be sure, yet this queering advanced not only heteronormativity but also the unspoken Latin Americanist racial project. Her maternal grief and any allusions to her personal feelings should supplement, not obscure, the analysis of her nationalist maternal discourse and how much it had to do with securing "the reproduction of the nation." While Mistral's official discourse celebrates the abstract qualities of the mother and the child, some of her other speech genres leave no doubt that certain women could never be mothers in this sense and that their children would never be counted as Latin American children. There are no necessary, certain, or predictable alliances between sexually oppressed people and racially oppressed people. Not only Mistral as a queer but also Mistral's nationally projected queerness helped articulate the state discourse about the reproduction of the nation, an example of Foucault's "right to life" within biopower. Between a prohibited sexual identity and a racist national identity lie the contradictions of Mistral as a race woman: proclaiming *latinoamericanismo*'s tenets, doing the work of its gendered and heteronormative formulations, and reproducing the racist and homophobic state.

CHAPTER TWO

Schooling and Sexuality

What led the state to highlight the dangerous liminality of the schoolteacher by choosing a *rara* [queer] to be its supreme representation? Undeniably, an aspect of the schoolteacher's role was to serve as a model of morals and virtue.[1] But is the assumption that "femininity" was a primary requirement necessarily correct? Indeed, if Mistral was the symbolic prototype of the schoolteacher—if this image became indelible in the minds of schoolchildren and their parents throughout Latin America—then sexual ambiguity arguably had a role to play in the psychic process of national schooling. Essential both to Mistral's rise and to the rise of the nationalism she helped spawn is the role played by her queerness and by the melancholic identification it enabled. Both Mistral and the state encouraged the national introjection of a sexually ambiguous woman in place of the mother, at the same time that queerness was despised and denigrated.

Scholars have regarded normal education in Latin America as a reformist development in the emancipation of women, a stage in their professionalization.[2] Certainly, it was: through the institution of the normal school, thousands of women entered the workforce and supported their families. These families, though, far from being the whole, complete, and healthy national family so encouraged in the discourse of hygiene and child care, were, more often than not, incomplete, partial, and feminine. Many schoolteachers came from families in which the highly symbolic male head had been severed; this was precisely the case with our exemplar, Gabriela Mistral. Yet women were forbidden to occupy this symbolic space, even as they sometimes assumed the helm of the family. Recent scholars might classify these families as "dysfunctional" because of the absence of the male provider or breadwinner. Indeed, in Chile several leading intellectuals of the day made such arguments. The figure of the *roto*, the fatherless mestizo (literally "the broken one" in English), emerged: the boy with an indigenous mother and an absent white father.[3] Therefore, the emergence of the schoolteacher, and of the woman schoolteacher in particular, arose in the context of the absence of the "national" man. Strikingly, Mistral's psychology is understood in these terms as well, a matter I explore in the second half of this chapter.

Contemporary scholars sometimes characterize the school as a machine of cultural transmission—a huge, unifying institution created to reproduce national subjects, erasing their differences and subsuming all into the ideal of the nation (i.e., Chile, Argentina, Mexico). One such example is included in Beatriz Sarlo's recent book, *La máquina cultural* [The cultural machine], specifically the essay "Cabezas rapadas y cintas argentinas" [Shaved heads and Argentine ribbons].[4] This testimonial narrative, in which Sarlo gives written expression to the words of an Argentinean schoolteacher, Rosa del Río, is accompanied by a scholarly interpretation; notably, it's characterized by a nostalgic appreciation of a past and by a desire to imprint the individual life with the calling of a collective. In this case, the collective is the Argentine nation, as defined by the modernizing project of the liberal state in the early twentieth century. Rosa del Río, daughter of poor immigrants, recounts her entry into the professionalized middle class in Argentina through the institution of the normal school. The normal school reproduced at a social level the program of the liberal state. Indeed, what makes the schoolteacher fascinating to Sarlo is precisely how representative del Río is—how perfectly she reproduced the state culture as part of a liberal army of schoolteachers.

Although Sarlo does not impute this fact to gender, she does partake of an unquestioned assumption that all schoolteachers in Latin America were women. Undeniably, many were, but not all. Mistral's father, curiously enough, is an example of a male schoolteacher, and there were many others like him. It would be more profitable to pinpoint the time at which the state joined the image of the schoolteacher to women or, more accurately, to "woman." It is also imperative to investigate why the transnational image of the schoolteacher was so masculine. The example of Mistral may allow for a more nuanced approach than the one taken by Sarlo.

The schoolteacher became a primary vehicle for the world-making project of the state. She was the first official image of the state the child received, and often she articulated the existence of a national public that was violent. The state destroyed any experience, allegiance, or feeling that it deemed "foreign" to the national temperament. Immigrant children, for example, suffered the violent destruction of their first identification with the culture of their parents. Indigenous children also suffered psychic violence in the name of "belonging." In fact, one of Mistral's contradictions is that she repeatedly insisted on the particular and the local, and tried to keep intact a sense of cultural differences even while she promoted the standardization of experience in other realms—clearly a vexed, if not an untenable, position.

In Sarlo's view, schoolteachers had so little potential for difference that they could carry out the rationality of the program to excess, thus exemplifying the state in all of its brute force. In other words, state culture was unified and succeeded in the creation of a unified subject. Sarlo is convinced of the success of liberalization. She takes for granted the smooth, though violent, incorporation of immigrants and other racialized subjects into national space. Although Sarlo admits that schoolteachers were paid little, she stresses that they might have been fulfilled at some modest level. Sarlo claims that because they reproduced the dicta of the state, schoolteachers "owned" something: middle-class culture, if not middle-class prosperity. As Sarlo writes, there was perfect success on the part of the state when it enlisted schoolteachers to do the work of social reproduction: "And this testifies to the efficaciousness of the State (something that appears incredible today) and to the fixity with which the State modeled public servants, introducing in the first place this idea: the repetition of an inflexible and intrusive task of forming identities and subjects" (76).

Mistral's characterization of actual teaching as tedium bordering on insanity suggests, in contrast, both lack of ownership and lack of identification with the state project.[5] At times, she severely criticized the Chilean government for treating schoolteachers, especially those in the countryside, like people in forced-labor camps.[6] Some of her more intimate thoughts on this subject appear in incidental writings or in draft versions of speeches that were not published during her lifetime. In the absence of a diary or of a journal of record, these texts acquire an enormous importance as a counterpoint to Mistral's public persona, especially during her early years.

In the draft version of the essay "Colofón con cara de excusa" [Colophon to offer an apology], published as "Comento a *Ternura*" [A comment on *Ternura*] (1941), Mistral poignantly and irately recounts the reasons she entered into education:

> *Children's* pedagogy, which is the most bitter to learn, was not tyrannical because it was a super-pedagogy, but precisely for the contrary. Its intentions were good: to take advantage of *that,* even of *that,* to make of the little ones exemplary sons and daughters and individuals. . . .
>
> By that time I was inside the prison or the trap. That is to say, I was an *official* schoolteacher, and I was one for twenty years, which means that I lived a saturation of that imperialism at once small and absolute. . . . Naturally I did not live there according to my heart's desire. . . .
>
> . . . I left teaching at the critical moment, at the best moment. They say that all crises are good, as liquidation. I left teaching at the point when the trap did not so much disgust me as anger me, so much so that the only option left was to leave, to change profession, customs, and residence. (Mistral's emphasis)[7]

From these remarks, it is apparent that the draft version of "Colofón" started out as an angry tirade against Mistral's own myth, showing that her early biography was opposite in nearly every way to the mythology surrounding her. Instead of adherence to, and admiration for, the national project of making "miniature citizens" out of children,[8] Mistral criticizes this imperative, suggesting that youngsters should not be indoctrinated into allegiance. She calls teaching a "trap," perhaps providing an explanation for why the final version of "Colofón" recommends an "escape" into a vaguely defined, soporific survival.[9]

Consider how Mistral speaks directly about her "personal" feelings regarding children:

> But I left behind my best years. I left behind my pretty material, the only element in this world that does not become misty, that doesn't wrinkle, that doesn't burn, the lot, the group, the mob of children. Well, better put, of the child, because I like them far better, I care for them more in the singular, and not in legion. I also like them when they are small like a flower's stem, or of the height of a three-year-old orange tree. Yes, exactly like I am saying: I like them alone, a few, and better yet, unique.

I left the schools. I did not see them en masse again, only occasionally. Little by little my eyes started cleansing themselves of the rows of seats, of the gymnasiums, of the geometrically-disposed classroom resembling a chessboard, of the responses written in "correct and complete sentences," of the school composition, like a farm of poisonous legumes, and the artificial realm of children. . . . (176)

If I had not had to become a schoolteacher at age 14 in order to more or less feed myself, if I had not had to later become a professor in order to eat, if I had not had to learn from my superiors to discard my language of my native Valley of Elqui, more Castilian than the Spanish of Santiago, of any capital, of Buenos Aires or Montevideo. It's my innermost tongue, which I learned from my mother. . . . That's the language I should have made my verses from. . . . It was too bad to have another language stuck on me like an arid seal, and to have to make moralizing verses with it as if I were a disguised Aesop. (177)

The complex discursive entity that is Mistral's poetic child should be understood as a narcissistic projection of Mistral, and not as the child that the state upheld at the symbolic level. It may be hard to believe, but most scholars still defend Mistral's pronouncements on children, sentimentality, and women and the home as a reflection of her personal feelings. Most notably, instead of happily choosing the teaching profession because of an innate desire for service, Mistral explains in this fragment that she had to teach to avoid starvation. The discussion of schooling and pedagogy as a completely bureaucratic language, not only devoid of but perhaps openly hostile to the world of feelings, is conspicuously absent in any consideration of Mistral and her writings.

Teaching, in the strict, empirical sense, was clearly a mode of survival for many of the women involved—understandably, given the harshness of the times. Less noticed is that the state promoted teaching in the discursive sense as a route to another type of survival—national survival and strengthening through nourishment of a national body, a historical fact that the testimonial collected by Sarlo starkly illustrates. Mistral, from the preceding passage, evidently knew that the schooling provided by the state was a program of normalization of social subjects; she points out the standardization of space, of speech, and of writing. Apparently, part of her intent in writing "Colofón" (excised from the final version of 1945) was to communicate the enormous sense of tedium and tiredness that teaching entailed, perhaps to explain why she claimed in the final version that "children's expression . . . fools sight and hand with its false clarity."[10]

Because of the advent of industrial society, schoolteachers were charged with the violence of effecting a break in which intellectual and manual knowledge were separated.[11] Teachers suffered a partitioning of mental labor into hierarchical levels. Sarlo's oral history concentrates on this aspect. The teacher herself never attended university. As historian Francesca Miller notes, "Women could not attend the universities, and secondary schools for women were scarce in most societies, nonexistent in others.... Normal-school graduates completed their certificates at the age of seventeen or eighteen, and they were barred from entry to universities, as their preparation was considered inferior to that of secondary, or preparatory, school students."[12] The schoolteacher was a transitional object, and a potentially murdered object, intellectually speaking. She was charged with shepherding a class of manual laborers through a bureaucratic training, while those designated for the faculties of "thinking" and "leadership" in the nation attended first preparatory or secondary school, and then the university.

Only in her overtly propagandistic work does Mistral present herself as a happy soldier of the state. (Sarlo actually refers to teachers as "state robots.")[13] More often than not, Mistral shows how schoolteaching led to a kind of hatred of the child. It's conceivable that this emotion—hate—was as central to the maternalist national project, indeed to the entire nationalist project, as was the more celebrated and dissected emotion of love.

State Suspects

Both the child and the mother were suspicious from the state's viewpoint. The difference was that the state cared much more for the child's potential than it did for the mother. As Ann Laura Stoler explains, what Foucault termed the "pedagogization of children's sex"[14] cannot be separated from the calculated management of life and from what he termed "the genealogy of racism."[15] The schools were an integral part of the management of sexuality for the health of the state; they were part of the state's preoccupation with the health of the race. As Stoler writes: "The historiography on nationalism and pedagogy, on patriotism and the moral training of schoolchildren suggests that there was nothing 'all of a sudden' about the concern for children's sexuality at all."[16] (Sarlo's piece implicitly emphasizes this fact.) Children embodied what needed to be "fixed" in the society. Stoler further describes the mother's role as being a model "of restraint of passion and individual self-control."[17] In the absence of any other view, mothers are cast as either passive or complicit with the state. They seem to identify with the state's role for them, which is to aid the state in "educating consent,"[18] cooperating with the creation of children as "heirs to the national patrimony and the race."[19] In this scheme, schoolteachers do no more than continue this role. Sarlo, for her part, exhibits a quasifuturistic fascination with the state as "cultural machine." She considers schoolteachers as pawns in this process, rendering them remarkably passive.

The smooth identification of schoolteachers with mothers, of mothers with the state, and of schoolteachers with the state posits women's role as being only about serving the repressive state.[20] Perhaps the state made an alliance with privileged mothers, but the alliance would be untenable if it were applied across the board. It's necessary to complicate this analysis if we are to grasp the complexities entailed in the teacher's existence and the place of sexuality in the entire scheme. It's important to remember that Foucault sought to investigate "the most immediate, the most local power relations at work ... with effects of counterresistance and counterinvestments, so that there has never existed one type of stable subjugation, once and for all," thus refuting the existence of any one Great Power and preferring to map a field of multiple and mobile power relations.[21]

Mistral was aware of the need to deal with the "problem of the mother." Historian Asunción Lavrin explains how the state specifically targeted the mother figure as the problem behind the development of the national child.[22] Mistral also believed that the various institutions set up to police the home and the child made sense in light of a fair number of "ignorant mothers." The state established Juntas Protectoras de Infancia [Protective Boards of Early Childhood], sent social workers called the *visitadoras de hogar* [literally, visitors of the home] to check on the welfare of children in the care of their mothers, and created *círculos de madres* [gatherings of mothers]. All existed to increase the chances of controlling the unpredictable variable that was the mother.

The relationship between the schoolteacher and the mother, Mistral suggests, must also be monitored. The system is established so that eventually the schoolteacher is bound to usurp the child from its mother:

I hesitate to accept the substitution that you desire—of the mother by the schoolteacher. This, for one reason: the teacher rarely is worthy of substituting even the most mediocre of mothers because she sees children as part of a mass; she sees serving them as serving a client; she may give them her knowledge, but she does not love them deeply and she cannot replace the other woman, for whom the child Pedro or Juan exist as individuals. . . . We have to help the mother, without usurping her little one. I do not know of a more marvelous human couple than that of a true mother and a true schoolteacher, inventing, through games and lessons, ways in which to bring out the best in a creature. With this couple in mind, we can create the new little man *that we desire.*[23]

Insightfully, in her discussion Stoler summarizes one of Foucault's findings that is relevant here: "a turn away from 'forbidden relationships' enacted to the production of new truth claims about individuals who now can be known not by their actions, but by what they desire."[24] The series of couples listed in the passage—mother-child, teacher-child, mother-teacher—fulfill different functions. The mother-child and the teacher-child are both sites of dangerous and antinational excess. One represents an excess of love that will hinder the process of extracting the child from the home and making him or her a national laborer. The other represents a lack of love that will alienate the child from the state, creating an obstacle to profitability as well. Both are "female" extremes. The strange couple that Mistral proposes—the mother-teacher—appears as the solution, the balancing of extremes, presumably because it joins the private and the social world for the child, without causing him or her to be caught exclusively in either. But this situation—of being kept exactly at the point of separation, permanently suspended between sets of needs constructed as incompatible—admits close scrutiny and may well have become the unarticulated target point of state education. (Notably, the father figure is completely absent from any of the couples.)

Traditional interpretations of Mistral's "maternal" figure, such as the desexualized mother, the stock matronly figure, and the avuncular figure, illustrate aspects of gender that apply to her. Although they all point to the question of her gender variance, the failure to take queer sexuality into account leaves the analysis short of interpretive power. They also fail because none of these figures evokes national desire at a mass level, and yet Mistral clearly did. If Mistral were simply a desexualized matronly figure, national identification wouldn't have been as efficacious. The riddle of Mistral's "maternal" discourse and the "queerness" of the figure of the schoolteacher demand and yield sharper arguments than those yet offered.

Mistral certainly utilized the ready-made discourse of maternalism strategically during her career. But ultimately her deployment of the figure of the schoolteacher—even if this was not her intention—entailed a repudiation of actual mothers as a threat to the state. Whether or not Mistral, the individual, was concerned about the protection of mothers, Mistral as an ideal of identification crystallized a more complicated process.

Instead of taking Mistral's official pronouncements on mothers, children, and schools as reflections of her own "feminine" sentiment, one should read them literally as state discourse on the problem of rearing future citizens. The subjectivation of women was critical to the projected path of the citizenry. The state could not simply relieve mothers of their duties, although at some points it may have contemplated whether it could do so. The state instead enlisted mothers, not because of a concern for their welfare or that of their children, but rather because of a concern for the needs of industrial society and because it simply did not have enough resources to make the schools totally sufficient centers for the administration of children's lives.

The state fully exploited Mistral's ambiguity in terms of gender and sexuality, because a public figure who was willing to occupy all the zones of attachment of the citizen would help inspire a melancholic identification in the citizenry. To be sure, neither Mistral nor the public was necessarily conscious at every level of this articulation, as both might have been with an explicit plan. Nevertheless, private and public understandings of queerness may have existed, and they probably involved rigid, binary ideas of "feminine" and "masculine" behavior, so that "Mistral as schoolteacher" both supplanted missing virility and was seen as a threat to it.

Additionally, one of the fundamental aspects entailed in the loss of the mother was racial loss. Mistral's assumption of the role of national mother, her supplanting of the actual lost mother through a mestiza pose, offset the state's racism toward many of its subjects and displaced it toward mothers, who were characterized as stupid or unable to cope with the developments of modernization—a sort of lost generation. Going back to the Chilean creation of the *roto* figure, the schoolteacher supplanted the lost white father, whereas the mother continued to occupy a denigrated, racialized role. Indigenous men disappeared from the picture.

Undoubtedly, the schoolteacher was involved in the deployment of dominant gender, sexual, and racial strictures: the right type of "man," the embodiment of the national "woman" through the "mother," and so forth.[25] This could have been accomplished by any teacher regardless of sex; these facts still do not account for why schoolteachers were figured as women en masse, when we know there were male schoolteachers. It is true that women were a source of cheap labor, and their entry into service sectors and professions like teaching did not destabilize the status quo of gender roles or of differential pay and prestige in a patriarchal society. Still, these realities do not explain, by themselves, the singular success of this ambiguous image at the transnational level. There is some aspect of the figure of the woman schoolteacher—who often seems to be not very "feminine" at all—that enables a national agenda of sexual identity. Mistral's permanently suspended sexual (in)difference is an important place for reflecting about these operations.

Mandatedly Queer

Compared to British or American studies, the school (elementary, primary, and normal) is understudied in Latin American studies when it comes to queer sexuality.[26] The queer sexuality of Latin America's schoolteachers is taken for granted in its popular culture; from spinsters, to the repressed, to the hypersexual, to lesbians, schoolteachers seem to be queer from nearly every angle—certainly never "normal." Jorge Salessi, in his elegant book *Médicos, maleantes, y maricas* [Doctors, thugs, and fags] includes a chapter on how the medical-criminological-pedagogical authorities constructed girls' schools as hotbeds of lesbianism; insofar as the teachers are concerned, it's clear that they were the subject of a similar inquiry on the part of the "experts" during their years of training. Salessi writes of a desire to curb the threat of the "lesbian professional."[27] Schoolteachers were suspended for a number of years in a limbo of sexual nonbeing, if they consented to the will of the state. (Conceivably, many did not, and were sexual beings.) Because age-standardized education was still in the process of being implemented, girls were often adolescents when they started to teach, as was Gabriela Mistral. Yet, regardless of their age, they were mandated to fulfill, in social or mass form, the role of the mother. And the mother was an equivocal figure, simultaneously tended to and despised.

According to Freudian theories of infantile sexuality, the mother must be a sexual figure for the child if the child is to become sexually differentiated. If it is true that Mistral was la Maestra de América [the Schoolteacher of America], a stand-in for all the schoolteachers of Latin America—that she crystallized the image of the national schoolmarm—then these women were figured as emblems precisely of ambivalent identification, as bodies that were oddly inaccessible to the child—nonsexual, closed, and impenetrable. If the child established a complete identification with the schoolteacher, he or she would risk remaining in a state of anaclitic attachment to the mother. This would, of course, run strictly counter to the state's desire to produce a legion of literate laborers who did not spend much time in school. The schoolteacher's body as image had to be a full body like that of the mother, but she also had to be a body with which not to identify, a nonsexual body. The child learned that he or she could survive without the teacher and that he or she must not only give up but even psychically lose the mother in favor of the nation's survival and thus his or her own survival. This was necessary in order for the state to erect itself as the source of anaclisis, the fulfillment of survival needs. Important to add is that this configuration must have affected the status of the mother and her sexuality as well.

Mistral's rise illustrates the vital role of this schoolteacher's body, disseminated as an image throughout Latin America. The descriptions of Mistral's body and physique repeatedly cast her as being at once inviting and discouraging. She was strangely masculine, "big," or imposing; and yet she exemplified, supposedly, maternal virtue and selfless dedication. The fact is that Mistral has always provoked attraction and repulsion, desire and fear, identification and disavowal.

Her pose meshes with the state project, in that the national school aimed to produce a subject mired in an incomplete identification; as Diana Fuss explains, the identification of melancholia.[28] National consciousness, then, is not an assumed ideal expressed in the bureaucratically defined freedom of the citizen, but something akin to introjection. The entire process of belonging to a nation can then be seen as melancholia or as melancholic in character. The state becomes a site of melancholic identification through a construct of national belonging, which depends on the (repudiated) figure of the mother. The role of sexuality is important, because, as Fuss has argued, sexual difference came to practically dominate the issue of identification and desire after Freud, but it is certainly not the only axis of identity in which these interrelated concepts thrive. Indeed, it's possible to see the schoolteacher figure—especially in her injunction to be "mandatedly queer"—as a linchpin in this takeover by sexuality of a subject's notion of his or her "difference" and proper place within nationalist schooling. Most, if not all, theories of nationalism within the context of a liberal, capitalist order explicitly assume that schools create identification with the nationalist project, thus aiding the state in creating the skilled laborer, responsible taxpayer, and loyal citizen-subject. However, hardly any of these theories have considered that, as Fuss explains, "identification is both voluntary and involuntary, necessary and difficult, dangerous and effectual, naturalizing and denaturalizing. Identification is the point where the psychical/social distinction becomes impossibly confused and ultimately untenable" (10). The cultural phenomenon of schooling is certainly an arena where national identification plays itself out, but not only in terms of immediate, linear relationships between individuals, such as pupils and teachers, which spark only affirmative emotions. National identification within liberal democracies also depends on less heroic and less uplifting emotions. As Homi Bhabha writes, "The function of ambivalence as one of the most significant discursive strategies of discriminatory power—whether racist or sexist, peripheral or metropolitan—remains to be charted."[29] Bhabha's notion of the "national minority stereotype" fits Mistral and this discussion. He speaks of the "stereotype-as-suture," commenting: "The role in fetishistic identification in the construction of discriminatory knowledges that depend on the 'presence of difference,' is to provide a process of splitting and multiple/contradictory belief at the point of enunciation and subjectification" (80).

Mistral, as stereotype, became so visible as the nonmother that this fact became invisible; or, more precisely stated, it was *disavowed*. This idea can be represented thus: "We know that Mistral is queer, but for us she is the Mother of America." Mistral's image is not merely display or an accidental hypervisibility stemming from her gender variance. It is an instance of deployment, with all the violence that deployment wreaks individually and collectively. Mistral, apparently, was quite conscious of this deployment and aware of this violence; her testimonial writings attest that she considered herself a victim of the violence of deployment, although they also suggest that she did not fully consider her own participation or the transformation of her personal subjectivity. In terms of identification, it's possible that the child makes an identification with the schoolteacher as queer, before disavowing it by proclaiming the mother's primacy all along. The schoolteacher is also an object of desire, in a world defined by the false opposition between identification and desire in order to produce the edifice of heterosexuality.[30]

The public fascination with Gabriela Mistral's ambiguous sexuality indicates national homophobia, but also a national investment in her sexuality that is stronger than straightforward prejudice suggests. No doubt, Mistral has been figured in terms of ambiguity, provoking a prurient, national "desire to know," with its flip side, the paranoid national statements of certainty as to her heterosexuality. The public discussion reveals a collective disavowal of Mistral's lesbianism as a known fact that must nevertheless never enter the official record. Disavowal entails the insistence upon a fact that all realize is untrue but that nonetheless is upheld as true in order to keep a psyche together—in this case, the national psyche.

Mistral's most original and forceful work shows a logic that is often intelligible in relationship to psychic processes such as those elucidated by Judith Butler in her book *The Psychic Life of Power*. Butler notices the complex tug-of-war between the subject's potential to resist state injunction in the logic of the unconscious, and the fact that the same unconscious logic "always already" ties the subject to the dominating force. She argues, along with Fuss, that homosexuality is not merely an external threat to the constitution of the heteronormative order. Interpreting psychoanalytic writings on melancholia, Butler concludes that psychoanalytic renunciation is based on the disavowal of homosexuality, and that this disavowal produces melancholic identification. Butler's complex argument is worth excerpting here:

It seems clear that the positions of "masculine" and "feminine," which Freud, in *Three Essays on the Theory of Sexuality* (1905), understood as the effects of laborious and uncertain accomplishment, are established in part through prohibitions which *demand the loss of* certain sexual attachments, and demand as well that those losses *not* be avowed, and *not* be grieved. If the assumption of femininity and the assumption of masculinity proceed through the accomplishment of an always tenuous heterosexuality, we might understand the force of this accomplishment as mandating the abandonment of homosexual attachments or, perhaps more trenchantly, *preempting* the possibility of homosexual attachment, a foreclosure of possibility which produces a domain of homosexuality understood as unlivable passion and ungrievable loss. This heterosexuality is produced not only through implementing the prohibition on incest but, prior to that, by enforcing the prohibition on homosexuality.[31]

Butler elaborates to conclude that the result of this situation is "a culture of gender melancholy," where masculinity and femininity exist to the extent that they have performed repudiations (140); that homosexuality is "not abolished but preserved" in its prohibition (142); and that "renunciation requires the very homosexuality that it condemns, not as its external object, but as its own most treasured source of sustenance. The act of renouncing homosexuality thus paradoxically strengthens homosexuality, but it strengthens homosexuality precisely *as* the power of renunciation" (143). Finally, Butler suggests that "rigid forms of gender and sexual identification, whether homosexual or heterosexual, appear to spawn forms of melancholy" (144).

In other words, Butler argues that homosexuality is introjected into heterosexuality and that it spawns gender melancholy because, as a loss, it is neither avowed nor grieved. Instead, she believes it is experienced as a renunciation for which there is no name. One might add that, if the connections with the mother and the schoolteacher are explored, this renunciation parallels the renunciation of the mother, also required in a culture with rigid forms of sexual and gender identification.

Fuss has demonstrated that identification is a process far more complex than mere imitation of a suitable model. The official "maternal" discourse alone, long held to be the defining element in Mistral's equation, could not have guaranteed national identification, because it presumes that identification works simply as imitation and that desire is always rewarded through satisfaction. It would be infinitely more productive to pay attention to the interrelationship between maternal discourse and the specter of female homosexuality that looms over it, that is, the potential collapse between identification and desire (women desiring [to be] women). The endless insistence that Mistral's supreme desire was to be a mother—a biological mother—reflects this unease well. There was also anxiety in the substitution of the mother for the schoolteacher, presumably sutured by Mistral's oddly reassuring masculinity. The schoolteacher, apparently, prolongs the desire for the mother, because, potentially, the schoolteacher desires the mother, too. Alternatively, it's just as possible that the schoolteacher desires to be a mother, but can't, as schoolteachers were often expected to be celibate. In either case, the child is inaugurated into national subjectivity by experiencing loss—either directly, via his or her own loss of both the mother and varied gender and sexual options, or indirectly, but no less powerfully, through the identification with the schoolteacher. In fact, the possibilities are endless, because "identifications are vehicles for each other," as Fuss explains thoroughly.[32] It is the call to create a culture where multiple forms of embodiment are available—including nonfemale and nonmale—that Judith Halberstam develops in her monograph *Female Masculinity*.[33] Halberstam details the effects of Butler's "culture of gender melancholy" while at the same time showing the resistance to this injunction on the part of certain social subjects and communities. A consideration of "female masculinity" helps to theorize Mistral's paradoxical status. Following Butler's and Halberstam's emphasis on the performativity of gender, I suggest that bracketing Mistral's masculinity and her same-sex desires misses the astounding subtleties of her performance.

Female Masculinity

Mistral was aware of the effect of her "queerness" in her day, as becomes evident in the letter where she celebrates her appeal to José Vasconcelos because she is *rara*. Judging from the testimonies of friends and contemporaries, Mistral was not self-delusional in considering the success of her equivocal image. Allusions to her strange or "queer" physique abound. A noted Mistralian, Fernando Alegría, writes: "Gabriela Mistral was a living legend in her own time, a personality of such charismatic force that people accepted her as a great artist solely on the basis of what she said or did, without knowing much about her art. Her voice, full of cadence and gentle rhythms, never failed to come through in all its complex density. It was a rare mixture of unrefined, ambiguous, and, at the same time, aggressive naiveté, the voice of a people, Mistral's rugged, simple folk of Chile's northern province." He adds a note about her physical appearance: "As we have stated, it was not so much her written poetry that elicited the admiration of her elders as her physical appearance and spoken words."[34]

Even though Alegría speaks of elders, he seems to be referring to contemporaries and peers: Alone (the pseudonym of Hernán Díaz Arrieta), Eduardo Barrios, Amado Nervo, and other well-known and notable artists and writers. Mistral is cast as the "younger" follower of an unspecified group of "elders," which presumably consisted of men who chose her as their national stereotype. She, in Alegría's description, is the chosen one—special, or queer—who was able to elicit, at both the intimate and mass levels, a type of attachment that can best be thought of in the complex terms of identification and disidentification. Arguably, Mistral came to occupy the space of the model, for children and for all those subjects put in the position of "child" at the symbolic level within the incipient nationalist project; mostly women and indigenous people, but also workers and immigrants.

Alegría repeats one of the maxims of Mistral's description—her size and "odd" sartorial habits: "As a matter of fact, it has not been poetry that people have associated with her voluminous and ceremonial presence. They have enjoyed making a legend of her unconventional ways of dressing and speaking. . . . One begins to suspect that the most profound and moving evaluations of Mistral's art are not to be found in critical, scholarly studies but in informal testimonies of persons who were exposed to the magnetism of her physical presence" (218). Alegría's slippage is interesting, because he seems to affirm that Mistral's performativity, her ability to rein in intimates and strangers and draw them to herself, is an example of "art."

Pablo Neruda's description of Mistral in his memoirs, *Confieso que he vivido: Memorias]* [Memoirs], adds some irony to the general perception of Mistral as physically "odd." She "appeared" to him when he was a small child, dressed in a long black skirt. She was very tall, he recalls, and strange-looking: "I saw her walking by, with her full-length clothes, and I was scared of her."[35] He recalls that many people in Temuco, where she was director of the girls' school, commented on her "unwed condition" [condición de soltera] (385). Neruda wrote about Mistral's resentment of the gossip but was never explicit regarding the subject matter. Instead, he referred to her "trabajosa y trabajada vida" [tortuous and crafted life] (384).

Cintio Vitier, a Cuban critic, also described Mistral in strikingly ambiguous gender terms. Vitier wrote a well-known article, "La voz de Gabriela Mistral" [The voice of Gabriela Mistral], which was published the year of her death (1957), as a poetic tribute to Mistral. Eventually it was included in his *Crítica sucesiva* [Successive criticism], a book on Latin American poetic "greats."[36] Vitier writes of "a secret, creative maleness that is necessary in women, in order to counteract their tendency toward pleasurable reabsorption or chaotic evaporations" (148). He goes on to analyze the poetic personality of Mistral's first book, *Desolación* [Desolation], an analysis deeply influenced by Vitier's Catholicism. He sees in this book a feminine quality, with occasional flashes of a more virile and impersonal brilliance in which the hand of the Father is clearly at work. His concluding remarks on *Desolación*, for all his admiration of some of its striking verses, is this:

> If she had not written anything beyond *Desolación* she would have been well situated within the group of Southern Cone poetesses that broke out with postmodernism and who were her contemporaries.... But the stubborn Chilean was joined to forces greater than contemporary feminism, and demonstrated a capacity for a different appetite, of unexpected growth. Neither hysteria nor sophistication were capable of engaging her. And so she marched forward, proving her stock's vigor, with a voice that became more vast with time and which accumulated a telluric essence. (159)

Vitier argues that women poets such as Alfonsina Storni and Delmira Agustini were "insane," "delirious," and "suicidal" (159). At best, when they were sane—like Juana de Ibarborou—they were "transparent." Predictably enough, all are rendered as having "feminine" qualities; in short, they appear as "femmes." Conversely, Mistral was gender-different— somewhat of a "butch." Vitier's description of Mistral literally revolves around size. The ability to "swell" was exemplified in her poetic voice, which was "vast," "cumulative," and "vigorous"—worthy, he claims, of her "stock" and capable of "telluric" greatness (159). It is not difficult to see a resonance with Alegría's insistence on Mistral's "voluminous" presence, her "charismatic" figure, and her "magnetism."

Vitier does describe Mistral in terms of an essential "femininity" at points throughout the essay; but one can hardly escape noticing that he constructs her claim to greatness on the basis of her "higher" dosage of masculinity in comparison to her female counterparts. Mistral has, Vitier asserts, "a spark of manliness" [una chispa de varón]. It is true that this insistence on the "manly" quality of her verse might be only a way to describe just that—her verses—and might not be related to her actual physique or bodily style.[37] Vitier concludes his article, however, with an instance of eyewitnessing. As a testimony to the power of Mistral's presence, he makes a third direct reference to her as "manly" [varonil]:

> I remember the only time I saw her. The Indian will of her hair, her male forehead and eyebrows, the utterly clear, desolate eyes resembling burning fires in the light of noon, the dazzling laughter of a child. All around her, a magical circle, a sacred space. That unbridgeable distance separated her from all. Her benign directness was not enough to dissipate the overpowering impression. I felt compassion for her, because there was not a single hand in this world that could alleviate her burden. She had been struck by lightning. (178)

What is memorable in all of Vitier's descriptions is how Mistral's masculine demeanor and physique emerge as the essential clue to her power to mesmerize or fascinate.

The last description appears melodramatic; it stresses Mistral's charismatic presence, sealing it as the definitive collective memory of Mistral. Vitier appeals to the reader's emotions to entomb this memory, which has had a very long life indeed. Mistral, the group leader, in this instance slightly recast as a *poète maudit*, fatally separated from "us," occupies the (male) space of the Great Poet, revered and alone. Vitier's descriptors align with Alegría's (quoted earlier): all directly pinpoint her physical appearance and her spoken words, magnetic and odd, as the reasons for her notoriety. Accompanied with Neruda's unsubtle hints of the gossip that trailed Mistral in Chile, an exceedingly clear picture of Mistral as an exemplar of "female masculinity" emerges.

Volodia Teitelboim, author of a well-meaning but ultimately sensationalist biography of Mistral, published in 1991, *Gabriela Mistral pública y secreta: Truenos y silencios en la vida del primer Nobel latinoamericano* [The public and secret Gabriela Mistral: Thunder and silence in the life of Latin America's first Nobel Prize winner], proffers the usual description of her, again harping on the physical: "When she was young she wore her hair in a pony-tail. Then she cut it off to a boy-cut. Most people regarded her as ugly and she repeated this with a proud sadness. Others looked upon her with an eye to discovering interior beauty. They did not consider her beautiful, but they could consider her attractive. And even majestic, visible from afar, all of 1.78 m tall."[38] Not only is Mistral's size an issue again, but so is her unconventional and antifeminine femininity, here rendered as ugliness. Teitelboim avows that she could be considered "attractive" but doesn't sound altogether convincing. Perhaps Teitelboim simply couldn't locate the appropriate adjective; perhaps he meant that Mistral was handsome.[39] This much can be stated with certainty: for Teitelboim, Mistral is asexual: "Her passion is, above all things, a platonic enthusiasm. She is afraid of sex, which, we can surmise, is a key to her intimate life" (29). As a consequence, Mistral substitutes passion for a sexual object with passion for an ideal of beauty: "Gabriela liked good-looking men, perhaps with some feminine features" (41). This comical attempt to heterosexualize Mistral's relationships at all costs, even if a little gender swapping is called for, illustrates the national desire to encase Mistral in the heteronormative sexual paradigm.

Is it possible to detect a cultural anxiety at work in these collective portrayals of Mistral's sexual aims? It certainly seems so. Interestingly, this anxiety is less apparent in another discursive realm, one set apart from the world of specialized literary criticism. Mistral's life in pulp writings is rendered by innuendo. Indirect references to material too "explosive" or "repulsive" to deal with up front assault the eye as a repeated feature of this discourse.[40]

Innuendo depends upon sources that can never be verified, and upon the desire to titillate. Authors who employ innuendo typically do not cite any sources other than an alleged experience that Mistral had, usually associated with a place-name, such as La Serena or Temuco; or perhaps a dramatic trauma, such as an episode of stoning in her childhood;[41] or a rape, again in childhood;[42] or the suicide of her male lover.[43] Supposedly, witnesses can vouch for the factual veracity of these experiences through the authority of their "personal" friendship with Mistral.

The point is that there are no hard documents of Mistral's heterosexuality, but it is assumed to be true even in the face of signs of queerness. These writers, allegedly regaled by Mistral with stories of trauma, take it upon themselves to pass on the accounts so that Mistral's image is protected.[44] Arguably, this desire could stem from a collective need. The import of these references is the existence of innuendo and scandal— that is, the persistence of the question, Who or what did Mistral desire? and not its definitive answer. The prurient obsession with Mistral's romantic and sexual life comes into sharp relief against the backdrop of national desire. In other words, it's not simply that Gabriela Mistral had a set of difficulties and perhaps one in particular that warranted a corresponding set of strategies, but that the discourses and practices that she mined for her official and poetic language can themselves become the object of scrutiny in terms of desire. Given Mistral's rise, and the restricted nature of her social milieu in Chile, it is apparent that the state enlisted Mistral notwithstanding any rumors of a despised queerness, and that perhaps her queerness was indispensable to her fame, although not in any straightforward way.

Determining the extent of truth and falsity in Mistral's biography is not this book's chief interest; rather, the point is to establish that the gaze on Mistral's sexuality is a queer gaze; that the insistence on the personal nature of highly bureaucratized discourse is a queer insistence; and that the desire to anchor an identity—presumably Mistral's own, but upon closer examination a national identity secured through the feminine role—is a queer desire.

A group, Freud notes in *Group Psychology and the Analysis of the Ego*, "thinks in images."[45] He adds: "Groups have never thirsted after truth. They demand illusions, and cannot do without them. They constantly give what is unreal precedence over what is real; they are almost as strongly influenced by what is untrue as by what is true. *They have an evident tendency not to distinguish between the two*" (16–17 [emphasis added]). If Mistral's image of being normatively heterosexual is "untrue" and, further, if her image contains this "untruth" and this "unreal" in a play with what is to be considered "visible" and thus verifiable, then a significant development occurs: the complex and interesting reasons why Mistral, and not any of the other available "models," was the state's perfect spokesperson and image become apparent.

Between Women: Family Arrangements

Mistral's relationships with women are not difficult to locate; they are universally acknowledged as life-sustaining. Whether they included a sexual aim and whether this sexual aim was queer are, for the time being, matters of speculation. Nevertheless, a genealogy of intimacy in Mistral scholarship points unerringly to critical discomfort surrounding Mistral's female companions. The insistent allusions to Mistral's "secretaries" epitomize precisely the mechanism of disavowal at work when a nation, a continent, and a discourse elevate a queer to Mother of America.

To begin with, the idea that a schoolteacher would have a secretary is telling. Of course, Mistral did not work as a schoolteacher after 1922; henceforth, she worked as a propagandist of sorts for the state, and as a consul, journalist, and lecturer. Certainly, given her busy schedule and the many tasks she had to accomplish, she required an assistant or secretary. In fact, she had several women assist her throughout her public career and, once she was world-famous, she frequently was assisted by more than one secretary at a time. Of course, this profession was considered feminine. Within this group of women, four figures stand out. Why did these potentially forgettable and replaceable figures provoke such attention and become part of Mistral's life narrative? The question begs to be asked: Were these women more than simply secretaries?

Jaime Concha sums up the list of companions as follows: "Laura Rodig, a Chilean; Palma Guillén, a Mexican; the Puerto Rican, Consuelo Saleva; Doris Dana, an American . . . and especially after her mother's death in 1929, her family will consist solely of her circle of [female] friends and secretaries, with whom she will form an exclusively female home, where the man will be merely a passer-by, decidedly a stranger."[46] Concha gives as an explanation for this strange female world the death of Mistral's mother. He believes that this event was traumatic enough to ensure Mistral's lifelong separation from men. Even though Mistral had many male friends and colleagues, and corresponded intimately with several of them, biographers insist that the creation of a home populated by women meant a separation from men and the masculine that belied sexual distress. Probably without intending to, Concha implies that Mistral's secretaries were substitutes for the lost mother figure and, as such, anaclitic, not sexual, attachments.

There is, absolutely, an ambiguity in the comprehension and classification of these intimate and life-sustaining relationships with "[female] friends and secretaries" [amigas y secretarias]. The absence of a man as a provider or in a sexual position within the "family" definitely provoked a thirst for an explanation, while also triggering a defense mechanism (although Concha at least recognizes these women's presence in Mistral's life as companions). The narrative of Mistral as a frustrated heterosexual and a long-suffering spinster would have sufficiently quelled this need to defend against one's own national mother as a queer. But there is another investment at work here.

Among the most entertaining in the list of mediocre books about Mistral is *Mi encuentro con Gabriela Mistral, 1912–1957* [My encounter with Gabriela Mistral, 1912–1957], a volume assembled by Isauro Santelices, a Chilean contemporary of Mistral.[47] Not astounding because of its literary merit, *Mi encuentro* is significant because it illustrates that Mistral was not bound to a feminine world; on the contrary, she was a full, sometimes bitter, and at other times witty participant in the machinery that fueled the desire to know about her gender and sexual difference. The volume is a hybrid composed of Santelices's personal reflections and letters he received from Mistral. This correspondence illustrates some of Mistral's vindictive personality, which directly contradicts her image as being saintly. Additionally, the volume passes judgment on her ex-companions, including condescending and damning remarks, respectively, toward Laura Rodig and Consuelo Saleva, and contains self-references by Mistral that are unusual given the climate of censorship during her lifetime.

For the first four chapters, Santelices recycles the well-worn commonplaces about Mistral's life, including her abnegation and spirit of self-sacrifice, her rise from poverty and paternal abandonment, her devotion to her mother and sister, and her adherence to her only and fateful love, who committed suicide in his early twenties. He also mentions key moments of consecration, such as the prestigious award of the Juegos Florales in Santiago in 1914 for Mistral's "Sonetos de la muerte" [Sonnets of death], supposedly written for her dead (male) lover, and the Nobel Prize in literature in 1945. At first glance, then, this book would seem to be one more in a catalog of praises to Gabriela Mistral, were it not for its strange undercurrent of doubt, gossip, and duplicity. This duplicity shows itself in chapter 6, entitled, appropriately enough, "Su carácter" [Her character]: "Conscious of my responsibility, I rejected even the shadow of a doubt when the case so required; I have pondered certain items at length; I have consulted what we could call my 'Gabriela Mistral dossier,' my archives, because nothing else that I own offers more volume and abundance" (37).

Gabriela Mistral, supposedly Santelices's personal friend, becomes an archive or an object for definition. Santelices does not describe the contents of his "dossier" on Mistral. It's impossible to gauge the process entailed in his deductions or the measure of his loyalty. This chapter is fascinating because it refutes, even as it pretends not to, the image of Mistral as self-sacrificing, self-effacing, and accepting of insult the Christian way, without any vindictive feelings.

Santelices's book insists on the threat of scandal or ridicule that plagued Mistral's life. It emphasizes the unpalatable and unflattering aspects of her treatment while she was still in Chile and continuing after she left Chile for permanent exile. The book makes much of her shame and difficulties at not having a university title, whereas most accounts would proffer this fact as proof of her distance from glory or upward mobility. It includes letters from Mistral that attest that she desired, logically enough, the comforts and recognition that would come with a degree.

A letter written by Mistral in La Serena, Chile, in 1925 illustrates her degree of self-awareness. At this point Mistral had begun what would become her lifelong exile from Chile, and was in her native region on a brief visit only. "You ask me if I know what people say about me. I know something about it, which reaches me through anonymous letters, which by now I read with perfect serenity."[48] One of the most interesting references in this letter is a rare allusion to Mistral's sexual status: "They say that my behavior is shameful. Let me tell you, Isauro, *I have taken far better care of my life than of my verses*. I have been, and am, honorable. If I have not married, it's because when I have loved, I have not been loved back; and when they say I have been loved, I have not loved back. A vulgar story which has reached the heights of stupidity, so much has it been told all over the world."[49]

Santelices put together his book decades after Mistral's death. He is significantly more performative than Mistral; he strives to work the curiosity of readers—provoking their prurience—without contributing any substantial observations:

> I can't help but transcribe this paragraph: "They say that my behavior is shameful. Let me tell you, Isauro, *I have taken far better care of my life than of my verses*. I have been, and am, honorable." This statement of hers, which she formulated a half-century ago, must be taken as an article of faith, as a commandment. No stranger has a place in such a meridian rectitude. Her loneliness drew support from herself, and, if on some occasion, with the passing of the days and the abandonment of time, ravaged by age and her declining health, she sought refuge, it was a refuge based on protection and support, on the need to exchange a deafening monologue with a fraternal dialogue. She wasn't always understood. She was often betrayed in the vulgar economic sense, or her good faith was simply taken advantage of.[50]

The coded words abound. Santelices refers to Mistral's marital or sexual status through Mistral's own allusion to not being married. The word *fraternal* suggests a vaguely erotic bond between two female companions. The mention of betrayal "in the vulgar economic sense" posits Mistral as breadwinner, provider, and center of a family unit. In a bourgeois world, the home is the "man's refuge," and Mistral, according to Santelices, "sought refuge." This is also a direct allusion to Consuelo Saleva: although the facts have never been verified, at various points in Mistral's personal correspondence to Santelices and others, she claimed that Saleva had tricked her into signing over the entire sum of her Nobel Prize earnings, leaving her destitute.

Interestingly, Santelices earlier makes an allusion to Mistral's lack of feminine graces, which he attributes to a sense of pessimism approximating shame. He writes, at the beginning of the section titled "Epistolary," as if to frame the book *Mi encuentro:* "Notice the trait of humor in somebody who, at age 25, proclaimed herself to be 'a good old lady.' Her pessimism toward her physical appearance was very destructive. It translated into a lack of coquettishness and wiles common to women, whether or not they are writers" (73). What is most curious about an already curious interjection of Mistral's physique—in a book adorned by a fair number of photographs of Mistral, obviously displaying this "unappealing" physique—is that last phrase, "whether or not they are writers" [escriban o no]. These words separate women who write from those who do not. Though the suggestion is elliptical, it is strong: Santelices insinuates that although writing may, in part, account for Mistral's disturbing (gender and sexual) difference, disguised as "pessimism," the personal and societal shame Mistral represents applies to all women, queer or not, who do not proffer the expected "coquettishness and wiles." And this shaming is most effective the more it is displayed, advertised, and consumed.

In an interview in Santiago, Chile, in August 2000 with the noted Mistral specialist Luis Vargas Saavedra, I asked him about the whereabouts of Mistral's correspondence to four women companions. He replied that its absence from the public record was one of the glaring gaps in the Mistralian corpus. He agreed that certainly these letters must have existed, and shared with me the hope that they still do exist, waiting to be read. It's probable that some of this correspondence is missing because of neglect or straightforward destruction, which undoubtedly constitutes an enormous loss.

However, the letters' absence does not preclude the question, Why did Gabriela Mistral, the avatar of the state family and the national family, have no nuclear, heterosexual family of her own? Obviously, as an individual, Mistral did not seek out or want this kind of family. Less obviously, it was not in the state's interest that Mistral, the national image, be an exact image of heterosexuality. It was in the state's best interest that she remain a sexually indeterminate subject—a queer subject—in public as well as in private. This is a hard insight to understand, because it seems counterintuitive, but it is possible that national subjects would form a stronger attachment to a sexually ambiguous icon than to a heteronormative one.

Even if new letters emerge, there is no way to anticipate whether they would actually reveal any "truth" about Mistral's lesbianism. Certainly, it is suspicious that they have never come to light. At least, the question needs to be pressed: Why does no correspondence exist between any of these women? But the scholar *can* consult the archive of letters Mistral received, in which one can find examples of the adoration that she elicited, among women especially—often smitten anonymous women who wrote Mistral in the hopes of attracting attention. Occasionally, a solitary jewel appears, such as a very poignant letter written in 1954 by Laura Rodig, a Chilean sculptor who was Mistral's first companion. In the letter, Rodig expresses a great sense of loss over Mistral, and approaches incredulity by her offer to once again provide Mistral with her company—after nearly thirty years of separation.[51] Notably, Rodig's letter is an account of a very specific loss: her loss of Gabriela Mistral.

It is also possible to scrutinize Mistral's very first writings and conclude that, in their *modernista* stress on the morbose, lurid, and disastrous—in short, on the perverse—Mistral may well have been seeking a way to assume an embodiment different from those the culture made available to her.[52] Interesting in this respect is the fact that these novice writings seem to be naively communicating messages to a female lover, real or imagined, in a sometimes ambiguous but at other times clearly feminine voice.

Apparently, some of the readers of the local newspapers in which Mistral published considered her to be mad. In 1905, one reader wrote to *La Voz de Elqui* that, "judging from the products of her imagination, she gives me the impression of an imbalanced mind."[53] The editors of a 1917 anthology of Chilean poetry, *Selva lírica* [Lyrical forest], wrote that "Gabriela Mistral's poetry is nervous and firm. There are no scared cries, mushiness or solemn attitudes."[54] In their exaltation of her "virile verses,"

however, they express a worry over the possible deviance of her pedagogical work: "It makes sense, of course, that Gabriela Mistral, powerfully absorbed by her teacher's preoccupations, sterilize and dilute the
exquisiteness of her poetic talent writing songs and stories for schoolchildren. Yes, they are truly beautiful, and of the highest humanitarian
caliber, but they distract her from applying her excellent disposition for
ample lyricism in all its manifestations and without the impositions of
a vulgar calling" (n.p.).

The young Mistral appears to have reveled in ambiguous sexual discourse through the appeal to sentimentality quite on purpose, judging
by her first creative writings as she began work in her native region of
Elqui. She wrote phrases such as "To her, who is much more than my
friend, and somewhat more than my sister."[55] Or this, signed in 1907
with one of her youthful pseudonyms, "Alma": "Let them fight us; let
them tie our hands together to keep us from caressing; may they keep
us apart so that every touch or intimacy becomes impossible; with our
hands tied we will caress, leagues apart we will embrace, with our mind
free, joyfully free." It might be considered a rather innocuous segment,
except that it is titled "A ella, la única" [To her, the only one].[56] Other examples from this first period are quite narcissistic, as Mistral tries on
the persona of the *poète maudit* addressing a "friend" [amiga], that is, a
female lover who does not represent the bourgeois prospect of settling
into castrating conformity. "Adiós a Laura" [Goodbye to Laura], published in *La Voz de Elqui* on 5 July 1906, is an example: "Other women
will enter your existence, other women will exercise my rights and will
give you this name, friend [amiga], that so many pronounce but few deserve or ought to."[57]

Mistral's first and only short story, "The Rival," revolves around an
amusingly transparent first-person male protagonist named Gabriel.
He has lost three female lovers to tragic circumstances and drunkenly
retells each of the painful occurrences to his implied listener. Gabriel
concludes that death itself is his rival. Significantly, with this short story
Mistral assumed her definitive pen name, which can also be read as a
masculinizing gesture, since the names belonged to two male writers
(Frédéric Mistral and Gabriele d'Annunzio).

Mistral's fragmented corpus bears the marks of self-censorship and
of actual censorship and points to a neglected historical truth. Judith Halberstam comments that queer methodology is a "scavenger methodol-

ogy,"[58] and thus far scavenging is the researcher's only alternative in the case of Gabriela Mistral, in practically all aspects of her life. A group of writings is not sufficient to qualify as a comprehensive historical record, but when combined with the descriptions of Mistral as an odd figure around which "all" revolved, as well as the presumably relieved but somewhat shaky assurance of those who offer "definitive proof" of Mistral's heterosexuality, Mistral's queerness appears difficult to dispute.

When I spoke to Vargas Saavedra about the reputed anonymous letters received by Mistral and asked him about their content, he replied that clearly they revolved around her nonfemininity and included accusations of her being *una marimacha* [mannish] and *una asquerosa* [disgusting]. Vargas Saavedra, who has devoted a lifetime to researching Mistral and knows more than any other specialist about her voluminous correspondence and prose, dismissed the official version that holds that all of these anonymous letters were written because Mistral did not hold the required degrees to head the prestigious girls' schools to which she was appointed starting in 1918. Still, Vargas Saavedra stopped short of endorsing any inquiry into Mistral's sexual identity and seemed swayed by his discovery of a handful of letters to Manuel Magallanes Moure that, in his opinion, prove conclusively Mistral's heterosexuality because they ostensibly indicate that Mistral had sexual relations with Magallanes Moure.[59] The letters will have to be judged when they are made public. But even the letters to Magallanes Moure can be an instance of queer performativity, seeing as how most specialists believe that Mistral and Magallanes Moure saw each other only twice, in social gatherings. Even if they shared a romance of any duration, it certainly seems queer that this fact alone could signify heterosexuality, as if lesbians and gay men never engaged in heterosexual sex or had romances with members of another sex.

Certainly, the existence of anonymous accusations confirms a general climate of instability and insecurity created in a society that surveyed, repudiated, and castigated family arrangements that did not conform to its values and economic interests. Irrefutably, Mistral lived her life with women and reserved her intimate passions for women. Although denigration existed and must have been very painful, at the same time one cannot help but notice how the public derived a kind of national pleasure from its fixation on this "oddity," suggesting that Mistral's queerness had something to do with the complex play of national identification/

disidentification made possible, to a large extent, through her figure. Mistral never entered a marriage of convenience, nor did she attempt to present herself as conventionally feminine. A more plausible hypothesis is that she came to deploy her queerness. Whether intuitively or not, she definitely understood the pivotal role played by identification, introjection, and melancholia in the national project. Whether consciously or not, Mistral queered the state.

CHAPTER THREE

Citizen Mother

Mistral is best known as a proponent of separate male and female worlds, a believer in separate-spheres thinking.[1] This fact is taken as axiomatic, just like her universally known persona: la Maestra de América, the "Schoolteacher of America." Essential to the idea that Mistral was a straightforward defender of "maternal thinking," "republican mother-hood," or the "cult of domesticity" is the view that the schoolteacher is the continuation of the mother. And yet, as I explained in the preceding chapter, the role of the schoolteacher was more complicated, entailing a degree of antagonism toward actual mothers and enlisting aspects of masculinity noticed in popular culture but timidly treated in scholarly discourse.

At times Mistral spoke of a community of women or of women's common bonds. At other times she did not engage in a gender-specific discourse at all. The standard feminist interpretation of Mistral's use of the "feminine" traces a progression from an early patriarchal conform-ity—necessary in Mistral's case to achieve a career in Chile—to femi-nine empowerment, which meant that once the discourse was "freed" from the clichés of maternity and child rearing, it moved toward the affir-mation of women's creativity and resilience.[2] In these accounts, Mistral upholds women and identifies with the feminine as "difference." A hand-ful of feminist critics want to pry Mistral from the chokehold of mater-nalism and domesticity, whereas others seek to reassign to those devalued domains a position of power.[3] To this discussion, we may add useful accounts of Mistral's role in education, especially during her tenure in Mexico.[4]

Up to now, queer sexuality has been addressed only timidly, if at all, by feminist revisionist criticism. This is surprising, for history avows a prurient obsession with establishing the "truth" of Mistral's sexuality, and this query extends to all women, marking the entire group as potentially "queer." Mistral's sexuality titillated people then, and it still does today. But thus far, feminist critics of Mistral, generally speaking, have shied away from the subject. There are notable exceptions, to be sure: Elizabeth Rosa Horan wrote a queer bio-bibliographical essay on Mistral, and Claudia Lanzarotti and Sylvia Molloy have mentioned her lesbianism. Eliana Ortega has directly criticized the presumption of heterosexuality.[5] But scattered mentions of queerness cannot do the work of a sustained analysis of gender and sexuality as they were mobilized by the state, and not factoring in Mistral's queerness occludes essential points about state formation in this period, as it pertains to all citizens.

Unraveling Mistral's participation in the dominant discourse, as well as in the social practices the discourse authorized, requires a departure from previous feminist readings that celebrate the Mistralian construction of a "community," "family," or "audience" of women.[6] Without lapsing into a lopsided condemnation of Mistral, it remains critical not just to reject hagiography, or even to rationalize it as strategy, but to examine its roots, causes, and functions.

There is literary greatness in Mistral, and she should be vindicated in the context of Latin American letters. But a revisionist approach to Mistral fails to examine the state uses of gender, race, and sexuality in which she was a participant. More specifically, it fails to consider how these multiple axes intersect.

The role of state architect was clearly very dear to Mistral. She helped to consolidate and uplift the rhetoric of democratic nationalism that was central to the constitution of the Latin American state in the twentieth century. The most obvious way was by serving as the "Mother of the Nation," but also, perhaps more crucially and in a less obvious fashion, by advocating a racialized form of maternal nationalism strangely sanctioned by her queerness. The relationship between the private and the public is essential; two regimes of power—race and sex—mutually constitute their presumed "visibility" and "invisibility" through gender discourse.

Within the context of maternal discourse, though, race is less visible than sexuality. Concretely, racial hierarchies are made invisible by Mistral's deployment of sentimentality and intimacy. To consider the subject of Mistral's iconographic use of the "feminine," this chapter will focus on two notable instances of the enunciation of the female "I" in Mistral. One is "Palabras de la extranjera" [Remarks of the foreigner], the preface to the book *Lecturas para mujeres* [Readings for women], her enormously successful primer for girls' schools, commissioned by the Mexican government in 1922. It is a fairly straightforward piece, articulated within domestic and sentimental discourse. Conversely, "Colofón con cara de excusa" [Colophon to offer an apology] appeals to the idea of a resistant "women's power" but is, in fact, a profoundly narcissistic text; coming full circle from the earlier, "state-referential" texts, it arrives at a self-referential discourse in which the preoccupation with women's social empowerment—what might be thought of as their citizenship— all but disappears. This essay is the afterword Mistral appended in 1945 to *Ternura* [Tenderness], her definitive compilation of her children's literature.[7]

Examining these essays provides a useful point of entry into the helpful evaluations offered by critics who practice the "separate spheres" logic, while stressing the need to become aware of the traps of that thinking. The main point to refute is that state- and self-referential discourses are instances of unrelated enunciations, respectively public and private. In liberalism, the state is supposed to arrive at a guarantee of the individual's freedom to pursue his or her own desires. For that to happen, subjects must first perform their duties as citizens in the public sphere. The public and private worlds abet the same system. Likewise, although Mistral's two essays certainly can't be collapsed, upon closer examination they should not be strictly divorced from each other either. As a corpus, they permit a critical examination of "women's discourse" as a less-than-straightforward proposition that straddles the difficult boundary between private and public existence that is necessary to liberalism.

Race and Sex

In this split between private and public, it probably comes as no surprise that "publicness" is figured in the language of nationalism and that it has strong racial underpinnings. In Mexico, for example, the status of the indigenous peoples came to symbolize Mexico's progress toward a

liberal order; the more they were modernized—that is, Hispanicized—
the more democratic Mexico became, for it could legitimately claim
one universal Mexican citizen. At the same time, the plight of women
was subordinated almost entirely to the creation of a discursive "Mexican
woman," specifically geared toward the definition of the Mexican home
and an ideology of domesticity. Both axes, race and gender, were deployed
to persuade global partners, and the United States in particular, to include the Mexican nation-state in capitalist ventures.

Therefore, it's quite interesting that the culmination of Mistral's domestic discourse should occur at that moment and in that place. She
was intensely involved with the self-study that the Ministry of Education
pursued under Minister Vasconcelos. Most scholars readily notice Mistral's role in manufacturing domesticity and the ideal of "citizen mother."
Fewer critics, however, have studied her direct involvement with the
fate of indigenous education and the spread of industrial-style schooling
to the countryside. Intellectuals and functionaries alike saw the countryside as in need of Hispanization, or cultural whitening. The primer
Lecturas para mujeres [Readings for women] was part of that project,
whether self-consciously or not.

While in Chile, Mistral had shrewdly positioned herself as the architect and representative of republican motherhood. When she was invited to Mexico, she was presumably expected to do more of the same.
But while fully taking advantage of the request to compile a reader for
women, Mistral immersed herself in other realms of education primarily
involving race. This enabled her to shift her self-representation consid-
erably. Instead of becoming the white doyenne of women's education,
which she would have been destined to be if she had remained in Chile,
Mistral became the national mother of racially mixed children. Mistral's
unrealized biological motherhood would have plagued her in Chile,
marking her as queer, yet it was perfectly suited to the Mexican endeavor.
Racial others would seem to betray the conception of nationality in
terms of biological intimacy, yet they had to be recruited into a state
project increasingly articulated in terms of familial ties among all. Thus,
the adoptive or "spiritual" model suited this state need quite effectively.

For all of Mexico's trumping of miscegenation as a sexual solution to
the problem of unifying the national subject, one would be misguided
to claim confidently that the Mexican nation succeeded in assimilating
all the indigenous peoples, as if they were rendered remarkably passive

merely by education and literacy campaigns. Certainly, Mexico wielded a racial ideology that was different from that of the Southern Cone nations, but this fact does not even remotely begin to dispense with the problem of Mexican racism.

The gains in women's access to citizenship must also be qualified. Taking into account their status as laborers alone, and bracketing purely political issues like the fact that the Mexican Revolution did not enfranchise women with the vote and emerged in discourse and practice as the work of a virile community,[8] still it is true that industrialization made more women self-sufficient as wage laborers. But Mistral's gender discourse promoted a new social conservatism that Minister Vasconcelos very much desired to see and, in effect, created gender divisions in Mexico's educational system that had not necessarily existed before. Mexico had been, up to then, a country with a coeducational approach to teaching, an approach that was continued in the rural schools but derailed in the urban centers. It's fascinating that "the indigenous mother" was, in effect, segregated from feminine schooling and also from the profession of schoolteaching, and that urban women, likely to belong to the white criollo class, were targeted as the future teachers of the nation. Women were enlisted, specifically, to make rational beings out of peoples presumed to be irrational, and therefore to inaugurate them into liberal membership.

In *El desastre* [The disaster], volume 3 of Vasconcelos's memoirs, he writes:

[I] established the Department of Indian Education. In it, teachers would imitate Catholic missionary action in the colonial period.... On purpose I insisted that this department had no other mission than to prepare the Indian for admission into the common schools, giving him notions of the Spanish language. I wanted to go against the North American Protestant practice that addresses the educational problem of the Indian as something special and separate from the rest of the population ... and this made possible for us to avoid the presence of terrible problems, such as those of the Negro in the United States. I told them, "if we create a reservation, then how could we distinguish those who are Indian from those who are not? All of us would have to enter the reservation. Fortunately, we cease being Indians here from the moment we are baptized. Baptism gave our ancestors the category of people with reason, and that's enough of that." So, following the Spanish, not the Smithsonian way, we organized our campaign of Indian education with the incorporation of the isolated Indian into the his larger family, the Mexicans. As soon as I left the ministry, though, they inaugurated the by now well-known Institute of Indian Education, imitating US policy on Indian education and so the Smithsonian anthropology triumphed.

The work of the Ministry, as I have pointed out, would be fundamentally three-fold, circumstantially five-fold. The three essential Directorships were: Schools, Libraries, and Fine Arts. The two auxiliary activities: the incorporation of the Indian to Hispanic culture and the literacy campaign for the masses.[9]

Mistral was recruited primarily for work in the effort to found nationwide libraries and to formulate their lists of holdings, responding to Minister Vasconcelos's desire to imitate what he regarded as the North American venture to institute a similar classic canon to cement a cultured, literate nationality. Initially, Mistral's gender intervention was secondary to this important and deeply racialized initiative. One imagines that she was regarded as a bastion of Castilianized identity by her Mexican employers, at least initially, and that her portrayal as mestiza evolved in Mexico. One also wonders whether, in the specular relationship to the indigenous peoples that she adopted around this time, Mistral was not exercising her liberal right to model herself after whom she pleased. Because Vasconcelos and Mistral were estranged by the time Vasconcelos wrote his memoirs, he yields little information on the subject. Nevertheless, the passage mentioning Mistral is significant enough to quote:

> The news that in Mexico a continental Hispanic movement had begun started to attract the curiosity of the continent's best. Mexico had a special calling to fulfill this mission, as the old metropolis of Spanish colonialism, but it had forgotten about its historic task. Through González Martínez, at the time our minister in Chile, I learned that Gabriela Mistral—whose fame as poetess and teacher had just begun to be spread—wanted to move to Mexico. Immediately I cabled her with an invitation to collaborate with the Ministry, and the date was set accordingly. On the other hand, Dr. Gastellum, our minister in Uruguay, tried without success to invite Juana de Ibarborou to visit Mexico. The celebrated poetess did not accept, but at least knowledge of her invitation drew attention to Mexico, and Obregón was delighted that his government was being spoken about abroad. (163)[10]

Although Vasconcelos ultimately presented himself as respectful of the indigenous peoples, he treated their culture as an antiquated remnant, aggressively championing their assimilation into the national project.[11] Coinciding with Vasconcelos's worries, Mistral's maternalist persona became more explicitly racialized around this very time. Some of the texts included in the primer verify this trend toward racialization: "A la mujer mexicana" [To the Mexican woman], a well-known essay, is an example.

Because the primer was intended specifically for the "escuela-hogar" [school-home], a phrase suggestive of a feminine, homosocial space, its call to consolidate a feminine labor force through the family appears logical. But apparently the *escuelas-hogares* were first mentioned specifically as a solution to the "Indian problem." They were created to acculturate indigenous children, separating them from indigenous adults and thus diminishing the presumably negative impact of the indigenous home, of the child's actual family and kin and, one must assume, of its mother—the same indigenous woman exalted symbolically as the origin.[12] Vasconcelos disagreed with the establishment of separate schools for indigenous children, yet it's difficult to conceive of his educational program as being superior to those of the people he criticized. In other words, although his program may have included a semblance of openness to Mexico's racial heterogeneity, it was consistent with the project of ultimately annihilating the last traces of "barbarism" in Mexico, helping Mexico to become a fully rational, and thus liberal, nation. Therefore, although Vasconcelos apparently did not endorse the creation of *escuelas-hogares* for indigenous children, and although the *escuelas-hogares* for women were not internment institutions like the indigenous ones, there is a curious link between the ideas of domesticity and its relationship to the development of true nationality.

Other cultural figures in Mexico, such as Manuel Gamio, favored a management model to Vasconcelos's acculturating project, and thus the Directorship of Anthropology was created in 1917, a subdivision of the Department of Agriculture. The project was also intended to homogenize the Mexican nation and to integrate the indigenous into the labor force, but, Gamio reasoned, knowledge about indigenous cultures would ultimately lead to a more effective way of governing them.[13] Mistral apparently chose this latter option as she materialized her Americanist projections. It's unknown whether the phrase *escuela-hogar* was borrowed from the presumably discarded project for indigenous peoples, but in light of Mistral's increasingly clear positioning and her imminent involvement with transnational formations such as the Institute for Intellectual Co-operation and subsequently the Declaration of Human Rights, it makes sense to ponder the connection.

Vasconcelos did not have, properly speaking, an infantilizing concept of indigenous peoples; he rather crudely regarded them as people without reason, unfit for the liberal enterprise unless they were permanently changed. Mistral, by contrast, adopted a familial approach to racial difference. All the projects regarding indigenous education and labor potential ultimately had the same goal: national homogeneity as a prerequisite for capitalist development. Aesthetic culture was regarded as primary in this endeavor and increasingly oriented toward visual culture. This language would eventually find its way into transnational organizations in which Mistral played a considerable role.

Castilianization and Hispanization were regarded as the only alternatives to homogenizing the Mexican nation, and female teachers participated in this endeavor. Conversely, women's schools, though presumably founded on the importance of keeping women aware of their family duties and reproduction, in actuality sent extremely young women to the labor force equipped with skills to make them laborers. It was a double movement of management that interrelated race and gender in intricate ways. Clearly, indigenous peoples were marked for assimilation. Notably, women did not fare essentially better; even those women who ascended to the middle-class as teachers, some of whom attended prestigious Pan-American conferences as delegates, still were routed into dead-end jobs in comparison to male-dominated professions. The feminization of schoolteaching, according to at least one expert, proved to be financially costly to women, because it segregated them into low-paying jobs with few opportunities for promotion.[14]

Without further information, this equivocation cannot be fully addressed. According to Claude Fell, author of a comprehensive study of education in the Vasconcelos years, many of the schoolteachers who taught indigenous children were men, and they were instructed to act as rather strict surrogate fathers.[15] In Mexico, the rural normal schools were mandated to be coeducational, thus refuting the misconception that normal schools were universally feminine across Latin America.[16] Throughout his memoirs, Vasconcelos himself thanks the men who served as teachers during the years of his educational reform, reserving most of his comments on women recruits to crude sexual allusions regarding his own attractiveness.

The casting of the national space as a national "home" has implications beyond the individual calculations or strategies applicable to Mistral as a literary figure. Here begins Mistral's complex and often confusing separation of the public and the private. It appears that in "Palabras" she recommends that women uphold the private values of the home and prepare to rule exclusively over families; however, what was really happening was that certain women were being trained to operate in the public sphere in order to transform it into a kind of national home, where the civilized would separate themselves from the barbaric (Vasconcelos frequently mentions this) and where national citizens would be created. These women were the teachers, not the students, of the Gabriela Mistral School. This school was classified under the rubric "technical school," alongside other vocational and technological schools designed to provide the economy with a skilled class of laborers quickly.[17] Vasconcelos, meanwhile, was vague on the subject of people who did not submit to this process of acculturation into "Mexicanness." Almost always he spoke of assimilation, emphasizing its beneficial aspects for the Indian. Some of the actual programs deployed to instantiate this acculturation utilized other terminology, such as "rehabilitation." Many times the actual programs were charged with separating schoolchildren from the elders in their groups, suggesting a rather violent experience. Even Vasconcelos shifted his original program, drafting, in 1923, a "Program for Indian Redemption," which was consistent with his idea of the teacher as missionary; he borrowed this notion from the religious language of the Spanish conquest.[18]

Domesticity and the "Women's Sphere"

Shortly before Mistral left Mexico, in 1924, upon completing her tenure with the Ministry of Education, José Vasconcelos asked her to compile a primer: "Months ago I received a request from the Ministry of Education of Mexico, asking me to compile a book of *School Readings*" ("Palabras," xv). This was not as informal a request as Mistral might have the reader believe from her introduction. In fact, it was specified in her contract that she would produce a primer for the girls' school that bore her name: "[Mistral would] write schoolbooks of a literary character for the primary and secondary school levels and, especially, one for the School-Home that is named after her."[19] Mistral recounts that she decided to produce a reader "only" for the girls in attendance at the Gabriela Mistral School, which Vasconcelos had opened in Mexico in honor of his guest: "I realized that a textbook should be written by native schoolteachers and not by a foreigner, so I have compiled this work only for the Mexican school that is named after me. I feel that I have certain rights inside it, and, in addition, I have an obligation to leave it a tangible souvenir of my lessons" (xv). Of course, this "only" was merely a rhetorical device; the book was published with a large print run by a Spanish publishing house, Callejas, and distributed internationally.

At first glance, this gesture may seem unremarkable and simply a practical measure intended to enhance Mistral's marketability by targeting a specific audience of middle-class women.[20] However, when placed in the context of Mexican state politics, discussed earlier, the gesture takes on a character more closely tied to the management of not only racially diverse but racially stratified populations. The reader "for women" was intended for middle-class women who would teach in girls' schools, not for all women. "Palabras," therefore, occupies a hybrid space. Instead of establishing identification with women, as critics have noted, Mistral's decision separated her from them, marking her as "group leader"—that is, as an exceptional woman worthy of a following of an exceptional group, specifically a racially privileged class of white schoolteachers and white schoolgirls.

Nevertheless, even Mistral's female audience is not so clearly delineated. Her book, designed to sell massively in the Spanish-speaking world, disseminated an image of bourgeois respectability. But, in fact, the school that bore Mistral's name was a technical school designed for women workers; specifically, it trained them in home-economics skills so they could occupy positions in manufacturing and service jobs.

Mistral identifies reproductive motherhood as the goal of the education of women, figuring the idea of education or pedagogy as the equation that unites woman and state and justifying her intervention in the national discourse. According to "Palabras," this is how the state achieves the reproduction of the good, female national subject—the mother: "*In my opinion, perfect patriotism in women is perfect motherhood.* Therefore, the most patriotic education one can give a woman is one that underscores the obligation to start a family" (xviii [Mistral's emphasis]).

Mistral, though, was arguably more interested in social reproduction—the reproduction of the national body—and not in individual reproduction. A sustained examination of her oeuvre yields an analysis in which spherical thinking has a place, but in a manner far more complex and shifting than what is normally assumed.

The aspect of separation from the sphere of women appears in "Palabras" precisely when Mistral deploys the nationalist rhetoric more straightforwardly. The rhetoric of love of country functions as a bridge to Mistral's social metaphor—the maternal body: "Feminine patriotism is more sentimental than intellectual, and it is formed less by the descriptions of battles and heroic deeds and more by the descriptions of customs that, in a way, woman creates and directs; by the description of the emotion of the native landscape, the sight of which, be it affable or strong, has instilled in her soul softness or strength" (xviii). The native soil and the female body unite in one emotion, love. The woman's abstract body functions as a compendium of the geography of Latin America. This ideal continent-body excludes the problematic axes of difference, as well as the structural inequalities of gender and race, by projecting them elsewhere—beyond the felicity of the clearly demarcated borders of "this miraculous land" [la tierra de milagro] (xviii). The land and woman's body as national symbols remain hidden as state sites of production and reproduction.

The essay indicates that Mistral is aware of her own body's status as a female body exempted from reproduction. Immediately after suggesting the equation between the maternal body and the geography of Latin America, Mistral defends her role as a spokeswoman for the nation from a vague, unnamed attack: "The Americanist nature of my *Readings* is not something that I invented at the last minute to please the government of one of these countries. The shadow of Bolívar has illuminated me with its doctrine for many years now. Ridiculed, deformed by sarcasm in many parts, [it has] not yet become a national consciousness in any of our countries, [but] I love it just like that, as the hope of a few, and as the disdain of oblivion in others. In this, as in everything else, I am in the minority" (xviii).

In fact, it is quite possible that Mistral became an Americanist only after leaving Chile. Before that, she had on occasion been a "tropicalist," part of a vanguardist movement writing anti-imperialist manifestos against the cultural dominance of the United States in the region while emphasizing the Southern Cone's preparedness for capitalist investment through extended pieces on geography and its inhabitants. Being an Americanist, though, required a shift of positions, particularly regarding the United States as capitalist superpower. More than a look outward to the United States as a threatening presence, Americanism became a look inward—a searching for inner threats that could stand in the way of the state project. Tropicalism was not a state discourse; Americanism was.

Mistral rescues an eccentric Bolívar who operates as a mirror of herself, in whom the threat of exclusion from the discursive "nation" produces a high level of anxiety. Why did Gabriela Mistral posit herself as both an object of attack and a constitutive part of this discourse? In fact, she was both. Decidedly, the nation was not about to become queer. Naturally, the spread of unmarried women living without children and in suspiciously same-sex households "without men" would not have been tolerated. Intriguingly enough, however, this does not mean that Mistral's queerness was rejected outright and that she had to hide it from view. In fact, the state exploited Mistral's queerness, and she became aware of its attractiveness within the state project.

In contrast to the abstract, felicitous, proper community that she delineated through references to the landscape, in "Palabras" she claims membership in a sort of "secret society" of persecuted, misunderstood male national heroes. The title of the introduction, "Palabras de la extranjera," suggests that from early on, Mistral wielded her status as outsider in response to real and perceived censure while simultaneously creating a persona as the universal female Latin American, in her guise of mother and schoolteacher.

With strong moralistic overtones, Mistral attempts to regain control of the enunciative situation, but the national imperatives are lost amid the repetition of nationalist rhetoric: "Lacking moral intent with the readings that we now provide to our teachers, we succeed only in forming rhetoricians and dilettantes. We supply leisure for the academies and the athenaeums, but we do not form what Our America needs with an urgency that on occasion, it seems to me, verges on the tragic: *generations with a moral sense; pure and vigorous citizens and women and individuals in whom culture becomes militant when it is animated by action and turns into service*" (xix [Mistral's emphasis]). Mistral adopts the tragic mode of speech and consciously posits herself as the guardian of José Martí's "Nuestra América" [Our America] replete with a prophetic tone and a messianic privilege of suffering that embodies the travails of an entire race. Women can achieve citizenship only by imitation ("ciudadanos *y* mujeres" [emphasis added]), and only in the arena that precedes the political one. From the beginning of her ascent into transnational fame, then, Mistral's imitation of the service and utilitarianism proper of the good national subject was marked as queer, genderwise. It was also conditioned by the national discourse's own anxieties about its allegedly compliant subjects. It is a curious inside/outside position, both for women in general and for Mistral in particular.

The *maestra-poeta* adopts the tragic mode to describe her own life at the conclusion of "Palabras." Mistral's oft-remarked strategy is to belittle herself and to aggrandize the men, like Vasconcelos and Sarmiento, who, as unquestioned citizens, possess the right to this discourse: "*Gratitude*. It has been an honor for this insignificant Chilean schoolteacher to serve, for a short duration, a foreign government that has gained the respect of the Continent, thanks to a work of construction that finds its parallel only in that of the great Sarmiento. . . . I will always be proud to have received from the hand of Minister Vasconcelos the gift of a school in Mexico, as well as the opportunity to write for the women of my blood in the only rest period my life has known" (xx [Mistral's emphasis]).

This passage warrants a closer look. There is no reference to the fact that Mistral is a poet; she refers to herself as "maestra" and, for greater effect, diminishes her prestige by use of the word *pequeña*, which denotes self-infantilization and self-shaming. Once again, she emphasizes her status as outsider by referring to herself as "chilena." Though ostensibly speaking on behalf of an America where literal national origin was secondary, Mistral did not hesitate to refer to herself as a foreigner, or Chilean, when it served another purpose: that of differentiation and of admission into a closed circle of privileged literary and political figures. By equating Vasconcelos's educational reform with that of "el gran Sarmiento" in the nineteenth century, she affirms her own participation in this male society of great educators and writers. The "ridicule" previously mentioned in connection to Bolívar only corroborates her membership in this select group; Sarmiento, for one, endlessly defended himself from one accusation or another. In addition, calling the school a "gift" is a clever way of personalizing a bureaucratic issue; it enables her to shrewdly point to her own importance. Mexico earned the respect of "the Continent" because it enlisted Gabriela Mistral—heiress to Bolívar and

Sarmiento and peer to Vasconcelos. The insinuation is twofold: first, that others should imitate this example and offer similar invitations; and second, that Mistral expects something in return for her "services."

However, Mistral carefully concludes the preface with a reference to "las mujeres de mi sangre" [the women of my blood]. In this essay, she clearly emphasizes and retains her earlier creation of a female reader-ship and a female community, begun in Chile, despite the fact that this community can be only imaginary or textual. By stating that her stay in Mexico has been her only "rest period," Mistral subtly indicates that leaving Chile, and her position as a schoolteacher, engendered not only tangible changes to the circumstances of her life but, most importantly, concrete changes to the circumstances of her writing (here elliptically referred to as "rest").

Subtly, Mistral indexes the trajectory of her own thought. She aligns her woman-centered discourse with a position she inhabited in the Chilean school bureaucracy—a feminized position. In contrast, she indicates that her increasing stature as an Americanist figure is linked to the transna-tional vistas opened by her trip to Mexico—a discourse identified with male power. It is not totally clear, even from this essay, which represents an instance of domestic ideology, that Mistral aligned herself with the "female world" because she actually preferred it. Though she certainly sought the company of women in the sphere of her home, her public world was not same-sex. But more importantly, though her desire may have been directed at the feminine, her identification was not.

Winning the Nobel Prize for literature in 1945 was the culmination of a process of consecration that was slow to crystallize. It granted ultimate recognition of Mistral's involvement in the conservative cultural and sexual politics of the Latin American states. She tailored her discourse to the state's interest in recruiting women for the workforce, particularly as schoolteachers. Mistral's status as the "schoolteacher-poet" suited the continental discourse's doctrine, which upheld the redeeming power of belles lettres and aesthetics in the formation of the "good national subject."[21]

The state was socially conservative not only because of religious and cultural reasons; it was also crucially invested in marriage and repro-duction for economic reasons. Additionally, women were a source of cheap or unpaid labor, such as in the schools. Therefore, the state had a direct stake in the persona of the schoolteacher-mother icon. The potential of such a persona lay in its ability to symbolize, strictly in the state's terms, both the continuation of restrictive social mores and the absorption of women into the labor force as *normalistas* and in other service professions. This followed the Argentine Domingo F. Sarmiento's program for educational reform, begun in the nineteenth century in Chile.

It is important to note that women were recruited as schoolteachers on the basis of their "natural" disposition toward motherhood, which was considered ideal for primary education. It is equally significant to note that normal education, aside from being female, was usually completed by age seventeen or eighteen, and that most *normalistas* eventually became primary and normal schoolteachers. Therefore, one must qualify the extent of educational reform in the nineteenth century as it applied to women. Although undoubtedly reformed in comparison to women's lot before, the normal system still created a sexual division of labor insofar as teaching itself was concerned and regulated the amount of education that women could receive formally. Thus, it curtailed women's advancement, effectively conditioning it to the needs of the state. Women entered the labor force in the name of progress, but only in patriarchal and heterosexist terms: their work could not disturb the normative status quo of heterosexuality and reproduction. Moreover, women's productivity was maximized, and at a low cost for the state.

Historicizing Maternal Discourse

To be sure, women who attended the Gabriela Mistral School were not about to become members of the elite. Elite women did not require any courses in home economics and domestic skills, because they did not perform those services. Did this new class of women owe their feeling of being more "empowered" partially to racial privilege as well?

Actually, maternal discourse as a complex and highly structured system arose hand in hand with social and scientific processes that, in the name of the nation's modernity and progress, fixated most of their attention on the mother. She was seen, in nationalist thought, as the receptacle for the reproduction of the nation, sometimes referred to as "race" and also "civilization." As previously mentioned, Mistral's ideas in the 1920s came quite close to those of eugenicists, and historian Asunción Lavrin explains that Mistral's ideas mirrored those of social-hygiene experts in the 1920s. Lavrin notes further that the state created a legal entity, "the mother-child dyad," to supersede the mother's individual authority over her children and to legally cement the carefully conceived state apparatus to monitor the activities of the home.[22]

This preoccupation for national health led to the creation of new domestic "sciences," especially those of *puericultura* [child care] and "scientific motherhood." Along with responding to pressing social problems, such as infant mortality and child abandonment, the experts associated with the home were undeniably motivated by other prerogatives of progress as well: they sought to demonstrate to the world at large that, far from being backward nations ruled by barbaric peoples, Latin American nations were up to date on the most advanced technologies of population management. Women were the targets of this specialized new knowledge.

But in order to create what Donna Guy aptly calls the "state-approved" mother,[23] the state had to effect a transformation in women's subjectivity, turning motherhood into a state of consciousness and thoroughly suffusing women with the belief that in order to be citizens they had to be biological mothers. When examining the Mistralian corpus, a distinction must be drawn between real mothers and this discursive, national mother created by the state. The latter is the one that was exalted.

Puericultura became a required course in some of the normal schools in Argentina and other nations as early as 1916, the same period Lavrin cites as the period when teaching emerged in the Southern Cone as a feminized profession. Teachers were expected to work closely with doctors to ensure the improvement of the "race" through the education of small children and to ensure that young girls were properly trained in their "biological destiny," to be mothers. Argentina proclaimed the following: "When all mothers know well their responsibilities toward their children, the Argentine Republic will have moved a giant step toward progress and the improvement of the race."[24]

Furthermore, Lavrin observes that

by the time the Fourth Panamerican Congress took place in Santiago in October 1924, there was a solid body of pediatric and health studies behind the concept of child care as an essential element of social hygiene, and women had been consecrated by feminists and nonfeminists as the priestesses of the new subject, though men remained the policymakers.... The advocacy of *puericultura* in national and international congresses boosted private and public efforts to offer adequate care to mothers and children, not in the spirit of charity as had been customary in the first decade of the century, but as a civic service to the nation.[25]

The state, occasionally aided by private agencies, established various institutions and professions that related to mothers and children in their capacities, respectively, as receptacle and future of the nation. These included milk stations, child-care centers, lecture cycles on child rearing and home economics, training centers for breast-feeding, *visitadoras del hogar* [social workers], educational programs on prenatal care for expectant mothers, and other programs.

In short, the language of mothering and child care was suffused with bureaucratic needs and ideas about national duty and had virtually nothing to do with any spontaneous, much less immemorial, feeling for mothers or for their children. This domestic world, usually conceived of as private, was in reality profoundly public and continually policed by the state. The state, no doubt, figured that it had every right to supervise this activity because it was precious to the nation's survival.

When Mistral wrote maternalist poetry, then, she was enacting this surveillance, whether consciously or not. No doubt, her ditties for children became a resource in the schools and day centers and were considered exemplary texts for mothers; it taught them the proper way to feel about their children. One suspects that Mistral may have felt ambivalent about the language she used; after all, mother's milk, the sanctity of the womb, rocking one's child, and other related matters were pure abstractions for her. But what is astounding is that this language, the most controlled of its time, could have been perceived as personal in any way. Citizen's affect—in particular, citizen-mother's affect—could not have been more dictated.

The historian Donna Guy effectively summarizes the state program with the example of Argentina:

> By the 1930's the bodily and symbolic nature of mothering had been challenged, reshaped, and redefined. Mothers were important not only for their wombs and breasts but also for their knowledge, emotional commitment, and awareness of patriotic duty. Initially absent from the body politic through patriarchal clauses of the civil code, women were written "into" mothering as a legal process by 1926. Earlier religious versions of the passive biological mother were infused with greater responsibility and activity through efforts of feminists and public health

officials anxious to lower infant mortality rates and encourage mothers to keep their children. The heart of the caring mother, along with the breast of the hygienized mother were embedded into the republican vision of motherhood. Children now needed their mothers' laps, their emotional nurturing, and their knowledge of scientific mothering.[26]

Mistral, it could be argued, performed a sizable amount of the cultural work needed to create "the caring mother" and to focus women's subjectivity on the reproductive body. She, quite possibly, inaugurated maternal discourse in Mexico; at least one specialist in education, Regina Cortina, believes that Mistral cemented the concept of the "female schoolteacher" in Mexico, and that previously Mexico's system had never been clearly articulated in such strict gender terms.[27] These gender shifts in education must have played a critical role in Mexico's racial politics.

Although Mexico erected itself on the basis of *mestizaje*, it nevertheless upheld as an ideal the assimilation of the indigenous peoples to a Mexican race that was suspiciously Eurocentric, at least judging by the work of some of its notable intellectuals, including Mistral's friend Alfonso Reyes. The link between gender and race is obviously reproduction and the new policing of sex. As Nancy Leys Stepan writes, tying this idea of racial improvement to eugenics in Latin America, the chief aspect that the diverse Latin American racial projects had in common was the notion that to exist as a nation, to erect a proper nationalism, there had to be a true nationhood "on the basis of a common purpose, a shared language and culture, and a homogeneous population"; "thus the Mexicans praised racial hybridization as itself a form of eugenization that would help consolidate the nation around the *mestizo*; the Argentinians condemned racial and cultural intermixture as threats to the unity of an Argentine nationality. In both cases, the eugenists aimed to use hereditary science to produce a biologically consolidated nation."[28] Stepan explains, of course, that eugenics movements in general were interested in reproductive science, but because of Catholic traditions forbidding surgical procedures and birth-control methods in Latin America, the region created its own eugenics, which Stepan labels "matrimonial eugenics." Stepan argues that this approach was even more focused on sexual reproduction and the control of women's behavior in particular: "Eugenists made it clear that women would become the object of eugenic care not as women per se but as mothers. Thus it was not the health of the individual woman that mattered but her health in relation to her

child, that is, to the future germ plasm of the nation" (121–22). States began to legislate in order to prevent the marriages of the "unfit" and called
for the registration of all pregnancies; prenuptial tests and certificates
for marriage were created as a result of the influence of the eugenicists;
and, instead of attending to problems such as poor working conditions
and decent living wages, the state became fixated on the body as holding the biological solution to the problem of the "race." In short, inher-
ent to all eugenic approaches was the reduction of the woman to her
status as mother.

Mistral's apparently contradictory poses might be due to their having
been formed in the thick of the transformation of women's subjectivities erected by the Southern Cone countries, and then her arriving in
Mexico to reshape them. However, the imperative toward the distillation
of a national citizen was essentially the same, and the role played by
women as mothers was pivotal to both projects and to all such nationalist projects across Latin America.

Women's Power and the Privatization of Feeling

The problem arises, then, when instead of a rigorous historicizing of
the emergence and context of "separate spheres," this critical tool mu-
tates to become a new mythology of Mistral and, by extension, women
intellectuals and activists transhistorically. Mistral herself was not an
outsider to state power. She intellectually traveled in a circle of men,
clearly considering herself a part of the group wielding power, not a
powerless person. Although she frequently spoke in the name of the
disenfranchised, many of her essays and her letters confirm that her
life, though same-sex in significant ways, was not necessarily a model of
the "female world of love and ritual."[29]

Mistral perpetually oscillated between representing the maternal body
as one of order and service, on the one hand, and of pleasure and creativity, on the other. Some of her earliest writings presented the mother
as an idiosyncratic, poetic figure.[30] However, women's pleasure continued to be represented strictly as a relationship with the infant child.
This turn to the "mother-child dyad" is the backdrop for Mistral's second
book of poems, Ternura [Tenderness]. This is the most critically ignored
and misunderstood of Mistral's poetry, partly because of Ternura's subject matter, the mother-infant relationship, and partly because of its
poetic form, the lullaby, or, more broadly conceived, literatura infantil

[children's literature]. Latter-day critics have been too quick to skip over these poems in favor of Mistral's more "serious" books of poetry.

Ternura was actually the most widely read of Mistral's poetry books. According to Palma Guillén, Mistral's secretary upon her arrival in Mexico, her companion, and her longtime friend, nine or ten editions were printed during Mistral's lifetime, many more than any of her other books of poetry.[31] This might be due to the poems' "popular" content or to their use in schools and educational programs. Parts of *Ternura* appeared originally in *Desolación* [Desolation], Mistral's first collection of poems; yet other sections of *Ternura* were published as part of *Tala* [Felling], Mistral's third book. This suggests that these lullabies constitute an integral part of Mistral's poetic production, underscoring their autonomy as full-fledged poems in their own right.

Mistral edited all her so-called *literatura infantil* into an expanded edition of *Ternura,* published in 1945, which became the definitive version we know today. In this edition, Mistral appended an extraordinary poetic essay, "Colofón con cara de excusa" [Colophon to offer an apology], to explain the creation of these "children's poems." Like the introduction to *Lecturas para mujeres,* this essay was requested by a male figure; this time, however, instead of the minister of education, her editor placed the request: "Now I have to digress, at my Editor's request" (106). Clearly, male control is still the condition for publication, but now the writing is literary and the output of an author, not a pedagogue. Mistral was firmly anchored in her position as author at this time; indeed, she won the Nobel Prize for literature that very year, 1945.

"Colofón con cara de excusa" plays with Mistral's positioning in the all-female world and points to a key aspect of Mistralian discourse not frequently studied: her narcissistic constructions of self. This narcissism at the individual level, though not collapsible with state narcissism, is linked to it. Familial relationships, the constant appeal to children and to mothering, and the feminine language of affect in place of reason play a critical role in the state's racial, sexual, and gender-related politics. Additionally, the rhetoric of intimacy and privacy, as Lauren Berlant has explored, supplants structural inequalities by helping transform the public sphere into a kind of national family, with its attendant feelings and fantasies.[32] Mistral was one of the chief architects and disseminators of this state-sponsored subjectivation.

The essay's tone is intimate, and it has abandoned the stance of the schoolteacher-turned-doyenne on the subject of women's education. Even sections pertaining to "the race" call attention to the violence, as opposed to the felicity, at the heart of Latin American miscegenation: "I belong to those whose entrails, face and expression are *irregular and perturbed* due to a grafting; I count myself as one of the children of that twisted thing that is called racial experience, or better put, *racial violence*" (109 [Mistral's emphasis]). By remarking on the "monstrous" birth of the race (109), Mistral partially distances herself from her previous role as the spokeswoman of the nation. She turns both her body and the abstract body of *Nuestra América* into a twisted, deformed creature that is born of violence—a far cry from "la tierra de milagro" [this wonderland] of "Palabras." Instead of an appeal to the abstract homogeneity of the common good in "Palabras," allusions to "the race" in "Colofón" call attention to Mistral's troubled relationship to the racial history of Latin America.

These allusions demonstrate that Mistral's idea of racial harmony requires a critique that it has not yet received, for the most part. "Colofón" was written in 1945, two years after the suicide of Mistral's adopted son, Juan Miguel Godoy. It appears to abandon or to lay aside her role as mestiza mother of the nation, in favor of taking up, once again, spherical thinking, with its racially privileged undertones. The folkloric "milk" that Mistral refers to in this afterword is clearly marked as European ("las leches de España" [Spain's milk]), reminiscent of the many poems in *Tenderness* that appeal to biological ties through the exchange of bodily fluids (such as milk and blood) between the mother and the child. The tradition to be recovered and vindicated is understood as philological, monolingual, and Castilian.

After the requisite nod toward male authority (in the form of her editor), Mistral states that lullabies are sites of exclusively female language. The mother, she claims, speaks to herself, not to the child, since the infant cannot yet engage in any kind of verbal conversation: "Once I told this story in Lima, about the sense that the lullaby genre would acquire *if it were regarded as a thing that the mother gives to herself and not to the child, who cannot understand any of it*" (106 [Mistral's emphasis]).

This striking opening sentence reverses the hegemonic interpretation of lullabies. It does not stress the lullaby's primarily utilitarian function.

The oral formula "conté" [I told] of Mistral's sentence downplays the significance of this reversal. The mother, not the child, is the object of the lullaby. The writing subject's attention diverges from the national imperative: the problem is no longer the nation and how women might best serve it. Mistral highlights eccentric aspects of women—how they do not conform, how they are able to be creative, and how they can be characterized as something other than merely the reproductive vessels of the national discourse, as mothers or schoolteachers. The subject of "Colofón" is women and poetry, even when it is ostensibly about lullabies in Latin America: "Why have we women been so daring with poetry, instead of music? Why have we chosen the word, the form of expression most loaded with consequence, charged with the conceptual, which is not our domain?" (106).

Here, Mistral is claiming something radical in a purportedly humble language. She maintains that women have always used words creatively, even though they have not had access to "higher" forms of the word, such as writing. Women, she implies, have always entertained questions of self. If the traditional interpretation of women's lullabies is that they are uncreative and poetically inferior, and that the mother is solely thinking of her child, Mistral's poetic twists appear to manipulate tradition in a way that empowers women. This is, undoubtedly, a movement of deterritorialization, as well as an inversion of categories, and a subversion of the traditional view of women as childbearers and caretakers.

But this is true only for the beginning section of "Colofón," which sets the stage for a more complicated set of maneuvers. Mistral once again masquerades as a mother and once again disguises the fact that she chose a markedly different route from that of most Latin American women. She criticizes "the slow decline of bodily motherhood" (107) and "the refusal of many women to raise children" (107), which she alleges affects the poetic quality of the lullabies (107). In short, she admonishes women for not doing what they are "supposed to do," while reserving the right to abstain from these very prescriptions.

At the same time that Mistral reaffirms women's creativity, she separates significantly from this female tradition. It's reasonable to assert that she did not ever really identify with it. One could construct a cultural-feminist "reclamation" of female tradition and a vindication of neglected feminine creativity, were it not for the inescapable fact that Mistral insists that she is a loner figure who does not fit into this idealized community of women. This figure surfaces not only indirectly, when she states that biological motherhood is necessary for the creation of "real" lullabies (107), but more directly, when she writes: "These songs are very removed from the folkloric ones, which I like the best, and I am aware of this, in the same way [that] I am aware of the vice of my hair and the disarray of my clothes" (108). Mistral creates a continuum that stretches from the aberration of writing and the abandonment of mothering and its detrimental effect, to her own "lullabies" and her figurative body (here turned into an indigent body). She unambiguously marks her separation from the tradition of women's creativity that she has just "celebrated."

In the next movement, Mistral states that her lullabies are poor, mutilated emblems of a love that has no language, a silent love: "The poor things were born in order to invite some musician to set them to music, even as they showed their crippled feet. I made them, half out of the love for the 'hums' of my childhood, half to enable the emotion of other women—poets undo knots, and a love without words is a knot, and it chokes" (108). Two things are significant in this passage. First, Mistral unambiguously, if indirectly, refers to herself as a poet. Second, it is unclear what kind of love she is referring to. Given that Mistral has observed that women have always used words creatively, addressing themselves and their children for centuries, it does not follow that the "love without words" is meant for self or child. Indeed, by now the figure of the child has merged with her own poetic self, and the tradition of oral lullabies has been left behind. Mistral concludes "Colofón" with a series of self-referential, ambiguous paragraphs in which the possibility of queer love might well reside in what is now that most commonplace of phrases: "the love that dare not speak its name."

The poetic "I" retreats into her "country," her "house," her "homeland," her "planet"—all metaphors of the self, of her subjectivity in a culture from which she feels alienated and exiled. The realm of dreams and sleep also escapes the economy of labor and the space of "acceptable" discourse: "In sleep/dreams I have had my lightest, most comfortable house; my true homeland; my sweetest planet. No plains strike me as so spacious, so slippery and so delicate, as those of sleep/dreams" (108). These metaphors relate directly to the discourse of the nation; in fact, they are its strange counterparts. The essay recommends, instead of an idealized, abstract community, an obsessive retreat from the collective consciousness. The sleep or dream induced by lullabies welcomes silence (the absence of speech) and love without words (the failure or impossibility of speech). In her official capacity, Mistral was the producer of speech, of discourse, as well as the embodiment of millions of women. In this poetic capacity, she is alone and silent; she presents herself as released from the body of order, as a destitute repository of that which must not or will not be said.

Once again, Mistral refers to her life as a hard one: "Maybe because my life was harsh, I always blessed sleep and consider it the most divine of graces" (108). In "Palabras," she also concluded with a reference to "rest" and the possibility of writing (for women). In "Colofón," Mistral relates women to motherhood, nighttime, lullabies, poetry, sleep, and dreams—an amalgam that she identifies, indirectly, when she refers to "my elusive homeland" [mi país furtivo] and "the escapade" [la escapada] (108).

Writing these "songs" figures explicitly as a way to access this homeland, where the conflation of sexual and maternal love is suggested in the complicity between the "I" and the "child": "Some stretches of these Songs— sometimes one or two accomplished verses—afford me that familiar exit to my elusive country, open the crack or trap door of the escapade. The musical counterpoint from which the child slides off leaving the mother tricked and singing uselessly; this last step I know very well. In this or that word, *the child and I turn our backs onto the world and escape it,* circling it just like the cape that hinders running" (108 [emphasis added]).

The subtle perversion of the official language of "family" and of "modesty" is particularly evident in "Colofón." In the passage just quoted, for example, the adjective "familiar" is used to describe the "exit" from the world into sleep and marks the chosen separation of the "I" from communal relationships. The topos of false modesty reappears in the reference to "one or two accomplished verses," the identity of which, however, will not be revealed to the reader, thus creating an aura of secrecy that further separates the "I" from the reader. Obviously, Mistral removes the language of reproduction and child care from an economy of reproductive functions.

The essay departs significantly from Mistral's prescriptive persona and contains a rare focus on her poetic self. It also, however, returns to Mistral's public capacities, albeit in a muted form. The last sections of the essay partially restore her self-deprecating stance ("an enthusiastic but failed artisan"[109]), her persona of the "Schoolteacher of America"

("May the schoolteachers forgive me for the outrage of my doing and redoing"[109]), and her position as the spiritual mother of Latin America's children—but the latter occurs with an important caveat. At the very end of the essay, she compares "children's expression" to a "crystalline and deep mystery" (110)—transparent, yet unreachable and inextinguishable, simultaneously simple and complex: "it fools sight and hand with its false superficiality" (110). This section was written, clearly enough, as a warning, to urge a close examination of her "children's literature" with an eye to discovering a hidden yet obvious meaning.

Could this hidden and obvious meaning possibly be queer desire? It is conceivable. Queer sexuality remains, at face value, as absent from this discourse as it is from the more strongly prescriptive "Palabras." A heteronormative discourse of woman-identification can hope to render lesbian desire only partially and, unless it is highly performative, probably not at all. Because lesbianism is excluded from the patriarchal, heterosexist conception of motherhood in traditional Latin America, it may seem, upon first glance, wholly invisible from Mistral's poetry, especially in her texts of motherhood. However, reading against the grain, with Mistral's sexual indeterminacy in mind, enables a radically different reading. *Ternura*'s lullabies have been interpreted as conservative statements on motherhood and womanhood, but, if read more carefully, some of these same lullabies can emerge as erotic poems. A close reading of "Colofón" substantiates this hypothesis; in it, Mistral provides the attentive reader with clues to initiate this other reading.

It is tempting to read "Colofón" as the essay that Mistral heralded at the beginning of "Palabras de la extranjera": "an essay that I will write someday, in my homeland, for the women of Latin America" (xv). Exactly what, or where, is this promised "homeland" for Mistral, who referred to herself as "la extranjera" [the foreigner] in "Palabras"? Might it not be located in an apparently heterosexual space, reproductive motherhood, but stripped of reproduction? Furthermore, might not this queerness be aligned with racial ideas of white superiority?

In "Palabras," reproductive motherhood was a site of profit, of the maximization of female bodies, and it emphasized the service sector as an extension of the home. In "Colofón," the emphasis turns precisely to the representation of a motherhood, so to speak, without maximization and, at times, literally without the child. The "home" of "Colofón" is a narcissistic home, one that signifies only itself ("Maybe I will die putting myself to sleep, turned into mother of myself" [108]). If this is an instance of "queering," then it becomes imperative to accept that queering is not concerned with the social, in some instances—that it can be resolutely against the social, enforcing regimes of privatization while disguised as purely "affective" discourse.

The discursive creation of a "feminine power" signifying resistance is a call to a different type of privatization from that of the essay "Palabras de la extranjera." "Palabras" advocated the creation of the nation as a home, with a role for women as its directors. Not explicitly articulated, but discernible nonetheless, is a racialized form of mothering in which white mothers would oversee the integration of racially marked children. More specifically, national citizens would be infantilized and the experience of citizenship would become akin to a state of familial intimacy.[33]

In "Colofón," desire itself becomes privatized and hermetic, and the racial project shifts once again to an unspecific state of white dominance, but this time removed from the egalitarian equivalencies attempted by the former "maternalist" position. An undifferentiated state of whiteness is encoded culturally by the signifiers employed in patriotic language once they become disembodied, free-floating, and universalist: blood ties, mother's milk as the transmitter of national ties, and the lullaby form as an intensely private encounter with the object of desire—whatever it may be.

"Palabras" authorized a process of domestication presented as desirable domesticity; "Colofón" straightforwardly abandons any concern for a public good and recommends instead a privatized version of "resistance" understood as self-making and not much more, a kind of "open statement" that could be phrased thus: "Women have been creative for centuries; women's creativity cannot be stifled." But in the process of schooling that Mistral spearheaded, some women's creativity *was* stifled, and other women were cast out of the national fold. Both essays are instances of female enunciation and of spherical thinking; both are ultimately conservative and abet privatization, although of differing casts.

Motherhood in "Palabras" is a social mandate; in "Colofón" it is a private affair. In "Palabras," the maternal discourse suggests that education preserves the importance of the mother. "Colofón," by contrast, posits the mother as a near-renegade figure, marginal and ignored. "Palabras," even as it deploys republican motherhood and female sentimentality, does not critique state rationality; in fact, the essay's tone is markedly rational and programmatic. To borrow the words of cultural critic Lauren Berlant, "Colofón" abandons the pedagogical imperative in favor of "a heightened state of affect and feeling"—presumably among women—but with no clear mandate or goal other than "a type of survival" and an "escape from suffering."[34] It proposes an exit from political life through its exaltation of dreaming and sleep. "Colofón" erases the public persona of Mistral and expresses a desire for the personal realization of this now emptied "I."

As Berlant (along with other critics) has indicated, such is the contradictory and self-defeating nature of sentimental politics: "The political as a place of acts oriented toward publicness becomes replaced by a world of private thoughts, leanings, and gestures. Suffering, in this personal-public context, becomes answered by survival, which is then recoded as freedom. Meanwhile, we lose the original impulse behind sentimental politics, which is to see the individual effects of mass social violence as *different from* the causes, which are impersonal and depersonalizing" (641). The racialization of the private/public split intersects with both poles of sentimental discourse: the nation as home and the self as home.

Mistral's writings on the subject of women's enfranchisement were articulated within separate-spheres discourse. She wrote that women had special aptitudes different from men's; she was cautious regarding the vote; she avoided the "feminist" label; she believed that men were rational beings whereas women were "affective." For instance, in a 1927 essay, "Feminismo" [Feminism], she proposed that human labor be divided into three groups:

> The first branch has room for contrasting pursuits: the brutish professions, as well as a task that could be called directing the world. Here, we would include the miner all the way to Aristotle, spiritual and philosophical counselor to all peoples.
> The second branch would be destined to pluck all men from light professions in which he may become effeminate, *losing his male dignity,* and appears as a true invader.
> The last branch would encompass various types of activities that we can't really define as feminine or masculine, because they require an average energy. So they don't entail the danger of exhaustion for women, nor the possibility for men of making a living out of a grotesque employment.[35]

Mistral was roundly criticized by feminists for these and other pronouncements made in the essay, which prompted her to respond angrily in that same year, 1927, that she was not an enemy of the working woman, that she was not against the vote, and that she was not an advocate of a separate morality for the sexes.[36] In "El voto femenino" [The female vote] (1928), she provided an analysis of her reservations about the female vote; for her, it was hazardous to vote simply as women for women, and she preferred having clear constituencies distributed by class or profession and represented by one of the group's own.[37] She resurrected the idea of guilds to illustrate this point. In the same article, though, she also lauded measures taken in fascist states as regards the women's vote, seemingly espousing an almost right-wing femininity and rendering her positions extremely difficult to decipher at times. But, returning to my earlier point, it's undeniable that Mistral, on several occasions, called for specific reforms based on a logic of separate spheres of action within the public domain, governed by gender.

Earlier writings concentrated on concrete social issues and called on the nascent liberal government to institute public education countrywide and to employ women in sectors appropriate to their feminine calling—in family courts or pacifist movements, for instance.[38] Unfortunately, many times these calls justified the placement of women in service professions without much hope of advancement. Still, Mistral was often focused on concrete social issues and, although essentially conservative, did espouse some positions that could be construed as feminist.

Later, when she was famous but not yet a Nobel Prize recipient, Mistral responded to a request from Uruguay's Ministry of Education to "explain how women wrote" with a description refusing the essentialist confession or testimony regarding "feminine artistry." In the speech "Cómo escribo" [How I write] (1938), she named the "radical disorder of women," presaging the argument of difference in which women escape the reality imposed through the state's program of rationality and partition of spheres according to sex.[39] This essay presents essentialist arguments about women, but its goal is markedly different from that of both "Palabras" and "Colofón"; it represents something akin to what transnational feminist Gayatri Spivak describes as "strategic essentialism," a self-conscious deployment of identity categories for defined political ends, understood as being immediately beneficial to a disenfranchised group.[40] (Spivak's reference is to progressive movements, but by its very structure nothing prevents strategic essentialism from being deployed in conservative quarters.) In fact, Mistral alludes to the strategic nature of feminine discourse when she writes, in "Cómo escribo," "To reduce to norms and a stable profile our common will, is a Roman enterprise that we can easily dismantle, by feigning to obey it."[41] And in the rest of the essay, she proceeds to describe, in a literal fashion, how she writes, without any recourse to identitarian concepts of the feminine.

Nevertheless, in Mistral's iconic capacity as "national stereotype," maternal discourse, in her case, cannot be separated from divisions, especially racial divisions, that are central to nationalist thought, whether nationalist thought be openly enunciated, as in "Palabras," or deployed in the language of absolute privacy and unintelligibility, as in "Colofón." Whereas the first essay, strictly speaking, is nationalist, reproducing nationalism's classic treatment of women, the second is narcissistic, exposing some of nationalism's dependency upon a paranoid state where all subjects are preoccupied with their extinction in the context of "national belonging." The following chapter turns to this relationship.

CHAPTER FOUR

Intimate Nationalism

National discourse in Chile during the first decades of the twentieth century became focused on, among other things, reproduction and the small child, even as it contributed to take over the idea of reproduction from the mother and to represent a state of parthenogenesis—the people beget the people—with the state's parental functions occluded. The despised mother, however, could not simply be eliminated from this affective landscape. Enter Mistral's lullabies, which represent, above all other things, the mother's body as a site of intimate national pleasure. This maternal body appears free-floating and self-sufficient. Often, it is separated from its children or exists in a symbiotic state with the child-to-be. Maternal plenitude's comfort exists more properly in the precarious safety of the dreamwork than as a representation of waking life. Indeed, *dream* and *sleep* are words Mistral used to describe her poems as well as her desires, often confounding the two.

From the time Mistral began writing children's poems to the end of their production, in 1945, the poems became increasingly self-referential. It could be argued that they already were so from 1910 to 1920, when Mistral was writing poems mostly for inclusion in textbooks in Chile. Her self-focus enabled her to bolster her career, since she was able to distinguish herself as a special and talented schoolteacher. The quality of remove was underscored by the fact that Mistral had no recognizable maternal body in strict social terms. (This was true even after Mistral became a mother, because her motherhood was nonreproductive.) Her existence as national mother might have related to her not representing the maternal body physically herself. This disjuncture explains why the lullabies examine, exhibit, and disseminate the idea of the mother's reproductive body but at all times oddly keep the mother's body separated from the child. Given that Mistral's lullabies and children's poetry were memorized in the schools, it seems logical to conclude that the children were memorizing a quandary: Who was the national mother? What relationship did she have to their actual mothers? How would she be apprehended? What would happen to her?

Mistral, it appears, was aiming straight at mass norms of affect through her extensive work in the children's genre. It seems curious that her lullabies have been interpreted as originating in her exaggerated sense of self-sacrifice. Produced for recital in schools (in part to foment linguistic standards and to increase literacy skills), they circulated widely in textbooks, stemming from an obligation to read, write, and be schooled into citizenship. Thus, their pleasure was linked to order and rationality, their privacy wedded to the publicness of the school. The mother, in fact, was an absence for these children, as they insistently became separated physically and psychologically from their own homes.

The mandate to represent "Chileanness" similarly revolves around absence and lack. Mistral wrote plainly about the dearth of creativity within the oral tradition of Chile. In "Sobre sus *Canciones de cuna*" [Regarding her *Lullabies*] (1938), she expressed reservations about the Chilean tradition:

My lullabies in *Desolación*... have a modest and happy origin.
The enormous Spanish folklore... never arrived in America, except for some very poor, ragged, one-legged versions. When I was in Madrid for two years, I busied myself with compiling folklore in its best texts and it was then that I realized, with pain and shame, that there was a mass of songs and lullabies that had not traveled to America in the three caravels, full of men, and that, when it did travel, it was plebeianized and unmade in our *mestizo*, disloyal mouths.
I only heard one lullaby in Chile, sung by the most disparate women; the nanny of rich people, peasant women, and urban mothers. It's almost grotesque.... It really sounds more like it was written for kittens.
In contrast, the melodies that it is sung to are often pretty. It's the law that dictates that music flies like an archangel over texts that are unhappy and bland.
My theory regarding lullabies is very simple. When one Chilean critic told me that my lullabies "surpassed" infantile understanding, I answered,

tongue-in-cheek, that the lullaby... cannot be understood by the three-month-old infant; that the lullaby is written for the mother and that's why it has to be tender, loving, and pointed so that she likes it, so that she repeats the verses and experiences her own love, her own tenderness. Therefore, this song is like a fruit that's been cut in half. Half goes to the child—the pure melody—and the lyrics go entirely to the mother.[1]

Mistral added that after the influx of her children's poetry in Chile, other women started authoring verses. Therefore, she credited herself very directly and literally with the birth of the genre, not only in Chile but throughout Latin America. This idea became the basis for the 1945 essay "Colofón con cara de excusa" [Colophon to offer an apology], examined in chapter 3, which states that the lullaby form was "dead," or rather "unborn," in Latin America, and that Mistral reconnected the cultural plug of America to Spain, thus saving the genre from extinction. This is, of course, a paradoxical idea. She implies that the genre never existed to begin with, so how could it have experienced dissolution?

Could it be that Chile's oral tradition was indigenous, not Spanish; that the descendants of the colonizers did not recognize oral traditions in languages other than their own as national patrimony? Indeed, Mistral's impatience with Chile and her expressions of thankfulness for Spain's rich oral tradition might be reconsidered in this context. Perhaps the familial arrangements of the native peoples of Chile did not correspond to the configuration favored by industrial society. There is room to speculate whether the status of the mother within non-Creole Chile at all favored the state's intimate play with family power, or whether the mother herself, as a creature of discourse, had to be invented.

Most scholars who have written about the children's genre have not paid attention to its racial aspects. As a practitioner of this poetry, Mistral was in a treacherous position. She became ensconced in the positions of mother- and child-lover, never quite able to free herself from these constructions. In other words, she became tied to these discursive domains. Moreover, because Mistral had to embody racial love, she also had to develop a language of love and intimacy for racial others for whom she may, in fact, have had little compassion. Thus, the public (read white) mothering of diverse racial children proceeded along two axes: on the one hand, an official language of love and, on the other, a private language much more difficult to decipher. Some of the lullabies hint at this private and ambivalent language.

The lullaby form expressed an apparently universal yet, upon closer examination, racialized love. When Mistral was still in Chile, she wrote some of the lullabies she is best known for, such as the memorable "Meciendo" [Rocking]: "El mar sus miles de olas / mece, divino. / Oyendo a los mares amantes, / mezo a mi niño" [The divine sea rocks its thousand waves; hearing the lover-seas, I rock my child]; or the more didactic "Piececitos" [Little feet]: "Piececitos de niño, / azulosos de frío, / cómo os ven y no os cubren, / Dios mío!" [Children's tiny feet, / turned blue in the cold, / how is it possible they not cover you when they see you, / dear God!].[2] Both poems reference God, but, significantly, "Meciendo," written in Punta Arenas but not part of the original *Desolación* [Desolation], evokes a divine power that is pantheistic and not necessarily Christian, whereas "Piececitos," part of the original *Desolación*, evokes God as a humanitarian presence in the context of social injustice and Chile's "war on poverty." "Meciendo" multiplies the reach of religiosity in the poem, possibly amplifying the meaning of maternal "love." This occurs through minor details not apparent in English translations: the substitution of a plural *mares* for the singular *mar*, and the addition of the word *amantes*, often mistranslated as "loving." By contrast, "Piececitos" has no metaphorical richness and was clearly written to represent the value of piety in a secular world. "Meciendo" shares with the best poems of *Ternura* [Tenderness] a dreamlike quality. Although some critics have detected an atavistic impulse toward the stock values of the countryside in Mistral (and this aspect is present), poems like "Meciendo" don't so much evoke a return to the past as present a preservation of a loved object in an uncanny time.

Before leaving Chile, Mistral saw many of her pedagogical poems published in elementary schoolbooks. Presumably, this substantiated the state's increasing exaltation of the official mother. Yet it is odd to notice that many poems stress separation from the mother at an age when separation is not desirable—that is, in early infancy. After 1922, Mistral began to expand the volume significantly, adding a fair number of lullabies, including those concerning racialized subjects, such as "Niño mexicano" [Mexican child] and "Cajita de Olinalá" [Little box of Olinalá]. This process would not end until 1945, when she published the definitive version of *Ternura*. By then, Mistral had excised all of her children's poems that had appeared in other volumes (*Desolación* and the first edition of *Tala* [Felling]), prophylactically separating them from the rest of her poetry into one self-contained volume. Between the two stages of composing the final *Ternura*, two visions of children come into play. These visions produce a type of battle for representation, coexisting only precariously in the final volume.

Although the lullabies are commonly regarded as expressing identical kinds of love, the first set of poems, written in Chile, deal with a child who does not appear very national at all. Indeed, the child is quite abstract, bearing hardly any regional markers, including those of Chilean Spanish. The second set of lullabies, written after Mistral's departure from Chile, consistently mark the child with more explicitly nationalist signs of the "popular."[3]

When the poems were collected in a single volume, in 1945, two things happened. First, the fundamental feature of their genesis—that they were actually produced for two markedly different audiences—was forgotten. Second, the initial poems experienced diverse lives. While accommodating the demands of an explicitly racialized public sphere increasingly articulated around familial intimacy, they nevertheless did not simply discard their original marking as white, Eurocentric poetry. Written as abstractions within the climate of a state wishing to legislate and police actual mothers, they were mixed later with other types of poems in which children, usually older ones, are welded to national origin and affiliated with a national, mythical mother. This hybrid mother was represented by the image of someone who was not a mother and not maternal: Mistral herself. The infant, in particular, evolved into a fetish for "America." Indeed, the poems themselves became fetishes, for the national imagery and also for Mistral herself. The emblem of a separation that had to take place but that could not be avowed and thus mourned, the infant child that Mistral identified so much with—a construction of hers and not to be confused with any actual infants—lived on in psychic time, dangerously close to the foreclosure of the social world and to paranoia, specifically in the Kleinian sense of paranoid-depressive position.[4]

It's well worth remembering that Mistral's own pleasures as a mother were completely circumscribed, and it is conceivable that her own dilemma found its way into the lullabies. Regardless of whether she desired children or not—something that seems impossible to know, as there is no personal writing to examine—it is certain that the strictures surrounding "acceptable" motherhood conspired against any form of parenting other than what was officially sanctioned. Within the national imagery, she had to present as childless. It seems, from her early "Poema del hijo" [The child's poem] that she was aware of this requirement:

¡Bendito pecho mío en que a mis gentes hundo
y bendito mi vientre en que mi raza muere!
¡La cara de mi madre ya no irá por el mundo
ni su voz sobre el viento, trocada en miserere!

[Blessed be my breast in which I drown my people, and blessed be my womb in which my race dies! My mother's face will not go forth in the world and her voice, turned into a miserere, won't ride the wind!][5]

The poem is apparently autobiographical; it speaks of Mistral's infertility in terms of age, but as Mistral was only thirty years old when she wrote it, infertility takes on a prophetic character. The identification between herself and the "race" ("mis gentes" does not yet evoke "the people" in the national-popular sense) is evoked by death; she claims literally that her race will die in her womb. She blesses both her breast and her womb, however, because they will preserve her "mother's face" and so prevent her mother from further suffering. Exactly what kind of suffering is being prevented is unclear.

Mistral's dismal outlook could be a pose, recalling her early desire to be, like the *modernistas*, a *poète maudit*, or it could be a feminine mask reminiscent of the accepted tradition of women's poetry as a catalog of suffering and defeat. The religious overtones clearly suggested by the phrase "Blessed be" indicate an allusion to the Virgin Mary. Mistral, however, blesses a rather different womb and breast: first, her own, appropriating, rather more than is comfortable, the stance of the Virgin Mary; second, her reproductive organs as receptacles to preserve the race, but only through death.

Mistral might have experienced both gender and racial discourse as stifling impositions contrary to her desires and feelings, though occurring at different moments. While in Chile, she chose to represent women through the symbol of motherhood. Once in Mexico, she took on racial aspects so that she could better represent mestizo Latin America. It is also conceivable that her intense focus on what she eventually labeled "the racial pulse of the people," as well as her preoccupations with origin, life, and extinction of the nation, might have had something to do with her own sense of persecution, thus accounting in part for the closed, protected space the lullabies ultimately create.

The lullabies appear to exhibit several classic psychoanalytic quandaries, including narcissism, melancholia, and paranoia.[6] Not coincidentally, Freud thought that these quandaries could lead to homosexuality if not "cured." Freud's homophobic and misogynist constructions have been amply critiqued. Following the lead of theorists like Eve Sedgwick, Judith Butler, and Diana Fuss, it's possible to utilize the psychoanalytic framework against its own grain.[7] Mistral's role should not be simplistically reduced to indoctrinating people into normative gender roles without being affected herself. But her participation in the reproduction of the state must not be minimized or rationalized as an effect of "oppression" either. Rather, it's more productive and truer to Mistral's own life to see these psychoanalytic struggles in the context of homosexuality's subjection to heteronormativity. If heteronormativity requires, as it does, that all women should be heterosexual; if it dictates that all women who want to be mothers can do so only through heterosexual relations; if it forces upon the subject a renunciation of homosexuality as a condition for acquiring heterosexuality, as Freud thought, then clearly Freud's characterization of these disorders would be intimately tied to his understanding of what homosexuality and heterosexuality were.

It's possible that Mistral was acquainted with these psychoanalytic interpretations of "abnormality." The poetic "I" she created for the lullabies—nearly all feature a first-person speaking subject—rehearses a number of primal fantasies that are commonly associated with narcissism. Bodily dispossession, a loss of body boundaries, and fantasies of merging with the mother figure often occur. An aspect of narcissism is its regression to a stage where the child has not yet separated from its mother's body—where it refuses to separate. This may be accompanied by the fetishism surrounding small objects or the idea of smallness, reminiscent of the mother's body and especially of her sexuality as the conduits to selfhood. (Freud considered part of narcissism the clinging to a clitoral as opposed to a penile sexuality. Boys had less difficulty with this transition, but for girls, apparently, it was next to impossible not to develop narcissism.) There is also the appearance of fluids, which emanate from the mother's body and signify plenitude and engulfment at the same time. Pleasure struggles with service, winning out in the final analysis; certainly the most memorable poems start from ideals of service and social life but quickly turn away to a world defined mostly by desire.[8] This is not an argument for a simplistic "desire for the mother" and consequent incest, but rather a sketch of the infantilized citizen. Trying to get away from asphyxiating mother-love, represented as anaclitic attachment, the subject stumbles upon the only other object-choice available: self-love, hence narcissim.[9] Citizens are offered two choices: the mother, with her extreme oscillation between good and bad, asphyxiation or abandonment; or equally polarized self-love, oscillating between delusional ideas of perfection and equally delusional debasement. In social terms, narcissim takes the form of a cathexis with another narcissistic subject—the leader, in Freud's view of group psychology.[10]

The lullabies exceed their strictly pedagogical purpose, if we understand this purpose to be merely the social reproduction of mothering. Clearly, the lullabies represent an especially complex example of speech genres. In contradistinction to the later *Tala*, and *Lagar* [Wine press], and to the posthumous *Poema de Chile* [Poem of Chile], where the pedagogical impulse is secondary or absent, the lullabies surrender to the nightmarish flip side of nationalism. Pedagogical in the perverse sense, they call national subjects to their duty, but only by reminding them of everything they have to give up.[11]

Mistral's lullabies go one step further than most Latin American lullabies. They create an intensely scopic scenario focused on the physical, primary functions of the mother's and child's bodies. The total absence of the father figure excludes any references to the social world, yet the lullabies were published and sung in schools as markers of national consciousness, preparatory exercises for citizenship. The lullabies represented a success story for Mistral, and they confined her to a nightmarish and infantile world, constraining her literary field of action. Inscribing fear of the unknown at times, they represent safety and pleasurable feelings at other moments. They record anxiety and pain (at times dismembering the child), and they speak to orgasmic release and joy.

In their play with the notion of the national family, the lullabies are both narcissistic and nationalist, recreating scenarios of regression while upholding a normative citizenship based on national allegiance. The writing subject engages public fantasies concerning mothers and children, or, more accurately, mother and child. The lullabies displace the "natural" world and the world of the state but borrow the elements of those worlds, particularly their biologistic, binary gender-sex constructions and the discordant world of race re-created in two distinct and competing regional contexts.

The language of narcissism possesses certain qualities. Among them are infantilism or a perpetual state of "childlikeness"; regression; self-pity and debasement; sickness; inability to project anything other than a desire for identification; fixation on the mother's plenitude, an inner world; absence of the father and rejection of the outside world;[12] recourse to a dreamlike world; madness; a pronounced fetishism of the small; a transit through diverse bodily, maternal liquids; and a loss of boundaries between bodies. Practically all appear in Mistral's lullabies. Could this indicate the extent to which Mistral's psychology and the state psychology became identified as one and the same thing, and the degree to which Mistral's excessive affect—paranoid and narcissistic—became the norm for mass affect in the dominant Latin American nationalism? Paranoia need not be only the state of mind wherein the individual fears annihilation by the malfeasance of another. Paranoia can also be the resulting psychic state of too much surveillance, visibility, encoding, and representing. Indeed, paranoia, as Melanie Klein observes, can also be the result of too much love.[13]

What is significant to consider here, then, is whether this paranoid imagery, this narcissistic world, entered a national psyche via the canon of pedagogical texts. Did the nationalist canon contribute to a sense of national belonging as, at best, a precarious existence always on the verge of threat? Mistral's double recourse to language simultaneously narcissistic and nationalist became not only confounded in her mind but also conducive to a strain of narcissistic behavior in the citizenry, understood not as a robotic duplication of state wishes but as a preoccupation with life and extinction characteristic of all narcissistic and paranoid subjects.

Clarifying in this respect is Mistral's fraught relationship with her own son, Juan Miguel Godoy, and her reaction to his death by suicide. Mistral assembled the final version of *Ternura* in the aftermath of his death. At this moment she finally put her lullabies "to rest." She could not, however, put her son to rest. In the refusal of mourning, the division between the official and private languages of love emerges. Their conflict is never more apparent than in the disturbing correspondence discussed in the following section, where the specters of nonreproductive motherhood and homosexuality also enter.

Stabat Mater

When Mistral became a mother, her very being became paradoxical. Until then, she had been the "Mother of the People," alone of all her sex, as Marina Warner's apt title goes.[14] Yet she chose to be a mother. Are these two positions reconcilable? To some extent, she was recognized only as Juan Miguel's mother figure, not his actual mother. Her image was that of the avuncular figure, a formulation resuscitated interestingly by Eve Sedgwick in relation to gay male figures, but not as enabling in this particular case.[15]

During her life, much was made of Mistral's probable biological parentage of Juan Miguel. Apparently, her decision to adopt Juan Miguel required an explanation. Consequently, an older half brother, Juan Godoy, appeared unexpectedly to meet her in Spain. He had married a Catalan woman. One legend goes that Mistral warned this young woman about the tendencies of the "men of her family." In the throes of passion, Maria Mendonza resisted the advice and became pregnant with Juan Miguel. Fulfilling Mistral's prediction, the older Godoy promptly abandoned Mendonza, confirming Mistral's prophetic qualities and, coincidentally enough, repeating her own life story (Mistral's father had abandoned the home). Selflessly, Mistral agreed to assist Mendonza, but before long the young woman fell ill and died. Juan Miguel was left in the care of his biological aunt, who, from that point, loved him like a mother but could not in actuality fulfill that role or fill in for the loss of the "true" mother. Mendonza's status as dead mother resonates with the precarious status of mothers in official discourse, at once alive and dead, discursively speaking. It also reminds us of the father's absence. Juan Godoy, unsurprisingly, disappeared, simultaneously ineffectual and exonerated.

There is no certainty regarding the numerous stories of Juan Miguel's origin; however, critics seem to favor this one as the most plausible. Perhaps soon a researcher will try to locate the birth records of Juan Miguel's presumed biological mother or the medical records of her stay in a sanatorium in Switzerland (a Thomas Mann–style twist that lends a literary aura to the story, underscoring its metaphorical aspect). It is intriguing that both the origin and the demise of Juan Miguel Godoy are so enshrouded in mystery. It's also interesting that the scenario of this story is Spain, the same country that Mistral repeatedly credits with keeping the oral tradition in Spanish alive, as opposed to the "meager" Latin American contribution. When Mistral wrote that she considered the tradition itself to be "in pañales" [in diapers], she borrowed the language of child care to classify Latin American languages as infantile and, one suspects, close to infirm.

Undoubtedly, Gabriela Mistral and Palma Guillén, Mistral's secretary during the 1920s and one of the women who fully participated in the project of educational reform in the Vasconcelian period in Mexico, considered themselves a "couple" responsible for the welfare of Juan Miguel Godoy. Surely, both assumed they were raising Juan Miguel Godoy according to his best interests. However, Mistral and Guillén confused the national prescriptions that they had ardently worked for with parental precepts about raising children. They confused "tenderness" or affect with citizen behavior, ostensibly driving the child to madness, not unlike that recorded in Mistral's *Ternura*. There, infantile happiness borders on a state of total symbiosis with the mother and thus becomes a claustrophobia bordering on insanity. Because the meshing of affect and citizen behavior had occurred around the articulation of Mistral as national mother, its repercussions were particularly acute in this family, an alternative family in which, surprisingly, Palma Guillén, the more feminine-looking of the couple, was the father-figure and Mistral, more obviously masculine, symbolized the mother.

Luis Vargas Saavedra published the letters Mistral and Guillén exchanged about their son's death in *El otro suicida de Gabriela Mistral* [The suicidal other of Gabriela Mistral].[16] The title unfortunately exploits the sensationalism of the event. Equally unfortunate is the fact that Vargas Saavedra reproduces, instead of critiquing, Mistral's evolving account of the suicide as a story of racial murder and xenophobia. From the account, Mistral collapsed world affairs and her own tragedy, experiencing them as one and the same. Thus, her nationalism betrayed a strong narcissistic component. This would be but a particularity were it not that this positioning, of nationalism as narcissistic, intensely affected Latin American pedagogy—schoolchildren in particular, and national citizens in general, as they were interpellated by the state.

Vargas Saavedra recounts that Palma Guillén gave him the letters contained in the book when she was very old, fearing that they would be lost when she died. When I interviewed him in Santiago, Chile, in August

2000, about this particular correspondence, he told me that he had expected to receive many more materials than he did—at least a box full of letters spanning a couple of decades, instead of the handful reprinted in the book. It is simply not known what happened to them. Guillén could surely have destroyed some of Mistral's and Juan Miguel Godoy's letters to her. As far as the bulk of Guillén's own letters to Mistral, their whereabouts or fate is also unknown. The entire circumstances of the women's relationship remain, for the present time, muddled and mysterious.[17]

I agree with Vargas Saavedra that Palma Guillén and Gabriela Mistral surely exchanged more letters than the few available in print. Because of the scarcity of materials and the lack of biographical detail about any of Mistral's companions, the triangular relationship between Guillén, Mistral, and Juan Miguel is truly hard to unravel. For instance, how much time did they live in physical proximity to each other, and when, exactly, did Guillén and Mistral separate, and why? Additionally, when did their differences over how Juan Miguel should be raised occur? I have sought some answers from Vargas Saavedra himself, and from Guillén's biographer, the Mexican historian Gabriela Cano. Both have responded that these details are simply unknown.

The handful of letters contained in Vargas Saavedra's volume are mostly from Guillén to Mistral, along with one from Guillén to Juan Miguel. During this correspondence, Palma Guillén resided in Mexico City, and Gabriela Mistral lived in Petrópolis, Brazil, in the months before Juan Miguel committed suicide by ingesting a lethal dose of arsenic. Guillén and Mistral were clearly worried about him, but their narratives exhibit two different and extreme poles.

Vargas Saavedra reprinted the available correspondence, along with a preface in which he recapitulates events according to the narrative of patriarchal absence:

> From my perusal of [Mistral's life] I have gleaned the sketches of a childhood in constant turmoil and uprooting. [Juan Miguel] changed languages, schools, weather, and friendships continually. He was intermittently deprived of his adoptive mother. He lacked the presence of a father or any man that could have served as an example and as a teacher. . . . Maybe he was spoiled because he was presented with two contrary directives: one, the discipline of Palma Guillén, the other, the indulgence of Gabriela Mistral. He tried as best he could to adopt the best aspects of both, as all children of incomplete households develop the psychological ability to accomplish. (25)

It's unhelpful to encounter Vargas Saavedra's negative rendition of the "lesbian family," as it doesn't really allow readers to arrive at their own conclusions about the correspondence. Nevertheless, in a way, Vargas zeroed in on an important aspect of the few letters that are available: that the women perceived themselves in entirely different parental roles and, moreover, that these roles did not correspond to the way their bodies circulated publicly in terms of gender. It would seem that their affect or tenderness toward their adoptive child of suspicious origins functioned as an occasion to reverse their public roles, a kind of escape hatch from the repressive normalization that, unfortunately, was brought to bear with uncommon intensity on Juan Miguel Godoy.

Juan Miguel was supposed to be the perfect (white) Latin American child, complete with a paternalistic "tenderness" toward his racially othered classmates. Instead, he became a kind of twisted cipher and playing ground for Guillén's and Mistral's affective struggle.

Palma Guillén expressed a great deal of negativity toward the young man and severely criticized what she regarded as his male tendencies, recommending militaristic solutions to his "discipline" problem. Most noteworthy, though, is her intense affect toward Mistral. Mistral, by contrast, had a tendency to describe Juan Miguel as perfect in every sense.

The letters indicate that Juan Miguel functioned as an emotional conduit between the two women. On 29 April 1943, Guillén writes:

> The kid is selfish by nature. Or maybe he's just in that age where selfishness is more manifest. He has no manners whatsoever. The things you recount in your letter . . . the insults he levels at you . . . What an idiot he is, comparing Malraux with Shakespeare and . . . well, I wouldn't know how to put it, whether it's idiocy or evil . . . of comparing you to Bordeaux. This has left me annoyed and dumbfounded. How can you allow him to talk to you like that and tell you such nonsense! I would quite simply shut him up. (32)

Guillén portrays Mistral as an entirely inept parent, especially because she is too "soft" with Juan Miguel. Her abrupt and punitive tone is coolly disguised in a discussion of high literary tradition and of Mistral's place in it. There is also a distinctive disdain for "Juanitos"'s French identity. Apparently, Juan Miguel had spent more time in France than any other country and had developed an attachment to that nation, which Guillén resented. Guillén was a fierce Mexican nationalist and subtly rejected

Mistral's Pan-Americanist stance. Their misguided way of "sorting out" ideas on nationalism was through claiming knowledge of Juan Miguel as "child."

In the same letter, Guillén is invariably cruel in her portrayal of Juan Miguel, clearly in an attempt to chastise Mistral:

> I thought Juanito was intelligent, but these things you tell me have convinced me that we were mistaken. Our excess love has made us see things in him that just aren't there. When someone is that vain, cynical and tasteless, he cannot be a real artist or even intelligent. His only hope—please listen to me—is work. Make him work at anything. . . . It annoys me that he does not obey you, that he insults you, that he's a lazy bum sitting around the house and you tolerate that. . . . He needs energy; to feel a firm, inflexible hand on him always; to know he has to obey. He never, ever resisted an order of mine, and he never insulted me. That cynical and insolent man who takes everything as a joke doesn't have anything to do with the child I had beside me before. Sure, he was a little indolent and careless by temperament, but noble and sincere. (32)

This particular passage partially concerns whether or not Juan Miguel is intelligent or a true artist. Guillén concludes that he is not, dashing Mistral's hopes that he will become an artist like her and vehemently denying Mistral's hyperbolic praise of him. One could argue that Mistral regarded her mission as a mother to create someone closely resembling herself. Guillén insists, rather, that "Juanito" be inserted into a "masculine" environment—where he be treated with the "firm, inflexible hand" befitting a male child. The insinuation is that Mistral is raising a spoiled, indolent, and feminized child who will be a dilettante. Moreover, Guillén abdicates responsibility by articulating that this disappointing young man "doesn't have anything to do with the child [she] had beside [her] before." And, although it's never explicitly expressed, it's not difficult to detect a stubborn characterization of Juan Miguel Godoy that revolves around his national status:

> It might be the crisis of puberty, sure, but it's above all your excessive leniency, your lack of firmness, the good treatment you give him which he does not deserve. In Mexico, such kids are sent to the Navy so they can become men, so they can be saved, yes saved because the way he's going Juanito will be lost. He will become lazy and depraved. I beg you, please come around on this. You, with your ideas on education (which I shared at one point), you think you have to make him come around, touch his heart, appeal to his sense of reason. . . . You have to issue

orders, you have to make him do things against his will, you have to punish him. If you don't feel you can muster the strength to do it, then send him to a military academy or to the Navy. Don't be afraid of him. The worst thing you can do with Juanito is to fear him. (32)

Here Guillén makes explicit her understanding of Juan Miguel's "solution" as nationalistic and, more specifically, Mexican.[18] Notably, she refers to Mistral's pedagogical ideas as "a thing of the past" that did not bear out its expected result, and she instead advocates a naked sense of discipline to obtain normalization. The poverty of her discourse on "men and their problems" is quite distant from the polished cultural discourse she deployed as a prominent figure in Mexican educational reform, when she addressed all citizens in one breath regardless of race or sex. This rudimentary and childlike nationalism is reminiscent of Mistral's unsophisticated, but deadly, private racial discourse. Also noteworthy is Guillén's self-portrayal as a parent who issues commands and is obeyed instantly—or else. Obviously, this was her fantasy, an image of herself that did not correspond to reality. But, translated into other registers, to the terrain of national fantasy, it is an entirely other matter, for the state took it upon itself to decide which of the two parental roles was to be enacted in the face of social movements and when.

Also in the letter of 29 April 1943, Guillén responds acrimoniously to Mistral's protestation that Juan Miguel's attitude is somehow due to his being more French than Latin American:

What does his behavior have to do with France? . . . This lazy loser that spends money left and right, who thinks he's a genius and doesn't study; who thinks he's a man and hangs out with loose women, is not the French youngster but the Latin American youngster—Mexican, Chilean, Argentine or any of our other republics. . . . No, my dear, it's not France's fault; it's yours, because you indulge him in everything, give him way too much money to spend and do not keep an eye on him at each and every moment so he won't stray from the good path that made him what he is today. (32–33)

The good path, one suspects, is Guillén herself, specifically her fierce discipline and no-nonsense approach to his upbringing—a decidedly self-interested account in which she is always right and Mistral always wrong. Guillén shows disdain for young Latin American men generally, labeling them self-centered, profligate, lazy, and oversexed, but the ultimate blame is upon Mistral, as she enabled Juan Miguel's behavior with reckless abandon.

Guillén's claim that Juan Miguel obeys her without pause is rendered unbelievable in the only letter in Vargas Saavedra's volume that is directly addressed to him. In contrast to Guillén's scathing criticism of Mistral and her otherwise emotionally disturbing characterization of Juan Miguel, she is markedly softer in this letter. In the letter, there is no sense of a man who has grown into young adulthood, who is no longer a small child. The roles played in Guillén's correspondence with Mistral are strangely static and oddly oblivious of the separation process that occurs between caretakers and their children. Indeed, in this letter, probably also written in 1943, her tone with Juan Miguel registers more as a plea than as an order:

> Dear Juanito: I receive very few letters from your Mommy; maybe some of them are getting lost. I receive nothing from you. Why don't you write me? I need to feel you close to me in some way; know what you are doing with yourself and feel you in some way until I get the chance to get over there. I can be unfair to you, Juanito, and get very angry at you without your really deserving it, or at least not deserving it as much. I can't believe you no longer care about this; I'd have to accept that you no longer care for your little Palma. (34)

Guillén emerges here as needy and dependent on the child to return her tenderness—something he is quite clearly either not willing to do or not interested in doing. Guillén's tone is vulnerable and childlike (she refers to herself as "little Palma"), far from the authoritarian, obdurate, and secure stance she sports in her letters to Mistral:

> In one of her letters [your mother] told me that in response to some-thing that you wanted to do, she said, "Unfortunately for you I exist and you won't be doing what you want" and you replied: "Tu l'as dit: mal-heureusement tu existes" [You said it: unfortunately you exist]. . . . Juanito, that kind of response will elicit a punishment from heaven. How could you possibly talk to your Mommy like that? She who has suffered so much for you and has done so much for you. . . . Where's your heart and where's your conscience and where's your intelligence? . . . Please reflect on this and tell your Mommy you're sorry, OK? And don't continue to make her suffer so. (36)

The mother-son relationship, if we are to believe Guillén, functions as one in which the parties cancel themselves out, setting up the need for the disappearance of one of them. Mistral had written, in "Poema del hijo," about blessing her nonreproductive womb that, it was implied, allowed the race to die. She also mourned the "face of the mother" who would not survive via her. This recipe proved deadly in the case of Juan Miguel Godoy, for it created confusion: he did not issue from her womb, but she was supposed to nurture him; he would not make his mother survive, because he would not survive Mistral's apparently narcissistic love in which he, above all things, had to resemble her.

Guillén employs the "missing man" theory in a letter to Mistral dated 16 June 1943, claiming that the absence of men is also responsible for Juan Miguel's rebelliousness. Neither apparently suspects that Juan Miguel's emotional state might have to do with their own asphyxiating and narcissistic love, in which they placed only demands upon the young man. They seem to be in a competition for his affection, as evidenced by the tense tone of Guillén's letters and by the air of unreality in Mistral's depictions of him as a perfect child. Guillén exhibits this competitive aspect actively, stressing her disadvantage in relation to Mistral because she is separated from him and can only write: "How's Juanito doing? . . . To be surrounded only by women is not good for him, trust me. . . . I have written to him and I'm affectionate but always firm and clear. He never answers my letters. Not a word; as if he never received them. What can I say? It's very sad to write and speak from a vacuum, especially after one has lived how I have lived with Juanito. . . . My dear, the more we prolong this situation, the harder it will be to correct Juanito afterwards" (36).

Guillén feels Juan Miguel is "damaged" because of his uncertain allegiances, both familial and national, an uncertainty due to the absence of strong male figures in his life that should be supplanted by state apparatuses such as military academies or hard labor. Mistral's reply does not address any of Guillén's concerns. Mistral writes that she feels utterly alone after the departure of her companion Consuelo Saleva and blames her loneliness on her childhood. Of Juan Miguel, Mistral says that he "has behaved extremely well in this new life [without Saleva]," crediting his company for her own capacity to survive loss. Yet, just two weeks later, on 31 July 1943, Juan Miguel committed suicide. Bizarrely, there are stories relating yet another lurid tale: that Juan Miguel was in love with Consuelo Saleva.

Vargas Saavedra copied a longish stanza from one of Mistral's notebooks, written just two weeks before Juan Miguel's suicide. The tone of this autobiographical stanza contrasts sharply with the letter Mistral sent in late 1943 to friends and acquaintances who expressed their condolences after Juan Miguel's death. In that letter, her life with Juan Miguel is depicted as perfect, and there is no earthly reason for his suicide. Though short and cryptic, the stanza is evocative, and powerful enough to denote the existence of several overlapping discourses and figures that give the lie to the idyllic vision:

> Yin Yin has abandoned me of late.
> To fall into oblivion is a great disgrace.
> Chileans hate me even though they have no reason to.
> Palma has forgotten about the war.
> Please help me arrange and file my papers.
> Please help me find peace.
> I have lived outside Chile for a very long time.
> I found a quiet town.
> They found a buried statue.
> I found my lost books.
> The plants are growing.
> France's offensive is growing.
> Yin Yin is growing.
> My hair is growing too fast.
> Each one of my books has notes scribbled on it.
> Each time I go to sleep I leave. (42)

Instead of registering a worry over any behavior that may have been a sign of her son's distress, Mistral feels "abandoned" both by him and by Chileans in general. Perhaps she expected Juan Miguel to be a caretaker figure and to supplant the feelings of alienation or depression she was experiencing. A tone of self-pity and loss pervades the entire stanza and touches upon many of Mistral's frequent self-constructions. She feels things—intimate matters, that is—are slipping out of her grasp. She feels that she's not in control and seems to hint that she is forgotten or hated, a "disgrace" for which she seeks peace.

Even though Mistral was very famous, she continually feared "oblivion" or being rendered "irrelevant." Chile appears as a major culprit in her life, a nation that disinherited her affectively, forcing her to live abroad for most of her life. Guillén is portrayed as being obsessed with purely regional and nationalistic matters; she does not realize that the Second World War is the most important event of world history in 1943. The idea of war and peace is collapsed into Mistral's own search for "peace," which ostensibly meant the devoted attention of everyone: Juan Miguel, Guillén, Chile, and the world generally, judging from the impersonal third-person perspective looming over the stanza. Juan Miguel's age and her own age are collapsed when she says he is growing and so is her hair. Finally, there is an elliptical reference to death in the ending: "cada vez que me duermo me voy" [each time I go to sleep I leave]. Juan Miguel's death is eerily presaged in Mistral's worry, but it appears as a worry about herself and her own extinction, both figuratively and literally.

Mistral's response to Juan Miguel's suicide is one extended denial. First she casts their life together as, literally, an "idyll" and begins the far-fetched rumor that a "tropical gang" poisoned him with a drug, although she does not expound on a motive until later. In response to Guillén's accusation that Juan Miguel was not intelligent or an artist, Mistral writes that "he excelled in his writing" and "did not use a single commonplace" (46). Although she appears to be exalting the memory of Juan Miguel, in the complete letter he appears as a vacuum filled by her grief but also by her narcissism. She feels God has punished her for the sin of idolatry. In other words, Juan Miguel's death is about God's resentment toward *her*, a score that God had to settle with *her*. Mistral's use of religion has a decidedly narcissistic twist to it, and the account of her son's suicide betrays the deeper implications of her paranoia:

> I know that God punishes idolatry severely and that idolatry doesn't only mean cult of images. (48)

> My sin was idolatry. My life was his. I did not have a personal life except for the hours I dedicated to writing poetry, no more. I am a pile of rubble, of logs, ashes and dirt. (49)

> Scripture condemns idolatry unequivocally, and I was guilty of this sin in respect to Juan Miguel. Life abroad causes this evil and converts it into a crime: putting everything into a single being of our own blood and separating from the world and all the rest. (50)

The letter's rationale for Juan Miguel's death is curious. Mistral introduces the idea of idolatry and the cult of images; in fact, Juan Miguel had become a (failed) image, and after his death, he could be "corrected" to the point of becoming heavenly, as evinced in the prayers she wrote for him. Mistral's idea of separation is not the separation that might possibly have benefited Juan Miguel, being allowed to be someone different from Guillén and her. Rather, other separations personal to Mistral, or the separations perhaps not achieved by Mistral herself in the psychic sense, seem to have governed his development. Arguably, the most important is her own separation from Chile, her homeland, which she views as having caused her sin of idolatry and therefore Juan Miguel's death. Juan Miguel's lacking a clear "nationality" was cited by Palma Guillén as one of the reasons for his lack of quality as a human being. The account that Mistral creates to explain the circumstances of his death, consequently, evolves into a paranoid accusation against countries, ethnicities, and races as personal threats. Religion and race converge in a type of fascistic nationalism. The fact that it appears in "personal" correspondence does not disqualify it from critical attention.

The tale of Juan Miguel's death narrated by Mistral in a letter to Alfonso Reyes, quoted in chapter 1, was widely circulated among friends and also appeared in newspapers and interviews. The identical narrative was sent, via Palma Guillén, to a conference in Morelos, Mexico, in 1948, and was reprinted in the Spanish-language newspaper *La Nueva Democracia* [The New Democracy] in New York City in 1949.[19] This version expands on the tale of Juan Miguel's tribulations, citing his extraordinary intelligence and the unease he felt as a white child in a "country with a fair amount of racial mixing."[20] Vargas Saavedra cites various versions Mistral gave of his death; clearly, the racial murder story evolved from disparate elements. Apparently, in 1943, Mistral believed that Juan Miguel had killed himself over mixed feelings of excessive shyness and unrequited love. She noted the gang's presence, but it was portrayed merely as a group of schoolchildren who taunted him. In one version that Mistral recounted to various friends and associates, she reported that she was fooled by an "Arab friend" of Juan Miguel's with whom she spent the afternoon watching a movie. Only when she returned home did she find that Juan Miguel had been taken to the hospital and lay in agony. Vargas Saavedra writes: "[There was] the suspicious attitude of Yin Yin's Arab friend, who took her to the movies almost forcibly. Why? Did he know that he [Juan Miguel] was to be killed and was he charged with the mission of keeping her out of the way so that her protective presence could not prevent it?" (52–53). Mistral claimed that this young man informed her of as much: "Since he [Juan Miguel] enrolled in our school, the gang had sentenced him to death. He was one of the ones who had it all: health, money, respect, comforts, maternal love ... too much for a single person to have!" (54). As part of this particular version, Mistral also claimed that this "Arab friend" somehow had Juan Miguel's suicide note in his possession. This belief apparently caused Mistral to realize that the note was a forgery and that Juan Miguel did not intend to die.

Another version Mistral told involved schoolchildren in Petrópolis who, before Juan Miguel's death, allegedly screamed on two occasions in front of her house, "Go back home, you German pig! We won the war, so go!" (52) Whether this taunting happened or not, what is fascinating is that Mistral described it not as an informal group of children yelling insults at her but as a round of children issuing insults in lullaby form, the same form that she herself used: "una ronda infernal de escolares petropolitanos"[21] "que, agresivamente, le bailaban en torno cogidos de la mano, mientras cantaban un extraño sonsonete de condenación"[22] [an infernal round of Petropólis schoolchildren, that aggressively danced around her locking hands while singing a strange sing-song of condemnation].

Another unclear and confusing point is what Juan Miguel Godoy's own alliances were. Mistral stated constantly that he was an "aliadófilo" [pro-Allied], but other parts of the biographical record indicate that he may have belonged to a pro-fascist group while they were living in France. Palma Guillén herself said that "what made [Mistral] decide to leave Lisbon and return to America was that Juanito, still a young boy, mingled with his friends at school who belonged to the 'Mocidades,' a fascist youth organization. Gabriela wanted to remove him from that environment."[23] It is possible that Juan Miguel identified more as French than as Latin American, and it is conceivable that his sympathies were with the collaborationist and not with the resistance government, much to Mistral's chagrin. Given this scenario, he might have espoused racist beliefs about his own racial superiority. Whether he did or not, what seems certain is that Mistral, in her self-absorption, would have completely denied these facts and would have offered, as she did, a portrait of a child so perfect he could not exist except in her narcissistic ego. After Mistral's improbable tale has undergone several quite sensationalist permutations, Juan Miguel, the white European-American child (as she describes him), is now pro-Allied, and the black and mulatto Brazilian children who "murdered" him have become pro-Nazi. Moreover, the children who formed the round outside her house taunted her as a "German pig," identifying her as white and a supremacist. In Mistral's world, it seems, everybody is a racial supremacist of some stripe.

Palma Guillén wrote, years later, that

> Juan Miguel killed himself so that he would not kill one of his classmates who had offended him, in one of those conflicts which are made bigger than they are in the imagination of a seventeen-year-old. It was made more serious by the fact of the war; it was also a conflict between pro-Allied and pro-Nazi students (Juan Miguel was pro-Allied). Juan Miguel died that night with Gabriela by his side, and from the pain that she felt that very night she got sick with the diabetes that eventually killed her.[24]

The explanations for Juan Miguel's suicide are undeniably peculiar. In the absence of any further documentation, it is impossible to assess when and why Guillén and Mistral began to be at odds over the best way to raise Juan Miguel. Obviously, both resorted to interpretations of his suicide that appealed to national and racial threats of extinction, instead of searching for the answers in the intimate reality of their lives. Apparently, this family experienced social and intimate realities as completely coterminous. But also evident is the fact that neither Mistral nor Guillén accepted any true responsibility for Juan Miguel Godoy's despair.

The dynamics of their family appear to have been rooted in infantilization. Certainly, Guillén infantilized Juan Miguel when she wrote to Mistral, and again when she addressed him condescendingly. Mistral similarly refused to allow her son to grow up to be someone different from her and an adult. Finally, Mistral infantilized Guillén as well: "Palmita arrived too late to save him with her camaraderie and her lucid love, so unlike my own. He knew she was coming. I can't understand why he left when he knew for sure she would be here in two weeks. He adored and trusted her completely—more than he did me—as if Palma were a girl his own age" (48).

For all the talk about children taunting and hurting the family from without, it seems more likely that the members of this family taunted each other from within, competing for each other's affection in a constant stream of affect equivocally named "tenderness" (in the letter replying to her friends' condolences, Mistral wrote of Juan Miguel's "unspeakable tenderness").[25] But Juan Miguel's suicide note begs the question whether this household was tender at all, or whether by "tenderness" they all signified something akin to affect in the psychoanalytic sense: "Dear Mother, I think I better just leave things the way they are. I hope there is more happiness in another world. Affectionately, Yin-Yin. Give Palma a kiss."[26] His laconic farewell letter appears to have been written precisely without any tenderness or withdrawing tenderness. The letter transmits an air of distance, resignation, and emotional numbness. Its reference to "happiness in another world" was evidently a reflection of Mistral's own preoccupation with both her extinction and her salvation. Perhaps, ultimately, Juan Miguel was hoping to find happiness in a world sans his asphyxiating mother(s).

Salvation or Melancholia? The Missing-Man Theory Revisited

After Juan Miguel's death, Mistral inhabited a space of suffering amplified by the prayers that she wrote for Juan Miguel's salvation, through which this personal experience of loss is cast as a divine test for Mistral's transcendence. There are numerous prayers to the Virgin Mary, Christ, and the Holy Spirit; many passages refer explicitly to Juan Miguel as the child of both Palma Guillén and Gabriela Mistral, suggesting that the prayers create a private space for the divine acceptance of this family.

Prayers come to replace lullabies. It is no coincidence that the lullabies "die" and the prayers begin with the death of Mistral's son. Mistral derived pleasure from her prayers, a type of comfort that emanated from the certainty that her "Yin Yin" could now be safely and only hers, and that he would indeed be forever a child: "I see, more clearly than ever, the certainty of eternal life. There is only one thought that soothes and puts me to sleep at night: I thought I would be leaving soon to go live alone in my other life, and now I have my other life in this earth with him, for a little while, in a short-term sense."[27] Through Juan Miguel's death, both of them are assured "life," in the Kleinian sense of preserving an object of love. Significantly, the family is not complete without mention of Palma:

> We [Palma and I] love you and look for you every day, Yin, our love. Both of us continue to love in your name and in your company, Yin, with no forgetting, with our eyes planted on your sweet and beloved eyes.
>
> Yin, our little one, you have not lost a single drop of our love; you will never lose us.
>
> You are awake in our memory, Yin, and also in our grieving hearts.
>
> You are in our spirits, that's where you really are, our little one, you are with us without any sadness or any painful complaint. (79)

Life of ours, love of ours, shame and joy of ours, small Juan Miguel, our flower. (80)

Bless this house where Palma and Gabriela work and pray for you. . . . Blessed be you, one and a thousand times, our love, blessed be you wherever you are, blessed if you remember us and if you forget us too. . . . We ask of God to be reunited with you, our little child, our unfinished and suspended feast, to be continued in that re-encounter promised to us by Jesus Christ, the Prophets, and the Saints. (82)

Even though when he died Juan Miguel Godoy was about sixteen years old, the prayers always miniaturize him, calling him "little one," "little child," and "little flower." Certainly, this is due, in part, to the grief Mistral felt, and expresses terms of endearment. Still, his infantilization is striking. The prayers recorded in her notebooks register conflict between reproductive motherhood and nonreproductive motherhood; this conflict, apparently, was embedded in Mistral's psyche. The prayers recur to the idea of the biological, as in one particularly intriguing passage in a cycle of prayers to the dead, which asks for their intercession on behalf of Godoy's salvation. This prayer is directed to his biological mother, presumably dead at the time:

Mother of Juan Miguel, mother that due to the will of the Creator he did not have once he could talk and comprehend what was going on around him, mother who departed before she could sing him his lullabies, affectionate mother who would have known how to give him the affection that I did not know how to give; honest mother to my mere mumbling, to my daily awkwardness; Catalan mother with milk from the Mediterranean, who would have nursed him with the sediment of olives and marble, giving him the strong sweetness, the energetic sparkle, and uncompromising ductility that I could not nurture him with:

Forgive me if I did not make him happy; forgive me if the law of Moses was broken by my fault.

Wherever you are, go where your child is. Recognize your flesh and recognize your blood, recognize your caste and your soul that uncertainly finds its way alone through the shadows.

Cease your eternal joy for a while and take him by the hand. So that when he looks at you, he knows he is looking at his mother, and recognizing you may feel that Mary, you and I, his three mothers, are keeping him company on heaven and on Earth as he journeys towards God. (103)

The objects of love that are preserved are threefold. First and foremost, Juan Miguel himself; second, the triangle Mistral-Guillén-Godoy, as a family; and third, the image of a biological motherhood that never applied to Mistral but that she, paradoxically enough, represented.

Mistral represents her motherhood as a "mumbling," in perfect alignment with earlier claims about the lullabies being merely "hums" and about Chilean lullabies as being poor vehicles for literature. The biological mother's European origin is stressed against Mistral's own origin, and she is constructed as having a direct and permanent link to the child through milk, a tie that Mistral could never establish. In a way, Mistral comes full circle to her literary representation of herself in "Poema del hijo": "Blessed be my womb in which my race dies!"

Mistral wrote of her own womb as a tomb for the race, and in her comments on the lullaby form in Latin America, she assumed responsibility for both "birthing" and "saving" it. Thus, the fact of death points to the death of a life option, national motherhood, and though the lullabies are related to gestation, strikingly, Mistral always represented the mother-child relationship as biological, and her own was not. In her literary representations of motherhood, the national "child" inhabits the mother's body before coming into "birth." Many lullabies thematize this "semiotic" relationship, to use Kristeva's formulation.[28]

Mistral's lullabies hold up an image of something that Mistral lost even before she knew she had it—the possibility of being a mother—given that national motherhood is defined in such strict blood terms as a result of heterosexual unions. Judith Butler, in *The Psychic Life of Power*, writes precisely of this type of loss, arguing that in order for heterosexuality to come into being, a previous disavowal of homosexuality must have occurred. In fact, she provocatively argues that a heteronormative order is founded on this disavowal, and thus its subjects experience themselves as melancholic.[29]

It's not that there isn't a level of synergy between accepted interpretations of Mistral's lullabies and their spirit, just that the critics have disavowed the ultimate implications of some of the poems' salient characteristics. Unsurprisingly, many critics have employed a psychoanalytic framework to account for the uncanny, personal nature of the lullabies and other child-inflected poems, even if this is not explicitly declared. The aspect of mourning is insistently cited, but only to indicate somewhat simplistically, and with no real historical data, that what Mistral "lost" was the male lover, which she sublimates as God,[30] as poetry,[31] or as femininity.[32] Interestingly, in all of the critical literature, Mistral appears decidedly self-absorbed. (Martyrs and saints often are; otherwise, how are they to maintain their intense focus on the divine and their relationship of desire for God?) But, I maintain, Mistral's mourning was not, properly speaking, of the religious or sacrificial type. Even when it is expressed in the form of prayer, it's not primarily about a Christian expression of faith.

Diana Fuss writes that "identification is not only how we accede to power, it is also how we learn submission" and, in discussing melancholia, reminds us that melancholia entails identification with the dead. All mourning initially does this, she explains, but in melancholia's case the ego is mistaken for the lost object and "commits suicide."[33] Mistral's prayers for her dead son are melancholic in this sense. Mistral, while mourning Juan Miguel, refused to let him go, and her identification with him became, if anything, consummated. His sad death strangely stamped Mistral as the sufferer, yet his own life is erased in most accounts, which offer Mistral as childless.

While asking for Juan Miguel's salvation in the next world, Mistral tries to collapse life and death and to experience salvation in this one. Only a secular understanding of salvation as the pursuit of individualized, worldly things can make sense of this desire. Mistral cannot wait to die to find out if she is forgiven; she cannot go through the religious steps one at a time. Instead, she creates a narrative to exonerate herself and establishes a relationship with the dead child.

It's not the missing man in Mistral's life that should trouble critics so much, but forced identifications, restricted choices of family and kin, and the raced and racist imperatives of nationalism. These are some of the core issues ignored by mythic explanations of Mistral's quandary, especially if we consider that some critical opinions are widespread in the world of the social (for example, Jorge Guzmán's belief that Mistral's tragedy involving the absent male figure accurately represents a national and continental dilemma, the absence of a strong masculine figure).[34] Our respect for grief and tragedy cannot keep us from assessing the implications of Mistral's racist stance toward the Brazilian schoolchildren that she came to blame for Juan Miguel's death. Neither can we ignore the ways in which Guillén and she constructed family life in terms of nationality. Both point to a kind of "intimate nationalism" that flows in from the supposed "outside"—that is to say, intimacy is constructed as much from without as from within—and flows out to this external place of the "nation," not insignificantly through the lullabies sung in the schools and also through other venues, as the second part of this book will point to.

The lullabies constitute an unexpected venue in which to find the exercise of "pastoral power." I believe this term, coined by Foucault, is very apt for a conclusion to the first part of *A Queer Mother for the Nation*. Foucault described pastoral power as a technique perfected in the West from the early years of Christianity. Even though the purely religious manifestation of such power has ended, Foucault contends that it has a secular life in the "pastoral function."[35] Throughout the first part of the book, we have seen how Mistral participated in institutions of pastoral power, from modern ones, like the school, to ancient institutions, like the family. As an individual she also exercised pastoral power, encouraging citizens toward ideals of salvation and sacrifice on behalf of the nation, mixing a secular "here and now" with a "beyond" of Christianity. As Foucault writes: "In a way, we can see the state as a modern matrix of individualization, or a new form of pastoral power" (334); and "The multiplication of the aims of pastoral power focused on the development of knowledge of man around two roles: one, globalizing and quantitative, concerning the population; the other, analytical concerning the individual" (335). Mistral's relationship to the state was, in this sense, a perfect fit.

Jean Franco writes that "Mistral did not write in a time period that allowed confessional poetry, except in rare cases. She did find, however, in the oral tradition a space which allowed exits into the irrational, what she called 'madness' or raving [desvarío]. It's through these 'desvaríos' that her writing attempts, in harrowing fashion, to breach the schism between rationality and irrationality, individual existence and mist"; "even though Gabriela Mistral assigns folklore an Americanist, pedagogical value, popular traditions open up another possibility for her: an exit leading to *non-sense* raving."[36] According to this view, the lullabies, in their madness, would still offer a degree of comfort and solace from an "outside" world. The foregoing discussion has attempted to expand Franco's analysis of the lullabies by tying their narcissistic world to Mistral's narcissistic view of her own motherhood, suggesting more intricate relationships between the "inside" of literature and the "outside" of her personal world.

A late poem by Mistral, "La dichosa" [The happy woman], alludes to a community of women living outside society's shackles: "We count ourselves among the happy few / who have left everything behind."[37] As part of the cycle "Locas mujeres" [Crazy women], this poem has special resonance within the discussion of this book. In this poem Mistral plays with self-reference, but she hides, too, in poetic language. She appears to have a "secret" or a "double life," which she accesses primarily through creative and private outlets. She also signals, through the title, that this closed-off (and somewhat persecuted) space is inhabited by women. There is an equally vague hinting at gender play. Speaking of a return home as a corpse or spirit ("When I am dead I will cross / the garden that saw me grow"), she ends the poem with a cryptic allusion to sexual love: "and the flying wind will possess me / it is not a husband." The play is with both the gender of the love object and an existence outside of the heterosexual ideal of marriage and reproduction.

As seductive as Mistral's own tale is, it's not accurate. It's tempting to construct Mistral as an outsider, one who expertly played the insider's game but remained true to herself and to an affective community (presumably of fellow women).[38] Where some have tried to uphold Mistral's private space of the feminine, the maternal, and the poetic as a clearing for survival in an intensely patriarchal society, I would interpret it, with Diana Fuss (when she discusses melancholia), as a kind of cemetery where all dead objects reside, objects emerging as a result of identification's submissive and subjugating double edge.[39]

In the poem "La dichosa," Mistral imagines returning to her village as deceased, as a spirit. She endlessly mourns herself; it is as if her life were about extinction. The poem evokes all the self-figurations of absence that marked Mistral throughout her life, at times rendering her a curiously empty figure living in the words of another one of her poems, "País de la ausencia" [Land of absence], in "the land of absence": "and in a nameless country / I will die."[40]

Indeed, Mistral was the embodiment of the maternal, but she was not the typical image of maternal piety. She was distant, often violent. This infantilization and violence took a particular toll on Latin America's people of color and its mothers—populations supposedly most protected by Mistral's public speech. Her eroticism at points regarding people of color and women as mothers is a challenge to interpret. Aside from the straightforward racism we saw in chapter 1, Mistral's polarized emotions often have explosive effects not dissimilar to state actions toward populations it needs but often despises. Perhaps Mistral embodied not so much the maternal as the repressed maternal, which, in psychoanalysis, is ultimately behind all mourning (and, if Fuss is correct, all identification as well).

Mistral's real-life experiences were, at times, truly distant from, yet intimately connected with, the official maternal discourse associated with her. That is to say, Mistral was the subject of her discourses in two opposing ways. She authored them and was their agent, yet they affected her, too. Mistral did not exist apart from her own recommendations for women or for citizens. Their effects on her, however, were manifested in peculiar ways that are not always apparent at first glance. Mistral's lullabies are supposedly preideological and intimate, or, more precisely, preideological because they are intimate, but this assertion misses the importance that the crafting of intimacy, or, more specifically, the "whiteness" of intimacy and privacy, occupies in Latin American nationalist thought.

On at least one occasion, Mistral experienced the trauma of real-life loss. Examining this incident, and Mistral's actual motherhood, is one way of speculating about the consequences of her assumption of the state's (queer) role for her. Because Mistral deliberately blurred the boundaries between herself and the transnational ideal she actively championed, she helped theorize a noticeable strain of narcissism within nationalism in Americanist discourse. Because so many of the national "threats" were figured in terms of family, home, and intimacy, maternal discourse must be taken to task for its reproduction not only of heteronormativity but also of white supremacy—even if on its face it champions the apparently all-inclusive emotions of tenderness, care, and love. It is these very emotions that couch, in fact, the tendency toward an unpredictable paranoia. Even as Mistral issued precepts and recommendations for disciplining children, she was also disciplined and infantilized by the state and her contemporaries. Race, gender, and sexuality were the essential axes of this normalization.

Part II
Queering the State

Cinema: consolation through the visual.
Music: consolation through the auditory.
Letters: consolation through our kin's love.
    —Gabriela Mistral, "Conferencia en la cárcel de Veracruz"
        [Conference in the prison of Veracruz]

CHAPTER FIVE

Image Is Everything

Gabriela Mistral was spectacularly successful as the image of "the mother," despite her description in masculine terms, and even though she frequently adopted a style of dress that was either outright masculine or "masculinizing," especially when compared to her female contemporaries. This fact indicates a productive or generative logic to be examined, not bracketed, within Latin Americanist narratives. Put succinctly, Mistral employed a masculine demeanor that was strikingly different from the femininity one might associate with the discourse of Latin American "national" femininity. The progression of Mistral's image demonstrates that she tried on different "versions" of herself, some of them according to international standards of taste and expectation in photography.

How did the state enable such complex and shifting identifications through gendered deployment of display, the display of a conservative yet rich visual culture? This chapter considers the progression of Mistral's photographic image as it began to circulate in mass form at the time, first in the Chilean context, then transnationally and internationally.[1] Mistral's massive and massified body is a case study. "Massive" refers to a body that is "big" to the spectator, independent of its actual size; "massified" refers to the widespread reproduction of this body in newspapers and books all over the hemisphere.

National citizens may have believed they saw simply a mother, but patently there was something completely mystified about their perception. As Jacques Lacan suggests, they saw themselves seeing something that wasn't there. Furthermore, they were aware that this something was not the individual who was actually photographed within the frame of the picture ("aware" in the sense of disavowal, a state in which the subject is oddly and simultaneously cognizant and unaware). In considering Mistral's photographic image, Lacan's central admonition is useful: "Must we not distinguish between the function of the eye and that of the gaze?"[2] The gaze constitutes an important way in which national subjects were schooled sexually, as national citizens, where the sexual entails their own apprehension of themselves as subjects.

There are literally scores of pictures of Mistral. For this discussion I have availed myself of the Mistral iconographic archive in Chile, housed in the National Library in Santiago. I have concentrated on photographs that are by now iconic. Some are studio photographs, after the manner of "celebrity" portraiture, and others are casual snapshots.[3]

In this corpus, Mistral is primarily photographed in three distinct contexts. The photographs up to 1922 hail from her native Chile and record her various educational postings, culminating in her position as director of three successive girls' schools. They are divided into two kinds: pedagogical portraits and portraits of Mistral in various "feminine" guises, underscoring the idea of intimacy and dreaminess; or moments "off" from professional duties. Photographs from 1922 into the late 1920s portray Mistral at her most iconic and unforgettable: cutting a strikingly butch, handsome figure, she manages to project an image both inviting and distancing at the same time. Later photographs, from approximately 1938 to her death, in 1957, reveal a prematurely aged woman but still retain her iconic appeal. Some viewers may regard these late pictures as matronly, but in my opinion they are still unmistakably masculine, especially casual shots taken away from international focus.

The photographic corpus demands that we revise Mistral's evolution as icon. Although standard biographical texts present Mistral as unified and unchanging, there was clearly some searching on her part for the proper "pose" to complement her ascendant fame and to accommodate her queerness. The photographs of Mistral while still in Chile reveal this fascinating development. They oscillate between the prototypical spinster figure and uncertainly "feminine" poses, probably derived from the influence of celebrity photography at the time, in particular the portraits of Alfred Stieglitz and Edward Steichen.

In these Chilean photographs, Mistral seems to be adopting the idea of the "masquerade" most prominent in her first figurations, a pose which eventually yielded to her more definitive butch appearance. After she assumed masculinity fully in the visual field, she became part of the state's official recording of its own activities through propaganda. Newspaper readers encountered her portraits often; they were pinned up in schools throughout the continent, a fair number of which began to bear Mistral's own name.

The project of this chapter is not to recuperate the photographs' "queerness" as documents of resistance, though other scholars may wish to attempt that particular project. That is, I make no attempt to locate queerness in the photographs as an autonomous space available for individual consumption. When I have lectured on this subject, I have witnessed many disparate reactions to Mistral's figure. Some viewers exclaim that she looks just like their own mothers; others are repulsed and ask why she was so masculine. It is entirely possible for individual viewers to construct their own relationships to these pictures, but this chapter attempts to analyze them in the context of their time period. I speculate how these images collaborated in the transformation of the public space so that it began to be experienced as a kind of familial intimacy, precisely at the moment when the school sought to distance itself from the familial home—and from the mother in particular. Consistent with this book's entire project, this discussion demonstrates how queerness was enlisted to perform state work.

Spanning her earliest years as a schoolteacher, to her engagement with the Vasconcelian project in Mexico, to her later years of fame, Mistral's image evolved tremendously. First she posed as a demure and hesitatingly "feminine" urban schoolteacher in Chile, presumably white, framed either in the context of her job, teaching, or in leisure time, where, in bourgeois fashion, she pursued her other activities, such as writing. Then she switched to posing as a masculine, rural, mestiza schoolteacher in Mexico who inspired awe and distance. Finally, she settled into the image of a transnational, supreme Mother of America, a kind of elderly stateswoman, the equal of any man—somewhat desexualized but still masculine.

The photographers for many of Mistral's photographs are unknown. Hernán Rodríguez Villegas has compiled a thorough register of photographers, photojournalists, and cinematographers in Chile from 1840 to 1940, and a perusal reveals that there were professional photographers active in every town where Gabriela Mistral lived, even in relatively remote areas like the Patagonian town of Punta Arenas.[4] Only an exhaustive research of regional archives within Chile and a survey of all the regional publications during Mistral's time will yield more precise information as to the authorship of these images.

Rodríguez Villegas summarizes the effervescence of the medium in Chile. The first daguerreotypist established himself in coastal Valparaíso in 1840. Many foreigners followed suit, establishing studios for daguerreotypes in numerous cities across Chile. In 1851 the first prints on paper were produced; by 1880 there was an extensive web of professional and amateur photographers working in a variety of formats; and by 1900, Rodríguez Villegas writes, "there are three well-defined fields in Chile; the professional, with a studio, who follows the formal practice of studio portraiture, producing prints of exceptional quality; the artist, an amateur or professional . . . ; the instant shooter, often amateurs working for journals or newspapers and who will soon become photojournalists." He adds that there were clubs, contests, and salons, sponsored primarily by print media; that photographers gained prestige in towns in Chile; and that every respectable family owned an album with snapshots instead of the more expensive and elegant album with studio portraits. Photographic activity, he concludes, became a mass activity.[5]

Some of the pictures of Mistral taken while she was still in Chile are, in effect, studio portraits, but many are snapshots taken by friends or acquaintances. Only a handful of prints are signed. It's unclear exactly who paid for the studio photographs, but it might not have been out of reach financially for the young Mistral to have herself photographed for important occasions, and she was probably photographed at others' expense when she won prizes or had become a regional celebrity. In regard to the school portraits of Mistral, taken in Punta Arenas, Temuco, and Santiago, it's possible that a pupil's parents paid for them. Mistral's ascending notoriety as the "schoolteacher-poet" might have influenced this decision, or it may have been quite simply a parent's desire to record his daughter's enrollment in a prestigious girls' school.

Whether the state had anything to do with Mistral's early iconography is a matter of speculation at this point. Opinions from experts such as Ilonka Csillag Pimstein, Pedro Pablo Zegers, and Luis Vargas Saavedra suggest that the state probably was not invested in visually circulating Mistral as an icon while she was still in Chile.[6] Chilean photographic practices at the time were heterogeneous, wielded mostly by a bourgeoisie capable of either paying a studio photographer or buying a camera and having their pictures developed. However, it could be argued that Mistral's later Chilean photographs—from about 1918 on—are invested with an official air missing from earlier pictures. Certainly, when a world-famous Mistral returned to Chile in 1938 and 1954, she received considerable visual attention linked to her iconic status as national mother.

Another vexed question among experts is Mistral's participation in the crafting of her image. Csillag Pimstein does not believe that Mistral liked to be photographed and that perhaps she even shunned it. Given the scores of photographs that exist, however, including ones taken before Mistral became famous, there is room to question that assumption. Furthermore, the photographs traverse conventions of portraiture that require a certain willingness to pose for the camera. Even early snapshots of Mistral in Chile often appear quite dramatic: Mistral pensively looks away from the camera, as when she is holding a tree bough or resting her arm against a windowsill. It's doubtful that Mistral was not manipulating her pose in these pictures, even if unconsciously.

Mistral's primary patronage in Chile was probably tied to an informal network of local notables, local civic institutions, and regional newspapers and magazines. Her photographs exist primarily because of her ascending fame, and secondarily because of sentimental or personal reasons. What seems certain, though, from a close examination of photographs taken after her trip to Mexico in 1922, is that, from that moment on, the state had an important role in the creation and dissemination of Mistral's transnational image. There are still, of course, personal snapshots and portraits taken by friends, the reel of a very masculine Mistral in San Francisco, the moving pictures of Mistral with Juan Miguel Godoy after his adoption in the early 1930s, and many others. However, there is a marked shift in the posed and studio representations of Mistral in Mexico.

Whereas photos in Chile might have been the work of amateurs or of paid professionals on behalf of private patrons, many of the photos in Mexico display the will to advertise and exhibit an official image of a strikingly masculine and certainly imposing public Mistral, identified visually not with women schoolteachers but with important male functionaries in the Mexican government. Additionally, these pictures—even the bohemian ones of Mistral engaged in conversation with writers—

no longer portray a woman in search of an image of femininity. Rather, as spectators, we envision a woman who does nothing to disguise her obvious gender difference. Furthermore, this woman is not photographed as a freak or monster of any sort. On the contrary, she is placed in a position of great power and influence.

"Masculinity" and "femininity" may signify very different things for any number of viewers. The problem is compounded when we recall that, since its inception, photography has played with the illusion that the spectator can accurately "read" the visual, something that is obviously not possible. Yet photography is not governed by total relativity either. Societal conventions governing sartorial expectations and feminine comportment make their way into photography, contributing to specifically visual conventions in female portraiture. Moreover, as the well-known *Screen* debates of the late 1970s and early 1980s established for the cinematic image, the gaze itself is gendered historically, and femininity often has been represented as the "negative" of masculinity or, from a psychoanalytic viewpoint, as lack in mass scopophilic regimes. In both of these formulations, naturally, femininity and masculinity have resided comfortably in the biological binary of female/male. Thus it obtains that female masculinity has found an affirmative aesthetics only in countercultural venues, where these rigid biological binaries are inoperative. As of yet, there are no historical studies confirming the existence of any sexually deviant countercultures in Chile at the time that Gabriela Mistral lived. This does not mean they did not exist, however, merely that we don't know about them. Nevertheless, schools were policed because it was thought that they were breeding grounds for sexual anomalies. Therefore, we have at least one indication that the homosocial world of female schoolteachers might have been one venue in which these binaries were contested.

The young Mistral was uncertain about how to promote herself publicly, both in print and visually. There appears to have been a disjuncture between her handsome, full frame and the demure or fetishistic images of the feminine that circulated in Chile. Mistral had herself photographed in a studio environment on various occasions when she was beginning to work in the La Serena area. Usually in these pictures, her hair is done up in a bun and she doesn't smile. She is photographed at a three-quarters-frontal angle, and the lines of her body and dress look as if they were blurred slightly by the photographer, making her contours appear soft. Her clothes have patterns and prints, and in a few instances there is a hairpin or a necklace to accentuate her womanliness. In one picture, from 1914, she was clearly instructed to look upward, and the result is an almost comical feminine drag. This early portrait features an amateur's use of contrast; exactly half of her face is in shadow, making her look very awkward (fig. 1). One wonders how this woman would have managed to portray herself as either demure or fetishistic within the narrow conventions of the time; one wonders, also, if this would have clashed with her self-perception or feelings in any way. It seems obvious that available cultural scripts of womanhood dictated a third choice, that of a desexualized matron dedicated to other people's children.

Since we do not have any journals or letters to testify to Mistral's interiority, it would be helpful to compare her visual image to other feminine images of her time, especially in those journals and editions in which she was actually published. A glimpse through their covers might afford an understanding of how at least two opposing constructions, the demure and the phallic female, permeated Chilean and Latin American notions of femininity. Global images of femaleness traveled to Chile and thrived as part of class and consumer society. In other words, it's impossible to speak of a pure, protected Chilean or Latin American femininity in Mistral's day that was different from North American or European femininity.

When I have lectured on this subject, scholars have occasionally observed that I impose onto Mistral notions of gender and sexuality that are not "indigenous" to Latin America: the femme, the butch, the demure lady, the woman as fetish. Not only were acceptable female roles promoted through popularized images, but also deviant types were assiduously policed in order to cleanse the population of any pernicious influences.[7] It's important here to note that the work of important sexologists had entered Latin America via translation soon after the original works were published; Havelock Ellis's *Sexual Inversion* and Richard von Krafft-Ebing's *Psychopathia Sexualis* were not unknown to Latin American pedagogues, criminologists, and psychiatrists. Indeed, there was a veritable army of sexologists, doctors, educators, and hygienists preoccupied with the spread of dreaded "diseases," including uranism

Figure 1. Gabriela Mistral at the time she won the Juegos Florales prize, 1914.

and fetishism among schoolgirls.[8] As anyone acquainted with these texts knows, it was generally thought that perverted types were readily identifiable visually, and Latin Americans were not an exception to this rule.

Additionally, the Latin American concept of the *raro* could well be translated as "queer," for in the public eye it often designated artists and intellectuals who were special or off-center, not because they were artists but because they brought forth the double possibility—both repulsive and fascinating—of deviant sexuality. There was an unerring sense of discomfort with, but also an attraction to, subjects who assumed a public role but were effeminate men or mannish women.[9]

The trials of both Oscar Wilde and Radclyffe Hall appeared in the newspapers in Chile and other Latin American nations. Far from being backward places untouched by modernity, many capital cities boasted newspapers of the highest quality, and their readers were accustomed to encountering dispatches from abroad from the likes of chroniclers such as José Martí, Rubén Darío (author of the work *Los raros* [The queers/The odd ones]), and, of course, Gabriela Mistral herself, who started writing for newspapers around 1930.

Stereotypes about "mannish" behavior existed. Mistral was aware, for example, of the classic tomboy narrative of failed womanhood, Carson McCullers's *Member of the Wedding*; she mentions it in at least one essay, and her personal copy is listed in Barnard College's Gabriela Mistral Collection. Having traveled extensively and enjoyed a wide circle of friends, it's impossible that she would not have read Radclyffe Hall's *The Well of Loneliness* and become acquainted with Stephen Gordon's memorable drama. She owned copies of several of Oscar Wilde's books; the Barnard College collection lists *The Importance of Being Earnest* and *Salomé*, but has no record of *The Picture of Dorian Gray*. Mistral must have owned a copy. Whether it was lost among her many libraries that were scattered and ultimately disappeared, or whether it was removed from the collection prior to its donation is simply unknown.

In Chile, feminine images displayed on journal covers sometimes appear to clash with their presumed intentions—to create the perfect housewife. Many resemble the "Gibson girls" of *Ladies Home Journal* covers from the time period. Given that some of Mistral's early pieces were published in the magazine *Familia* [Family], one would expect a different rendition of Chilean womanhood than the one that often appears on its covers (stressing, perhaps, maternal duties and virginal qualities consonant with traditional Catholicism). Instead, a July issue of *Familia*, probably published in 1913, features the classic fetishized image of the woman (fig. 2). Feminine, but wearing with fashionable boyish dress signaling a tantalizing gender-crossing (and always holding or displaying a phallic symbol such as tiny binoculars pointed slightly upward or a long, erect

Figure 2. July cover (probably 1913) of the magazine *Familia*, where Mistral was published.

feather in her hat), the woman here is not plenitude but a reassuring lack—the kind that confirms that the phallus is indeed in its proper place, in the spectator's eye, and that women want it at all costs.

It is fascinating to consider the implications of this image for women. Presumably, they had to identify with the narrative of femininity as being about not threatening men's possession of both the phallus and woman. Undeniably, Mistral's appearance was not of this sort. Initially, she did appear as a matronly woman uninterested in marriage. It's reasonable to assert that this was the sole available cultural script—bourgeois cultural script, that is—for Mistral to occupy.

One has only to look at the description of the 1914 Juegos Florales, portraying the "queens" of high society, to verify the discordant note that Mistral must have sounded in this context (fig. 3).[10] Nine young girls, probably between the ages of thirteen and fifteen, are presented as

Figure 3. Announcement of the "queens" of the 1914 Juegos Florales competition, when Mistral won the "Flor Natural" prize. This appeared in the July 1915 issue of the magazine *Familia*.

simultaneously demure and available, looking for a respectable "man." They are excessively made-up and adorned, are photographed half-lit, usually from the side or the back, never smile with an open mouth (as that was considered quite uncouth for a lady of their position), and sport classic fetish accoutrements, like lace or fur shawls. They adopt varying poses such as offering an outstretched arm or extending an uncovered shoulder or a lily-white neck toward the camera, suggesting availability and also a femaleness freed from labor. Noticeably, they all appear white.

We can further compare Mistral to the image of the woman that adorns the cover of the Juegos Florales commemorative bound edition, in which

Mistral's "Sonetos de la muerte" [Sonnets of death] appeared, having won a prestigious prize (fig. 4). The image is that of a flapper, her hair carefully coiffed to suggest carefree boyishness but not a substitution for the man. The image could not be further from that of Mistral herself in the official portrait of the competition (fig. 1). The flapper's eye is coquettishly averted but looks upward as a sexual defiance, however muted. She smiles knowingly in a moment of anticipated intimacy, mixing the lure of unspoiled innocence with its opposite, a worldly, cosmopolitan knowingness. In her own, official portrait, Mistral, by contrast, looks upward, as if to the heavens, divorced from the world and uninterested in those who regard her. Already she is constructed as a figure mystically—and soon to become mythically—separated from the world, a narcissistic, (because possibly arrested) woman.

Finally, the February 1913 cover of *Elegancias* [Elegance], a journal edited and published in Paris with Rubén Darío as literary director, and which published some of Mistral's early poems, confirms the ubiquity of the imagined fetish woman and her status as male object in dominant circles at the time (fig. 5). Notice, once again, the symbols of the "phallic mother": the long, pointed umbrella, at a slight angle, the erect feather of the woman's hat. And, of course, the fact that this female image adorns the cover speaks volumes about the centrality of the imagery in male-dominated literary venues.

When Mistral published in *Elegancias,* she was still quite young, and her letters to Rubén Darío reveal how she had to work herself into an image of womanhood sanctioned by bourgeois society and art. She essentially pleads with Darío to notice her, assuming a feminine voice:

Poet: I, who am but a woman and therefore weak, being a schoolteacher have something of our grandmothers in me, loss of brains, I have stumbled upon my weakness for writing stories and verses for my little girls.

I dare—oh, how I dare!—to ask you to read what I'm sending you, to wit, an original story of mine and some verses, with my sole authorship.

I dare—oh, daring it is!—if you would be so kind as to smile at me with a paternal sweetness, if you read them and perchance find a few seeds here and there, a hint of a promise for the future, I dare ask you to publish them in *Elegancias* or in *Mundial*. . . .

Rubén, if in my story and little stanzas you should find no more than hollowness, useless and vulgar strands, just write this in a piece of paper: bad!, bad! And sign it. Devoted as I am to you today, I will be even more after that![11]

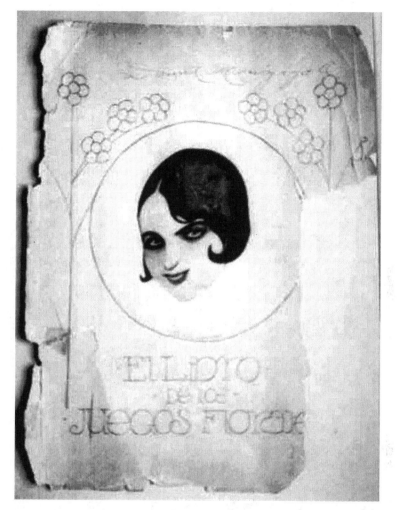

Figure 4. Cover of *El Libro de los Juegos Florales* in 1914, where Mistral's "Sonetos de la muerte" [Sonnets of death] was commemorated.

How different would Mistral become, once outside of Chile! Here, however, it is clear that she wanted Darío's recognition and that she knew he would accept her literary submission only if she assumed an exaggerated stance of feminine humility and devotion. It's clear that Mistral admired him as a poet. She probably was aware of the space afforded male poets in her day but rarely extended to women. Therefore, in her earlier years, she tried to adopt a hyperbolic feminine pose but, given her masculinity, could not do so in sexual terms. As with so much lesbian

Figure 5. February 1913 cover of *Elegancias* (no. 28), a journal published in Paris with Rubén Darío as literary director. Mistral was published in nos. 29 (March 1913) and 30 (April 1913).

discourse of this period, Mistral's language became that of biological filiation. Here, she casts Darío as a "father" and herself as his daughter.

Stepping back in time, we discover that the child Lucila Godoy Alcayaga was enrolled in school circa 1896. A group picture taken in Montegrande, which is now preserved as a museum and stands not far from Mistral's

Figure 6. Gabriela Mistral enrolled in the Montegrande School, where her sister
Emelina was the schoolteacher. In this photograph, circa 1896, Lucila is standing
almost directly behind Emelina, who is seated.

grave, records the emerging public school in Chile (fig. 6). The setting is
midway between rustic and modern. Mistral's sister Emelina is the schoolteacher and is seated at the far right. Slightly behind her, Lucila is standing up, somewhat stiffly, and looks uncomfortable in her best dress; her
shoulders are tight, and her expressionless face signals what might be
discomfort at being held so firmly in the camera's hold. This photograph
reproduces the new discourse on children that was crafted during this
period. The children stand outside in orderly rows behind the authoritative schoolteacher, who is not set up as a particularly maternal figure.
Emelina does not stand with the schoolchildren; she does not touch,
much less embrace, them or gaze at them lovingly. The schoolteacher
cannot be interpreted as a loving, maternal figure; she stands for discipline, perhaps "tough love."

Emelina was probably not a deviation from the norm. Schoolteachers
were instructed to be strict with their students and to encourage discipline above all things. If Mistral's own writings on the subject are any
indication, the school was a place where children had to abandon the
permissiveness and disorderly conduct ascribed to the home. Recall Mistral's own admission of the tedium involved in teaching—of having to

put children through the mill of boring compositional Spanish removed from any regional markings—or the mandate to seat children in a row.[12] Consider also excerpts from her precepts for teachers, "Pensamientos pedagógicos" [Pedagogical thoughts] (1923); "All the vices and the lowliness of a people are the vices of its teachers" and "only the aristocracy of culture exists within a personnel. By this I mean the capable."[13] From these statements, one may surmise the degree to which the schoolteacher's proximity to students, especially any kind of permissiveness or close physical contact, became strictly policed as the national school organized itself on institutional lines. Just as evident, the female schoolteacher became an agent of surveillance: "Make the superior's vigilance unnecessary. If you are not surveilled, you are trusted."[14]

In order to avoid any semblance of inappropriate feeling or affection, the schoolteacher was ordered to keep herself at a distance and to become a strict disciplinarian. Probably real life did not always proceed in this way, but certainly official representations of teaching did. This representation also served to promote the child's radical separation from the home and specifically from its mother, as I noted previously. Nevertheless, the official discourse suffered from its fractures on occasion. Perhaps it promoted occasional slippages such as this: "It is dangerous for a superficial teacher to talk with a schoolgirl. Likewise, it is beautiful that a schoolteacher that has something to teach outside of the classroom be next to the schoolgirl always."[15] One cannot but wonder who would adjudicate that line between the superficial teacher and the teacher who was given latitude to break the strict inside/outside demarcation. In this light, a photograph inscribed with Mistral's dedication to a pupil is particularly evocative; it points to that unknowable quantity, the actual affections of the teacher, that the state wished to penetrate (fig. 7). The inscription reads, "To my noble and dear ——— your teacher, Gabriela." Interestingly, Mistral signed this gift picture with her pseudonym, not her real name.

Some early pictures of Mistral between 1914 and 1916 are taken outdoors. She appears relaxed and inviting, with a benign smile as her arm rests on a tree bough in one, and looking pensively downward while her friend Barack Canut de Bon is shown slightly profiled and looking ahead in another. Another early picture, from 1914, depicts Mistral holding a feminine accoutrement in her hands, possibly some knitting work in progress (fig. 8). This object seems small and distinctly feminine. Mistral gazes directly at the camera, as if surprised by the photographer's intent

Figure 7. "To my noble and dear ———, your teacher, Gabriela." Circa 1910–1920, probably between 1910 and 1914.

to capture her in a "private" moment. These photographs reveal a plain girl given to the pleasures of homemaking, more than they do the stern professional who would soon replace them; but it's important that they appeared in a newspaper, advertising, as it were, this "domesticity."

Some of the photos taken while Mistral was still in Chile depict her as an urban schoolteacher. In these portraits, Mistral tries on the image of a young professional surreptitiously "caught" in her moments of "leisure time." But, unlike early pictures where she is the image of the modern schoolteacher, having come in from outdoors and soon to be in her office, Mistral appears, in these Steichen- and Stieglitz-like portraits, completely unaware of the lens—self-absorbed, impenetrable, and

Figure 8. Mistral as a schoolteacher in Los Andes, Chile, 1914.

unknowable (Figs. 9–10). Her dress is plain and dark-colored but not masculine as such, and her figure, though imposing, does not occupy the entire frame. Generally, the background is either invisible or there is a window that indicates the existence of another space. Her gaze is directed toward an unlit area of the photograph or follows an area of light that is not accessible to the spectator. The classic picture of the enigmatic woman, Mistral usually appears half-lit, shot from either the side or the top. Occupied in her own reflections, she looks away from the camera, never smiling.

Already within Chile, Mistral underwent a transformation from her early years in La Serena, beginning most forcefully with her appoint-

Figure 9. Mistral in the southern town of Punta Arenas, 1918–1920, where she directed her first girls' school.

ment to direct a girls' school in the southernmost town of Punta Arenas. As she increased in fame, she was less dependent on a feminine discourse and abandoned an attempt to appear visually feminine. After she is photographed in the towns of Punta Arenas and Temuco, with her pupils in the girls' schools, it's quite apparent that Mistral is moving in a different direction. It's also clear, though, that she has not discovered her mestiza pose. At this point, Mistral has not yet written any defense of the indigenous peoples, nor any poems exalting the mestizo or indigenous child or mother. Mistral's earlier portraits were constructed around respectability—the image of whiteness. The photographs of her with her pupils in the girls' schools similarly lend visual evidence that in this regime of visibility, racial difference appeared only in anthropological fashion, and racial diversity, in general, was not photographed among subjects within the same frame.[16]

Two pictures offer a contrast and point to this transition. They epitomize Mistral's image as the emerging schoolteacher in Chile. A photo of her at her desk shows a figure occupying almost all of the photographic space, looking to her side (fig. 11). Compared to an earlier, similar picture in Los Andes, her gaze is stern and uninviting, almost businesslike. This

Figure 10. A portrait of Mistral resembling the celebrity photography of Edward Steichen, possibly photographed before she left Santiago for Mexico in 1922. She was probably in her mid-thirties.

photo, in the opinion of Pedro Pablo Zegers, was probably taken close to 1920, as she was about to leave Punta Arenas for her next assignment, the Temuco girls' schools. Before that, photographed with her pupils in the Punta Arenas girls' school in 1918, Mistral is seated squarely in the center of three rows, flanked by girls in uniform (fig. 12). The uniforms are black, and each girl wears standard-issue ties, blouses, and skirts. Mistral is with them, but not of them. Looking away from the

Figure 11. Mistral at her desk in Punta Arenas, around 1920.

camera and down at the floor, Mistral wears an equivocal expression. Is she uninterested, aloof, alienated, or perhaps lost in a private reverie? Although physically in close proximity to the schoolgirls, she neither touches nor gazes at them. And though one of the schoolgirls drapes her arm over Mistral's knee, Mistral does not adopt an expression or pose that might be interpreted as maternal, loving, or reminiscent of a caretaker. The schoolteacher is photographed on the same plane as the schoolgirls, yet their relationship appears both ambiguous and ambivalent. Mistral's expression is unreadable, her feelings completely veiled.[17]

Figure 12. Mistral *(center)* with the pupils of the girls' school in Punta Arenas, 1918.

The potential of that ambiguous and ambivalent relationship to the schoolchildren did not emerge in the context of the privileged girls' schools, created for the national bourgeoisie. In Mexico, not only did Mistral encounter a situation that was more personally profitable than the one she struggled to create in Chile, but there was also a rich visual culture catalyzed by the state. Perhaps no photograph better epitomizes this turning point than one of Mistral taken around 1922, ostensibly with Mexican schoolchildren (fig. 13). Only some of the children in this group were actually enrolled in school. The setting combines various elements of previous photographs. It recalls the outdoor, orderly rank-and-file format of earlier school portraits, and presents a facial expression midway between the harsh, annoyed stare at the camera of Mistral's years in Temuco and the benign, embracing, surprised look of the early pictures in Los Andes. Interestingly, Mistral's shoulders are not quite as rigid as when she was the child Lucila, who had them tightly pressed against her body.

Again, Mistral is not totally accessible; there is a quality of removal, perhaps a hint of self-absorption, in her positioning. Her shoulders drop slightly, and her arms and hands don't touch or embrace any of the children. Still, she does seem more present in this picture than in the picture taken in the Punta Arenas girls' school. Although she is not smil-

Figure 13. Mistral *(center)* in the Mexican countryside, circa 1922.

ing widely, there is a hint of a smile. She looks directly at the camera, but not intently, almost as if she has been momentarily interrupted, possibly preparing to leave and visit another school in the countryside. She is the center of the picture but functions more as its vanishing point. She is, as Roland Barthes might argue, the picture's *punctum*.[18] The attempt to create order in the countryside by bringing the modernizing project to Mexican Indians, evident in the school-portrait structure of the photograph—the rank and file, its obvious appeal to cultural hierarchies—is disturbed by the central figure of the group.[19]

The picture of Mistral with the Mexican "schoolchildren" neatly encapsulates the state's attempt to shape the gaze of its nationals toward Mistral's indeterminate figure. Other photographs are not as ideal in this sense, but as a corpus they confirm Mistral's primacy as the privileged object of the nationalist gaze. A visual aura enveloped Mistral, not only as a static image in a frame but also as she circulated in her multifaceted public presence—in ceremonies, in universities and schools, and in the United Nations and other international organizations.

In one example, from 1923, Mistral is seated with her arm against a table and an unidentified man standing behind her (fig. 14). Mistral's pose and his pose are nearly identical. Shoulders thrown back, chin up,

Figure 14. Mistral in Mexico, 1923, with an unidentified man.

and gazing directly at the camera, Mistral exudes confidence and a certain air of impatience. Notice her typical man's suit and shoes, and how
the crook of her elbow mirrors exactly that of her male companion.
Here Mistral is much closer to male masculinity than she is to female

Figure 15. Mistral *(third from right)* in Chapultepec Park, Mexico City, 1923. Seated to her right is the minister of education, José Vasconcelos.

femininity. In fact, she is not even remotely portrayed according to the conventions of bourgeois womanhood: sitting up straight, hands folded across the lap, knees held together, generally wearing a lighter-colored dress or a tailored women's dress with adornments and probably a small purse.

A wonderful photo taken in Chapultepec Park, Mexico City, in 1923 shows Mistral seated to the left of Minister José Vasconcelos at the center of a male group (fig. 15). Her hands are folded much like the man to the right of Vasconcelos, and her legs are crossed, mirroring Vasconcelos's own. Her head is bent to one side as she listens or perhaps waits for the official event to begin. More likely than not, this photo was taken by a journalist, or a photographer paid by the Mexican government, and not an acquaintance. Compare Mistral to the only other woman clearly shown in the picture, who wears a hat (as was becoming for ladies when they were outdoors, lest the sun darken their pale skins), sits erect with her head up straight, and holds her purse in the lap of her dress.

Still another group picture taken in Mexico, in 1922, has Mistral seated in the center (fig. 16). Although the exact occasion for this picture must be identified, it's obviously an official portrait, with priests and mostly male dignitaries in the first row, and a couple of dozen women, along

Figure 16. Mistral *(front row, fourth from right)* in Mexico, 1922, probably in the Ministry of Education building.

with one man,—probably all schoolteachers—in the back. The setting is grand, probably the Ministry of Education in Mexico City. What interests us most is that Mistral is at once part of the female group in the back, positioned as she is in the center, but is also separated from them by an air of higher rank, obliquely confirmed by her being flanked on both sides by the majority of the men in the photographic group. Additionally, she is, once again, in dark-colored clothes, wearing a somewhat arresting cape in contrast to the women's dresses. She is clearly a powerfully attractive, charismatic figure, not precisely feminine and definitely not subordinated to the feminine space of the photograph.

Another photograph, of Mistral standing in the center of a group of Mexican schoolteachers in 1922, might be considered a conventional "group portrait" of national schoolteachers posing with their Latin Americanist icon, Gabriela Mistral (fig. 17). A casual examination doesn't reveal much more than the illusion that these schoolteachers modeled themselves after Mistral. Examined more closely, however, there isn't a smooth continuity between Mistral's smiling figure and the rest of the women depicted in the group. The schoolteachers, without exception, are noticeably more feminine than Mistral, wearing dresses, high-heeled shoes, and the occasional necklace or bracelet. They all pose demurely for the camera, with a hint of coquettishness. The spectator cannot see the lower half of Mistral's body, but details of her dress are discernible. She is wearing her usual *traje sastre,* a tailored dress in thick material, similar to menswear. Other photographs of Mistral reveal that she wore a long, shapeless skirt with men's-style shoes. Interestingly, these are occluded in this picture. Mistral's hands are posed reassuringly on the

Figure 17. Mistral *(center)* upon her arrival in Mexico, with Mexican school-teachers, 1922. Mistral's hands rest on the shoulders of Laura Rodig, her companion.

shoulders of a woman seated in front of her, who happens to be Laura Rodig, Mistral's first companion. Of all the women in the group, only Mistral is smiling widely. This wide smile, showing all the teeth, is not a style of posing that respectable middle-class women adopted during this period.

One of Mistral's favorite portraits of herself shows her in profile against a light background, staring straight ahead (fig. 18). According to her, it showed the blossoming of her "indigenism," but in truth its composition resembles rather closely Renaissance portraiture more than it does any indigenous image. It's not unlikely that this photograph was modeled after the great mural paintings of Mexico, which stressed monumental, abstracted types, and which adapted classical poses to Mexico's idealized vision of its racial history. The original portrait, made in 1922, is full-length, stressing the resemblance to a mural. Other pictures of Mistral employ her profile as a sign of her mestiza identity. While indigenous peoples were being taught in the schools how to become more and more Castilianized and Hispanicized, Mistral began to fashion herself as indigenous-looking.

Another head shot, taken in Mexico in 1922, portrays an unmistakably masculine, strikingly butch Mistral (fig. 19). She fills almost the entire

Figure 18. Mistral in Mexico, 1922. According to her, this photograph showed her "indigenism." The original is from the waist up.

frame of the picture. She is blindingly lit, looks away from the camera without the slightest trace of a smile, and appears stern and uninviting. The photo exhibits a harsh quality and the same obliteration of space within the frame as in figure 11, at her desk in Punta Arenas; Mistral appears both imposing and masculine. She is also, clearly, photographed as a person of great importance. Her gaze does not meet the viewer's eye, but neither does she appear self-absorbed in leisure time, as in some earlier portraits. Instead, this picture is suffused with power and clearly posed to create that impression. It appears disarming, as opposed to a later portrait of Mistral, taken in 1946, after she won the Nobel Prize and after Juan Miguel's death (fig. 20). This is also the portrait of a stateswoman, and it is also masculine, but its power varies; in this latter portrait, Mistral is smiling and appears benign once again. The photograph combines two contradictory messages. Contrary to the portrait of 1922 (fig. 19), this portrait invites more intimacy, yet there is still a boundary. As in 1922, Mistral looks upward, in a gesture that signifies leadership. She is also looking slightly to the side and not directly at the lens. Therefore, the viewer cannot make eye contact, and the figure is

Figure 19. Mistral in Mexico, 1922.

still unapproachable and elusive. In figure 19 the effect of this boundary is a sense of clear superiority and strength, whereas figure 20 constructs Mistral as more saintly. Other pictures of Mistral taken in the 1940s and 1950s depict a disheveled, strongly masculine woman, usually serious and often smoking.

Figure 20 is significant, because it was reproduced in many newspapers across the hemisphere and has by now overshadowed the other photographs in its iconic capacity to seal Mistral's memory as mother. Also, it seems important to include in this discussion one picture of

Figure 20. Gabriela Mistral, 1946.

Mistral being greeted by children, as she was often photographed that way in her maturity (fig. 21). In this 1945 photo, she appears with Brazilian schoolchildren, probably at an airport or at an official function organized by the government. During such occasions, children were given a day off from school so they could form the backdrop to Mistral's pictorial "motherhood." Compare Mistral's visual stance toward the children with her virulent remarks about the Brazilian children who, she alleged, murdered her son, Juan Miguel Godoy (as discussed in chapters 1 and 4). The open space in the upper left-hand corner suggests a warm

Figure 21. Gabriela Mistral, with schoolchildren, Petrópolis, Brazil, 1945.

acceptance, and the group is bathed in natural light. The lighting gives the impression of instant recognition between the two parties, the children and Mistral. In truth, they were total strangers and probably had no real affection for each other. However, their embodiment in the visual frame forces them to symbolize national affection and communion. Furthermore, our position as viewers places us squarely amid the group of children, as if we too were "welcoming" Mistral at some level. We also look up at her; the lens makes us part of an anonymous mass, erasing our faces and rendering us as partially as the children of the photo, who do not exhibit any individual markers of personality.

Mistral's most masculine portraits, the ones that declare very "visibly" her difference with respect to the national ideal of femininity, are all flooded with light. These photographs leave little room for the spectator, because Mistral fills the frame and because her expression in nearly all of them is severe, almost punishing. The spectator, presumably, expected to see in portraits of Mistral a confirmation of her femininity and thus of national femininity. In other words, the spectator might have expected a confirmation of a heteronormative gaze. Instead, these blinding portrayals depict femininity's lack.

For decades, critics and readers alike have assumed that Mistral—that is, the icon we take to be Mistral—embodied a Catholic construction of femininity as a celibate abstraction, or that she modeled herself after an asexual mother figure who does not evoke desire. The fact, for example, that Mistral's clothes are not "revealing" in the conventional feminine way is often cited as proof of these interpretations, and Mistral has been understood as simply a cloistered body, like that of a secular nun. These interpretations, however, cannot account for her charisma, her success as image, and the passions she provoked nationally and transnationally. They also tend to de-emphasize her masculine dress, her penchant for endless cigarette smoking, and her preference for whisky—a style that was part of her widespread appeal, even if it was downplayed in official photographs.

In this chapter I have aimed to convey a sense of the collective investment in Mistral's image, from her entry into the visual field to the period of her rise into transnational fame. State processes came to manipulate this iconography, and thus it contributed to shaping citizens in an affective or psychic register, through filiation with a massified mother figure which both could and could not resemble their own mothers. What else could individuals "see" when they "saw" the photographs of Mistral as the national mother, but themselves not seeing, to borrow a Lacanian formulation?

The Chilean writer Leandro Urbina recalls his encounter with Mistral as a schoolchild in Santiago thus:

> I have a hazy image of a woman in a man's suit, traveling through an avenue in Santiago in a topless car. She is smiling and waving at the tightly knit web of children along the way, children waving back with little paper flags. . . . I can't really affirm that I was there with my kindergarten class, or if I saw it in a newsreel while at the movies. I see her from above, when in truth, I should have seen her from below. She is tall and smiling. Did we shout anything? Miss! Miss Gaby! Long live the Nobel Prize!, or, Long live Chile!
>
> Miss Josefina tells us more about Gabriela Mistral. A woman poet is depicted on the wall, receiving a bouquet of flowers from a little girl in public school uniform. Miss Josefina coifs herself like Gabriela Mistral, Miss Josefina is Gabriela Mistral. She jerks us from our seat because we are talking when we're not supposed to. She yanks us by the ear to the pariah's corner. The best poet in the world is Gabriela Mistral. The King of Sweden gave her the prize personally. And where is Sweden?[20]

The adult writer knows that the encounter may or may not have happened. Furthermore, there is no way to know whether the memory of the encounter coincides exactly with reality. It makes no difference. In this scenario, as in mass media, the spectator need never to come face-to-face with the perceived object, for the massification of the visual image ensures that the encounter will still be staged. The teacher was at her most effective when she reproduced at a minute level the encounter with the icon, replicating what happened at the national, transnational, and international levels. It didn't matter when the local teacher failed at reproducing the image of Gabriela Mistral; still, the child was interpellated through "schooling" to guarantee his existence within the nation as a deserving national subject. Gabriela Mistral was the perfect image. The local teacher didn't need to be.

Mistral's image as mother was cemented from the point where it instituted a type of transnational equivocation, as it was disseminated and staged repeatedly throughout Mistral's hemispheric career beyond the national confines of Chile. In conversations or interviews away from the written record, seemingly everyone agrees that Mistral was markedly masculine, but no further consideration is given to this issue. Mistral's sexual indeterminacy—the permanent suspension of her sexual identity—held the national scopic relationship in place, for, ultimately, the relationship of the national subject as "seer" was to his or her own sexuality, and sexuality was a precondition for national existence. This is why Mistral was the Mother of America.

It's necessary, then, not to dismiss Mistral's status as the mother figure but rather simply to factor in the missing half of this equation: an appeal to the masculine. Gendering Mistral straightforwardly as "feminine" is patently not possible from the way she was photographed. And yet, in this chapter I have noticed the insistence on this gendering in the face of visual representations that appear to indicate otherwise. Perhaps what might be entailed is a structure of melancholia, a return to the object that, while promising plenitude, offers up lack.[21] Melancholia is one example of the mechanism of disavowal; the mourning subject knows the object is lost but doesn't want to accept it. Therefore, he or she introjects the object, making it live forever and confusing identification and desire. Mistral's image was successful because it evoked this national affect consistently and, it would seem, effortlessly.

CHAPTER SIX

Pedagogy, Humanities, Social Unrest

Mistral's politics of the school were not confined to the assumption of a normative gender discourse, although, naturally, this was one of the most important facets of her role as educator. She had a broader focus. She was interested in the question of literacy and, as previously explored, was recruited by Mexico specifically to review and make recommendations for the holdings of school libraries. Furthermore, in pedagogical writings, she manifested concern with the elementary curriculum.

The route of Mistral's ascent to national icon in Chile was possible only through the public-school bureaucracy. This fact is evident in highly anthologized prose works like "Oración de la maestra" [The schoolteacher's prayer] (1919), which correspond with the construction of Mistral as dutiful schoolteacher. Alongside other exemplars of her practice of female education and the training of teachers, such as the 1917 "La enseñanza, una de las más altas poesías" [Teaching, one of the highest acts of poetry], there are several essays on primary education that are of an altogether different nature. These bear scrutiny and help correct the view that Mistral's time and energy were spent only in formulating "separate-spheres" rationales.

Related to this subject is the occlusion of Mistral's politics regarding the university and the actions of older students. Mistral never held a full-time position as a professor, but she was a visiting professor at several universities during the 1930s, and she received various honorary degrees. This aspect of her career has been neglected because of the emphasis placed on her so-called fixation on small children and their schooling.

But pedagogy doesn't stop at the age when a child becomes an adult student, and the state was just as interested in having a policy to influence the actions of universities and university students. Sometimes, in fact, it sought to dictate such a policy and assign the university a role such as what Foucault labeled the Panopticon's role in discipline and punishment.[1]

Foucault's Panopticon is, importantly, an analysis of the workings of several sight- and vision-related events, or, more specifically, a metaphor of the shift from a corporeal discipline to another kind of discipline based more on self-policing. The subject who eventually comes to police him- or herself needs an agent from without to stand for the awareness of somebody looking in not only on the subject's actions and thoughts but also on his or her desires.

Accounts of schooling tend to separate the various stages of schooling and to accept, at face value, the naturalness of categories that were invented just before or even around Mistral's time. Chief among these were the creation of grades separated by ages, and the division between the "child" and the "adult" student, with corresponding authorities and power structures founded to administer the new, age-based institutions. Mistral's involvement with education was not confined to primary education but extended to university education as well. These two realms of education should not be divorced from each other, either conceptually or temporally, but should be considered as inextricably linked and interdependent. That is the work this chapter will survey, as I focus on the pedagogical imperatives that Mistral engineered.

Pedagogically Speaking

As has been explored throughout this book, in her early years Mistral entered the educational arena through the assumption of a normative gender discourse. The previously analyzed essay "Palabras de la extranjera" [Remarks of the foreigner], which is the introduction to *Lecturas para mujeres* [Readings for women] (1923), is the most notable example of this deployment.

The essay proposes a slight adjustment to the nineteenth-century insistence on the redemptive quality of literature and aesthetics in the formation of citizens.[2] Mistral's justification for the reader that she compiles under contract to the State of Mexico is the need to instill in female students the love of literature and the humanities. The essay demonstrates

Mistral's awareness of the changing nature of humanistic studies in the context of modernization, as evident in the opening paragraphs:

> I have crafted not a schooltext as such, but rather a book for graduates of a particular section. We are dealing first with a near industrial school, in which language instruction is merely a detail. Second, the heterogeneity in the ages of the students—from 15 to 30—calls for a similar heterogeneity in the selections.
>
> On the other hand, my students will not study the humanities in any other venue. Therefore, they run the risk of never knowing the most beautiful pages of our literature. It is a good thing, then, to give them in this work a minimal part of the artistic culture that they will not receive in its entirety, and which every woman should possess. The love of grace, cultivated through literature, is a very feminine thing indeed.[3]

Mistral claims the redeeming qualities of humanistic discourse for women. However, she recognizes and compensates for the partial nature of this education; not only are students' ages heterogeneous, but the texts will demonstrate similar diversity. Notably, this education will be incomplete. Though it is not explicitly mentioned, one can conclude only that the female aesthetic subject—through lack of a complete education—will be a poor rendition of the original (male) model.

According to Mistral, the literature curriculum has to be abridged, and other methods must supplement the function once served by a protracted study of the humanities. Therefore, books as objects must be "beautiful"; they must condense the aesthetic effect primarily through visual material: "So-called educational literature to which we have become accustomed is only 'educational' in its intention. *Inferior material never educates anybody.* We need pages of true art in which daily life is elevated to the level of beauty (as in Dutch painting of interiors)" (107 [Mistral's emphasis]).

The aesthetic recourse is also a stopgap measure. Society is in the process of transforming itself, homogenizing the ages and the cycles of productivity of its workers. Because standardization cannot be achieved overnight, the present heterogeneity is treated practically. Simply put, pedagogical materials require efficiency: they must be digested in what seems like a photographic instant to create national adherence and sentiments of belonging that are infinitely and quickly reproducible. The goal is to create compliant and literate laborers out of individuals who will not require much time in school. To use a Gramscian formulation, the goal is "to educate consent."[4]

Laborers could not afford to spend too much time in school, as their years of productivity had to be maximized. Women urgently needed to work full-time to support households that frequently included one elderly parent and sisters, as well as the head of the household's own children. Male absenteeism was high at this time, and women were often the only source of stable employment; they learned to administer their homes efficiently, as resources and time were scarce. This reorganization of women's productivity was very much a prerogative of the state. It is remarkable to see this inscribed in the early introduction to *Lecturas para mujeres* as a turn toward the visual within the curriculum, something that Mistral would develop more in later essays, which I will examine presently.

The concept and practice of condensed time informed, as well, the "science" of folklore, paving its way for use in schools. Folklore shared this instantaneous, ready-to-consume, quick-pill effect on potential national citizens—or so the state hoped—in a world marked by movement, migration, and uprooting. Orality and its melodic aspects came to occupy a role secondary only to the visual in the shaping of pedagogical subjects, especially children. Even though Mistral claimed that her own folkloric ditties were targeted at mothers who had to sing their children to sleep, many of these texts experimented with her desire to capture the power of the image and the gaze in her poetry, which she thought she could do, not so much through metaphorical language (as is customary in poetry and literary genres) but by audaciously mimicking the visual through the auditory. As I will explore in chapter 7, the import of these moves went beyond the renovation of Mistral's own writings, influencing as well the management of citizens, who were understood as populations in what Foucault labels "biopower."[5]

Mistral writes in "Poesía infantil y folklore" [Children's poetry and folklore] (1935):

> We have reconsidered a number of things; also what we have been calling, up to now, children's literature.... The failure of the genre could not be more total, because there is a surplus of works written with no pedagogical intention whatsoever, which means they have been written for

adults or better yet, for peoples. Which means that we have not missed the mark: when we thought of the people, we zeroed in on the child. We come thus, to this valuation: the most or only valid children's poetry would be popular poetry, or more properly folklore.[6]

In this essay, Mistral makes clear that, however much her earlier work on the genre might have had to do with an escape into "another world," she considers folklore's major virtue to be pedagogical, not personal. Additionally, her views on folklore exceed the actual collection of tales, writing of ditties, or preservation of the "popular" as national patrimony, though all of these aspects are important. It's clear that folklore is aligned to a way of seeing, a way of teaching, a way of schooling, finally, that can penetrate the public sphere and introduce a component of identifications that can be employed by the state in arenas beyond schooling. Among the virtues that Mistral assigns to "popular poetry" are directness, gracefulness, vivacity, and, above all, brevity and condensation: "The poem must not be too long, except in those cases where the subject is heroic or religious. It should limit itself to songs or portions full of the senses; it should have the exact rhythms of its melodic archetype and its themes should be as naked in emotion as an entrail" (278).

Likewise, in this new organization of society, visual materials or prose that is actively visual and expressionistic must come to replace expository prose whose consumption requires a high degree of specialization. To this end, Mistral underscores visual materials. She recommends that all textbooks adopted for use in Chilean schools have a visual content—sometimes primarily a visual content—which will be interpreted by the teacher for the students. Her insistence is extraordinary and resonates with the ascendancy of the visual in other national contexts. In Mexico, for instance, as is well known, Mexican muralism flourished under the tutelage of Vasconcelos and the newly formed modern Mexican state.

On the surface, Mistral proposes to diminish the importance of literature and to relegate the qualities most associated with literature to the realm of high literature—literature for specialists. However, aesthetics, or, simply put, "beauty"—of which literature and high art are the supreme manifestations in this scheme—can and should be marshaled for mass purposes. In "La geografía humana: Libros que faltan para la América nuestra" [Human geography: Books that are missing in our America] (1929), Mistral emphasizes the visual, photographic, or painterly aspect of the textbook. She also highlights the status of the pedagogical book as an object of consumption:

> With the beautiful rubric of "Human Geography," a selected collection of books is being published in France. These books should convey, at one and the same time, the landscape and the people of a region, in brief but substantial sketches.
>
> Two years ago, I included in the budget of an Indo-Spanish series of books, from the Institute of Intellectual Cooperation of the Society of Nations, a volume by the name of AMERICAN LANDSCAPE. But... who will write the books? Soon we shall start searching for those who will write the sections for each country. We want an expansive frieze, divided into national segments, of the physical appearance of our America; twenty portraits boiling with panoramic veracity and in which, as in Gozzoli's frescoes, the typical tree, the patron mountain, and the heraldic beast jump to the eye.[7]

The state must educate a large number of people in order to transform them into literate workers in a short period of time. These students should emerge from the classroom with a strong sense of attachment to their country of origin and to the Latin American continent. They must learn quickly, as in shorthand, one or two characteristics that will encode the national character of an entire people. What is at stake here is a transformation of the most basic pedagogical materials and a manipulation of the attention span of the student. The idea of geography is enlisted to produce this ideological effect; description becomes secondary to image. High literature remains the model, but in a mass-media form.

This is also a model, albeit a tentative one, for the "national writer." There will be, Mistral suggests, one such writer for each Latin American country: "I wish one writer in each country would dedicate himself to writing a synthesis of his plain, valley, or mountain. Then we would have that extraordinary work. The land is always more precious than the literary creature" (137). This may appear to be patriotic conviction but is born out of a profound resentment, for Chile did not make Mistral its hallowed national writer, forcing her instead to adopt a transnational and abstract belonging that is oddly transposed into the sense of totality with which she imbues the image.

Mistral writes: "I would counsel more engravings, lots more, as many as possible, for this edition." She speaks constantly of "omnipresent engraving" (138), "lithographic generosity" (139), and so forth. The visual image championed by Mistral carries with it a constitutive ambivalence, the oscillation between love and hatred of country, a polarity Mistral herself occupied, at least with respect to Chile. This polarity also manifests itself as an ambiguous and conflicted relationship to the written word.

Reading: A Love/Hate Relationship

Apparently, Mistral tried to resolve this polarity with a very peculiar definition of the act of reading, important to consider given that reading was the central action of students. By the time she wrote "Niño y libro" [The child and the book], in 1935, at the height of her turn to folklore, Mistral had established the relationship between pedagogical books and visual culture as a kind of "competition" in which books that were bereft of images were bound to lose. The child, she wrote, was born with "a passion for the image," which needed to be addressed. In "Niño y libro" Mistral recommended joining "educational cinema" to illustrated pedagogical texts as a way to not "lose" the child.[8]

Backtracking a bit to the 1929 essay "Contar" [Storytelling], Mistral wrote:

> First we have to create printed images—as many as possible—abundant, numerous printed images. Without them, there will be no true object in the classroom to which the child can add any knowledge. Next, above the image on the page, I'd place the adventure or story of the habits of animals, with lots of coloring. This can be excerpted from a good zoophile anthology or any animal tale that the professor may know about. Only after having given the student that double image of the little beast, the visual and oral ones, would I delve into the technical information, making it vigorously slender, imitating the traces of the watercolorist, because it's wearisome to the child. Finally, I'd cover the topics of order and family of the species, since these are very boring to the child.[9]

Although the educator presents as facts her opinions about the attention span and interests of small children, there is nothing natural about these characteristics. That is, the child is being forcefully stimulated by the image and discouraged from conceptual challenges and temporal engagements. Just like "Niño y libro," "Contar" presents the conflicted relationship between reading and visual culture as emerging from the "natural" disposition of small children. In a decidedly secondary and supplementary relationship to image-based education, critical reading is displaced, presumably to the space of adult leisure time in which high-aesthetic practice will find an outlet. This, even as a creature of "leisure time"—cinema—would substitute for pedagogy.

Returning to 1935, Mistral exalts the hallowed status of the book as an object of passion and pleasure in the essay "Pasión de leer" [A passion for reading].[10] The book becomes dependent on the originality and talent of the writer. Mistral's prototype is the Mexican Alfonso Reyes, one of her most important correspondents, as discussed in chapter 1. In this essay, pedagogy is posited as the "savior" of the act of reading and of the object of consumption, the book. No mention is made of the fact that Mistral herself, in a different context, called for the reduction of words and the condensation of actual reading. Here, though, she retains her emphasis on orality, discovering the future of the book in its capacity to integrate orality. In "Pasión de leer," orality emerges as the necessary hook to seduce the child, who's supposedly resistant to reading and more inclined to visual and auditory media. Mistral proposes orality and, more specifically, folklore as the mediators between word and image.

Manufacturing books with images and color is fairly expensive even today. Public-school systems across Latin America had to provide children with their supplies. If we take these two factors into account, it is understandable why audio materials were valued: they were cost-effective and achieved many of the effects required of pedagogical books. Orality holds captive both the individual child and groups of children, instilling patriotic feelings and a desire to adhere to the homeland. The state must have reasoned that the task of establishing a homogeneous canon was facilitated by an appeal to the senses and not to cognitive faculties. Concomitantly, formulaic instruction suited the constant movement of workers within the national confines and across to other nations: "May the first act of reading for the children be that which most nearly approximates the oral tale. . . . Folklore, lots of folklore, all the folklore that we can muster, of any genre that we like. It amounts to the moment in which the child goes from the womanly knees to the dry school bench, and any nourishment that we may provide, must carry within it the color and the odor of that milk of yesterday. This folkloric milk is wasted in many races" (101).

Through folklore, students can achieve belonging within and across borders, and folklore is less dependent on the manufacture of books, as folkloric ditties can be memorized and sung. Additionally, in folklore the figure and faculties of the mother often recur, particularly in the arena of anaclitic needs and their attendant pleasures. In considering folklore, it becomes vital to assess its double character as socially conservative yet simultaneously based on primary erotic impulses. The state, obviously, uses childhood as a metaphor for the origins of a national culture, but there is more. If we take Mistral as an indication, the state not only used childhood metaphorically and not only sought to create the national child in the schools, it also extended folklore to signify a relationship with the citizen by taking at face value the identity between the "child" and the "people."

Folklore was concretely enlisted in instruction, being sung or recited by children under the watchful eyes of the schoolteacher. The teacher hoped to fill the children's time (even as she became desperately bored herself). All this entails a founding paradox. Folklore is at once national, public, and social, and also intensely bound up with bodies—or, better put, with two bodies, those of the mother and the child. The mother, though, is severed from the child as soon as s/he enters school, but the memory of the bond is exploited and preserved instead of redressed, through the teacher's body. The status of books and of reading is ensnared in the same double bind, with the teacher as its inevitable agent.

Mistral figures reading as an act that is possible but unlikely. The student can aspire to read, and so can experience this as desire. He or she, however, faces continual postponement of reading, constructed here as an act of gratification:

> A passion for reading . . . May the eyes dart to the printed page like a dog to his master; may the book, just like the human face, call us to the storefront and make us plant ourselves in front of it, in a true spell; may the act of reading become in us veritably an impetus of the flesh, may the noble book industry exist for us to the same extent to which we make a noble expenditure in it. . . . May the writer become a creature present in everybody's life, as important, at least, as the politician or the industrialist. (102)

Whereas Mistral previously enthusiastically championed the use of cinema and image in the schools, in "Pasión de leer" she shifts her position to an ambivalent one. Cinema now directly threatens the book's extinction. The new medium has to be incorporated and outsmarted in its own game: "Cinema is making children accustomed to a quick, urgent danger. . . . We have to take advantage of this event and draw from it all possible benefit. . . . The only thing that matters is to take care of the beginnings; not to tire the newcomer, not to bore him, not to discourage him by making him read an arduous piece" (103). Mistral structures the reading experience as parallel to watching television or going to the movies. The page becomes a screen that enthralls and seduces. The commodified pleasure of leisure time invades the pedagogical scene, replacing critical thinking instead of contributing to it. Folklore also seems to steer the child away from the investment in critical reading, constraining orality in a substitute position for the dazzling image. Folklore, in other words, is "the poor man's image."

Mistral's interest in orality underscores her belief that sound, along with visuals, effectively shapes the child. It also points to her own stature as the savior of orality in Latin America; Mistral actually considered the Latin American oral tradition dead, and she believed that folklore entailed the manufacture of a new national orality. Folklore presents a discursive or national child, eventually producing the subjective state of the adult citizen. In "Recado sobre una maestra argentina" [Message about an Argentinean schoolteacher] (1944), she wrote:

> The genius of storytelling, which for me is much more valuable than that of writing... is a rare virtue among our people. Our oral tradition has slowly been bled away and is now in agony.... If the Normal Schools would award the oral genius the carats that it has in schooling; if they understood that to handle children you first have to win them over, through the solar thread of beautiful speech, their *resistance* in the schooling battle would dissolve and the climate of the classroom, currently one of tension and boredom, would change completely as in a prayer.[11]

Here Mistral addresses the normal school as an institution, chastising it for not understanding the nature of children and for not recognizing the need to entertain them with things of beauty, in this case "the oral tradition"—meaning folklore. Downplaying writing and favoring storytelling, Mistral creates a narrative of doom and gloom in the national school in order to justify her own selection of educational philosophy.

In truth, Mistral's embrace of visual culture was prescient in many ways, but also misguided. Her attitude toward the image was suffused with individual and social ambivalences exhibited as melancholia. The image became a savior of the word, and the many problems entailed in the increasing commodification of society, from its labor to the culture industry and its schools, were bypassed. Furthermore, orality stepped in as a partial solution to not only pedagogical but also political issues.

What kind of citizen can intervene productively in the public sphere of industrial society without the tool of reading? The older Mistral was forced to address the consequences of replacing prose with image and, to an extent, sound. In "Biblioteca y escuela" [The library and the school], written in 1947, for example, Mistral laments the fact that "culture" has been drained from books and warns against the "suicidal" tendencies of the book industry. She mentions specifically that "deformed and bastardized books" [engendros] seek to imitate cinema, which she (belatedly, perhaps) characterizes as "another realm."[12]

Image-Based Education

The written word and the act of reading become obstacles to the school's imperative of stripping the child from the home while preserving the child's primary identification with the home. Visual and auditory media are marshaled to compromise the child's allegiance to the mother. Of course, all of these processes are ambivalent, fraught with feelings of remorse and grief, and colored by an exaggerated sense of a mission whose goal is life—the life of the nation.[13] In a 1934 essay, "Una mujer escribe una geografía" [A woman writes a geography book], Mistral links the book to the developmental stages of the child: "If attentive parents care for and pay special attention to the matter of selecting a wet nurse for the child, then it's incomprehensible that they would ignore and not care about the schoolbook, which is, as with the wet nurse, their successor in the care of the child."[14] Clearly, Mistral has merged the book to the wet nurse [nodriza] that the parents hire to take care of the child. In this way, she underscores the connection between anaclisis and schooling.

In chapter 2 I analyzed the transitional existence of schoolteachers. The state interpellated them as indispensable to the national project while simultaneously phasing out them out of that same project. In the schools' treatment of the visual image, the same logic of replacement is at work. The printed word and the conceptual tool of reading compete with the newer possibilities of the visual image. Mistral often writes about these elements as if they were engaged in battle, as if only *one* of them could emerge as the teaching tool for children: "A formidable competitor has arrived in the Home of the Word. We call this home School. The competitor is the Image. . . . Visual teaching is giving us something admirable for adults and a true feast for the schoolchildren, who delight every day in the company of those schoolteachers with a capital S, called Image, Color, Spoken Tale and enjoyable Vision."[15]

Mistral teeters between this idealization of the image and the fear that it will eliminate the printed word or render it a mere curiosity. In the following passage, her life-narration coincides with the modernizing possibilities of the image. This is not surprising. The identification with the image holds out the promise of continued life. The image is cast as collective, whereas identification with the printed word marks the individual as fated for extinction. Note that female schoolteachers [maestras] cling stubbornly to the printed word, whereas Mistral associates with the image:

> I have recollections that date as far back as my first years as a schoolteacher. Since then, I always regarded the image as an entity vastly superior to the word. However, I never had the good fortune of securing for my primary school, or my girls' lycee for that matter, a big and qualitative supply of engravings or even of mere photographs, with which to persuade some of the teachers and professors [maestras y profesoras]. They were very stubborn, not because of any ill will, but simply because of an exaggerated preference for the word. They looked down upon the image because they considered it mere entertainment. It was very hard for me not to be able to convince them that, when it comes to children and young students, the image is much more effective than even the best oral lesson. (200)

Because the child symbolizes the life of the nation, there is an intimate sense of urgency over the fight for the child's attention. The entire discussion of pedagogical materials and the impending alliance with the nascent culture industry, signified primarily in this essay by cinema, mask an underlying anxiety over individual life: "What was born with cinema was the alliance of the Word and the Image and this fusion has quite obviously benefited the great matter of literacy" (200). Notable here is the image of birth, and also the imprecise but looming, mournful aspect that engulfs the printed word.

Finally, it is fascinating, if paradoxical, that a wordsmith like Mistral—whose most cherished pursuit is poetry—should write the following: "I always thought of the Image as a kind of super-word, one which avoids all error and that convinces much more than the mere written or spoken word. Our generation, not to mention those to come, is living under its power, its triumph, and its beauty. Even more: the image has triumphed in the cinema and is now making its way into our homes through television. Some professors and teachers are alarmed in the face of the undisputed victory of the Image" (204).[16] If the word dies in the triumph of the "superword," the image, then what is the place of the poet in this scheme? What about the schoolteacher? and women? Who will have access to this mastery, to the technology, to the market? As with the idea of "beauty" espoused by Vasconcelos, Mistral's idea of the beauty of the Image is predicated on the elimination of what does not belong. It is a homicidal concept of beauty.

Mistral was aware that in order to "survive," physically but also intellectually, she had to cast her lot with the state. But there is more: this identification did not afford her an untainted space to protect her own "life" as a subject. This identification transformed the terms of her own subjectivity: "I confess, even against the opinion of its illustrious detractors, that in this discussion, now a battle, I will vote for the image, even if I scandalize my colleagues, the defenders of the word" (204). The "confession" here is certainly rhetorical, but it also indicates a tone of guilt and loss that pervades many texts Mistral wrote.

These excerpts are noteworthy because they express a complete faith in the image's potential to do state work. The Image with a capital *I* will make the children literate—an odd assignment, considering the absence of words. "Literacy," then, has changed its meaning. Ostensibly, literacy is about learning how to read; not just recognizing letters and putting together simple words and phrases, but also the capacity for comprehending sustained arguments and expressing critical thinking through writing. However, as we have witnessed throughout this section, literacy has been transformed into something altogether different. Mistral's discourse represents the child as lacking an attention span; literacy is that instant of identification between the child's gaze and the object of the gaze—the image or illustration in the book. Literacy can also mean the moment of thrall when the child listens to an auditory message. Literacy runs the risk of no longer meaning reading or critical thinking. And the public universities don't appear to be exempted from this reality. "Image and Word in Education" is one of Mistral's late speeches; it was delivered in 1956, a year before her death. The last few lines indicate that the program of schooling included plans for the public universities: "All the school levels, from the unhappy primary school to the universities of poor countries, can aspire to the efficacy and accomplishment of their goals so long as a large cohort of these magnificent educational aids arrives to help them: Radio, Cinema, Television" (205).

Culture and the State

Universities and university students have long played a critical role in the state's management of the social body in Latin America. The standard interpretation is political, but it's useful to consider the psychic implications of identification when theorizing student acquiescence and student resistance. Before examining one of Mistral's essays that clearly stakes out her position regarding the university and its role in national life, it's worth recalling the complicated levels of Mistral's successful and unsuccessful identifications.

A repeated allusion in biographies of Mistral is her lack of professional credentials, from certification by the La Serena Normal School (which she belatedly obtained in Santiago) to a university title of any sort. I have mentioned how the schoolteacher, by definition, did not attend university. It's relevant to note that most normal schools either were annexed to a university or were the originary institutions that gave rise to state universities. Although Mistral and other schoolteachers, as individuals, may be considered to have lost definitively the option to continue on to institutions of higher education, public institutions of higher education may be considered to have been, at least on some occasions, "birthed" by the normal school and so intimately related to it. In certain circumstances, one may even speak of an introjection of the normal school by the university. Individual melancholia, as epitomized by a female schoolteacher like Mistral, might be correlated to a kind of social melancholia experienced by a larger collective.

Turning first to individual melancholia, Mistral exhibits her identification with university professor Margot Arce of Puerto Rico, in a letter to Alfonso Reyes in which Mistral asks Reyes to place Arce in a job in Brazil:

> I am following the tragedy of Puerto Rico, which is exacerbated with every passing day. I love that Island and I love it especially because there is no other country as unhappy as this one amongst us—although many are—and the worst thing about its unhappiness is that, same as in the South, we have given it up as a lost case; its people do not have our attention, which, even if distracted, would still serve as a comfort.
>
> It would take me too long to outline the political situation there. The last two bits of news are the hunger strike of a University professor and

the movement for statehood for the Island. It's not a State and the hopes and honesty of the University and the service sector resided in that fact, as well as the hopes of all Nationalists. There are only two Nationalists in the University: the hunger striker, and a professor, the best they have, a literature professor, Margot Arce.... She's thirty years old. She has a serious, thinking intellect; there is an elegance about her; she is a careful reader, in fact, your best reader, after Palma; and, in a childlike fashion, she has a heroic sense of life. I could have been like her, if I had gotten books in my Elqui mountains. A lot of the sad tenderness I have for her comes from the fact that she reminds me of my youth. If she doesn't make it in the University, no one else will.... I feel I have an obligation to help her sort out her life. I have not only motivated her, but I have pushed her along the path of many things that are done without thinking in that place.... I am sure I am asking you on behalf of one of the finest creatures of our race.... She is working with me on a selection of folk poetry for the children in our schools.... She will do more for her country once she is away from it. There, she only has poverty and desperation because of the silence surrounding the political situation.[17]

Mistral wrote this letter to Reyes in the period just before Inés Mendoza wrote Mistral the letters that will figure in chapter 7. In this period, this soon-to-be first lady of Puerto Rico was a schoolteacher and a Nationalist Party member; she had not yet met and married Puerto Rico's first elected governor, Luis Muñoz Marín. This period was certainly one of frequent violent upheavals, as Mistral mentions; but, far from indicating a "tragedy," it pointed to a oppositional political culture that was alive. It is telling that Mistral names Arce, who was pro-independence and anticolonialism but also essentially a cultural nationalist, as the one salvageable element from all the destruction that she associates with Puerto Rico. It is also significant that Mistral discusses the issue with Alfonso Reyes, denoting that a select group of Americanists will anoint and "train" their chosen, solitary intellectual heirs to serve as their own trace or reflection amid an already doomed culture. Arce, as Mistral expresses clearly, represents what Mistral could have been if only she had had access to the university and its intellectual resources, but since Mistral was a schoolteacher, she was forever cut off from higher education. Mistral, it seems, was also a melancholic, and her vision of nationalism reflected this. Her identification with Arce was also an identification with cultural nationalism, always preoccupied with loss.

This identification with an institution Mistral never attended—because she couldn't—accounts, in part, for her hyperbolic vision of the university's role. Mistral viewed the university as pivotal and wished to identify with it much more than with the normal school, which she continually criticized. This, as well as the display of a kind of genderless or asexual discursive stance, is evident in many of her speeches. When directing the fortunes of normal education, Mistral assumes a conventionally feminine and pedagogical voice. But when positioning herself as the equal of statesmen and politicians in the university setting, her stance is unmarked in terms of gender, and sometimes it appears masculine. Mistral, the living embodiment of Americanism, would come to serve as the occluder of state force.

One of Mistral's most important speeches, "La unidad de la cultura" [The unity of culture], delivered in Guatemala in 1931, reveals the perpetually vacillating nature of her identification with the state.[18] It also demonstrates that Mistral's championing of the primary-school system was laced with resentment. She had a clear idea of what her public role had deprived her of. Undoubtedly, these emotions toward both the school and the university were experienced as identifications, and her hatred of the school and love for the university were but two sides of the same coin:

> My friends, I carry a legend around with me, with absolutely no desire
> to. People say I am the enemy of the University, insofar as I am a friend
> of popular education. Our mind, addicted to antagonistic siding, not
> attracted to conciliatory unities, has seen in the followers of Sarmiento,
> in Vasconcelos, in me, hatred of the superior culture balancing out a
> passionate love for primary education. This is a good occasion to clear
> up the conscience of those who have not taken pains to observe me
> before they define me. You will understand if I use this excellent
> opportunity to do so. (192)

One obvious element of the speech is Mistral's conversational tone; she was a master at blending the vernacular with a more magisterial tone.[19] She addresses the audience as "my friends," thus allowing her to "use this excellent opportunity" to complain about the public's perception of her. And what, according to Mistral, did this public "see"? The public saw, erroneously, too much love of the primary school, an excessive attachment to children, and a straightforward assumption of the woman's role. Notably, Mistral takes pains to equate herself with two of the most important statesmen of Latin American history, Domingo F. Sarmiento and José Vasconcelos; both prototypically masculine in public, they also took an active role in primary education in Argentina and Mexico, respectively. Mistral expresses impatience with her role as "woman" and desires to be regarded as more virile. The university becomes the space where she can exercise some of this virility:

> In my view, the University carries with it the entire spiritual business of a race. It is with respect to a country much like that which the Egyptians called the double of the human body. That is to say an ethereal body that contains the complete features and members of the material body. The University, for me, would be the moral double of a territory and would have a direct influence, from agriculture and mining to night school for adults, including under its purview schools of fine arts and music. (192)

Mistral's references to a unified Latin American citizenry as "nuestra raza" became a constant feature of her prose and correspondence. When she says, then, "the entire spiritual business of a race," this is not merely an allusion to a civilization or a nation but a true racialized understanding of what it means to be a Latin American citizen—an unsettling mix of José Martí and José Vasconcelos.

A second feature of this paragraph is the characterization of the society as literally a body. The state and the university are inseparable, and, in Mistral's view, the state fulfills the corporeal needs of the social body, whereas the university directs its "spirituality." Those familiar with Latin American intellectual history will certainly recognize echoes of José Enrique Rodó's argument in *Ariel* (1900). Rodó evacuated any trace of the body from his vision of the Latin American intelligentsia. In his scheme, the true student was Ariel, not Caliban—and Ariel was lightness, air, and spirit. Mistral characterizes the university much like the "superword" of the Image. She claims it is an ethereal body that contains or subsumes the material body; further, she asserts that the university is "the moral double" of the territory. This recalls the nation-state, a creation of space that corresponds to political needs and that draws, as well, on affective and psychic registers.

The prerogative to represent a race—indeed, subsuming individual will in favor of group psychology—and the assumption of a "moral" role over a territory indicate Mistral's belief that the state university should have a political role and also the power of censure over not just its enrolled students but the entire citizenry. Herein lies, perhaps, the nature of Mistral's "maternal" inclinations: "It is then that we would call the University 'mother.'"[20]

In her speech, Mistral visualizes the university's takeover of national culture from the state: "After a century of preparation, the State would take over all administrative matters, all financial matters, and the university would govern all that which is not related to material assistance." Her extreme prediction and the extreme role she assigns to the university appear to be linked to the uncertain stature of national writers. Mistral laments the fate of writers in "countries [that] pay homage to mountains and rivers" but not to the spiritual realities embodied in high-aesthetic pursuits (195). Her speech attempts to marry a culture-based concept of national identity to a high-culture understanding of leadership, despite the fact that in other speech genres her rhetoric is more populist. Here, she is clearly speaking to those she considered her own. The speech's subtext is an ardent defense of her public existence as leader.

At this point, in 1931, Mistral was just about in midcareer. The decade of the 1930s coincided with the full launching of her transnational career, which set the stage for her numerous interventions in world affairs. Additionally, during the 1930s she traveled extensively and her career as a journalist flourished. In effect, this decade can be seen as pivotal in two important respects. One concerns Mistral herself; she transcended definitively the regional spheres of influence she had achieved, of which Chile and Mexico were the most important, and reached a position as Latin America's cultural ambassador to the West. The other has to do with her ideas on education and on affecting the public sphere through educational policies, which translated into her role in the development of UNESCO and married the educational viewpoint to social policy.

If we keep the Institute for Intellectual Cooperation in mind, and also the fact that it provided the model for the eventual founding of UNESCO, we'll realize that Mistral's articulation of the role of the arts was not simply about an individual positioning for power in order to have the time and financial support to pursue her craft. Generally speaking, the relationship between writers and the state in Latin America during the twentieth century has been understood as that, a securing of patronage. Mistral's case for the arts is different, however.

There is, presumably, no ambiguity when Mistral writes, "We will not accept any dualities, save the fundamental one, body and soul, State and University," and "A fortifying unity, a theological unity, let this be the guiding slogan of our cultural enterprise.... Nothing shall live its greatness outside of the doors of the University. Nothing national will be allowed to survive severed from the trunk that has been assigned to sustain and feed it."[21] Mistral's vision is couched in terms of the "spiritual" needs of the nation, and this essence agrees with art's essentially redeeming nature. None of this should obscure the fact that Mistral's vision is of the university as Panopticon, as the singular site for the production of a unified national culture and the agent charged with the nation's "spirit." Also, although it is a self-assured discourse, it clouds the issue of who will make the decisions about the nation's "spirit"; is it that the "people" will already be endowed by this spirit from their years in primary school, and that they will bind to it specifically through their attraction to the image? In this university, Mistral appears to create a new kind of "home" and a new kind of "maternalism." These positions evolved from earlier and more personalistic or "feminine" discourse. In fact, her "genderless" or even "masculine" positioning, on the side of power, resonates with her earlier, possibly failed masculine identifications.

The "university" as a creation of discourse provided a convenient locus from which to fashion an abject receptacle—students—who could quickly turn from objects of unconditional "love" and caretaking, to de-idealized objects of hate to be eliminated and silenced. It is telling that the university became the space where the antagonisms of the caretaker relationship set up by the state were played out; indeed, the state used the university as a screen for its own shortcomings by constructing dissidents as wayward instigators of "social unrest." Students were targeted as a threat to the organic existence of the social body, an unease or illness, and were not considered subjects with the faculties of critical thinking. Endowed with the "new" literacy, they were expected to identify with the state project and the state's vision of the nation.

Student Dissidence

Perhaps one of the most dramatic instances of the university's role of Panopticon is the student strike at the university of Puerto Rico in 1948. The event unfolded with inevitably violent consequences, given the university's mandate as described by Mistral. When events spun out of the colonial state's control, Mistral lent her powerful discursivity to "educate consent" and to avoid unsightly solutions to the conflict—such as beatings and university occupation by the police.

It was April, and the Popular Democratic Party was ready to assume power in the island's first democratic elections that November. The party's victory was assured. Its leaders had created a vast and powerful political machine, and its head, Luis Muñoz Marín, had been involved in a complicated round of negotiations with Harry S. Truman's cabinet. These negotiations concerned Puerto Rico's colonial status and its continuing relationship to the United States; they centered, as is well known, on Puerto Rico's role in the creation of a Latin America ready for and willing to receive enormous injections of U.S. capital, and on the military's need to keep Puerto Rico as a stronghold for the U.S. Army in the face of the cold war.

The founder of the Nationalist Party, Pedro Albizu Campos, had returned from an Atlanta federal prison in early 1947. Of course, his return was perceived as a major threat to the political process, which the Popular Democratic Party had gone to great lengths to ensure. By midsemester, a group of Nationalist students had planned a university event to honor Albizu's return. (Albizu, it should be noted, enjoyed tremendous support from students of all ages.)

As early as 1936, Jaime Benítez, then a professor, had recognized the serious attention Albizu paid to students: "Those who would complain that the youth follow Don Pedro Albizu Campos aren't helping matters by complaining. If they want to avoid this, they have to take an interest in youth in the same way that he has, and give them faith in ideas offered, while putting them into practice."[22] Benítez had expressed admiration and respect for Albizu, as Luis Muñoz Marín also did. In the 1930s, Benítez was a member of the Liberal Party and an outspoken defender of Puerto Rican independence. After he was appointed chancellor, in 1942, he singlehandedly and decisively changed the university structure. By 1948, his positive assessment of a political rival had vastly changed. Benítez denied the student organization permission to use university space for its event, and he claimed in 1948 that Albizu was a dangerous and criminal influence over youth.

From a psychoanalytic viewpoint, one may think of Albizu as an object of identification for both Muñoz Marín and Benítez. The three men shared *la patria* as an object of love. In a way, Puerto Rico's politics revolved around a central cultural dynamic "between men," to borrow a phrase from Eve Sedgwick.[23] Benítez and Muñoz Marín ostensibly fought for control over the same object, constructed as feminine—the mother-land—but they came to reserve the highest intensity of their endeavor for the purposes of eliminating, both literally and figuratively, another man—Albizu—whom they had turned into an object of hate.

Benítez wrote Mistral that Albizu had accused him of delivering a speech written by the U.S. Department of State. In this letter, Benítez claimed that he could not deliver the speech because it included attacks on Albizu, and that "a Nationalist fanatic could assassinate [him] be-cause [he] was participating in a plan against Albizu."[24] Oddly enough, he sent a copy of the speech to Mistral, who was a friend of Albizu. When Benítez addresses Mistral in his letters, they often read as if he is seeking a stamp of approval—as childlike. Benítez is engaged in the similar process of melancholic identification, that is, an anxiety about loss.

Mistral's position on Albizu, as with so many of her positions, seemed ambivalent. On the one hand, she clearly admired him, initiating efforts on his behalf during his prison stay in Atlanta.[25] On the other, she did not defend him from men who had power in Puerto Rico—Jaime Benítez and, especially, Luis Muñoz Marín.

Before the student attack on the chancellor's home, on 14 April 1948, Benítez formally invited Mistral to give the commencement address. Ac-cording to a letter dated 9 March 1948, Mistral had offered to be the com-mencement speaker in conjunction with a Puerto Rican plan to invite her to the country indefinitely as resident writer (a plan that never material-ized). As is well known, Benítez championed the Western tradition, con-sidering Western culture to be the culture of Puerto Ricans. Puerto Rico, he stated, was "multiracial" but "ethnically homogeneous" and "Span-ish."[26] Benítez hoped that Mistral's speech would affirm his reform of the university, which was a critical part of the political project of the Popular Democratic Party. The plans for the University of Puerto Rico closely mirrored Mistral's comments in the speech "La unidad de la cultura."

However, outraged that Benítez had denied permission for Albizu's lecture, students attacked the chancellor's home, declaring a strike. Benítez responded by repressing not only the Nationalist students but all stu-dents who demonstrated any sympathy for dissidence. Inundating the campus with undercover and uniformed police complete with riot gear and tear gas, he canceled classes and expelled students. These images filled the front pages of local newspapers for weeks.

On 21 April 1948, Benítez sent a telegram to Mistral, characterizing his actions in this manner: "Thank you, Gabriela. Nobody could help the University more in these moments. Feel free not to participate in these matters. I have never acted with greater honesty and democratic conviction. Commencement exercises scheduled for May 30."[27] Benítez was convinced that he could eliminate the troublesome students without losing control of the university. Barely a week after sending the telegram, he wrote Mistral again: "The disturbances recently created in the University, which you know about because my office and others have sent you the news, have been placated, at least for now. I feel comfortable telling you now not to miss the graduation. . . . We'll celebrate Commencement on May 31 and we await your speech. You, more than anybody else, can help us to raise the level of university life and to make the attitudes more magnanimous."[28]

Most noteworthy is how Benítez glibly exonerates himself from any responsibility for the strike, describing the students' uprising as a "disturbance" and suggesting that it was "created" from nowhere by an insignificant faction that somehow took hold of the entire campus. The encounter was certainly lopsided, but it was state force that sought to crush a group of students, not the obverse. Throughout the correspondence, Benítez consistently portrays himself as a moral character and as a victim of fanatics, valiantly struggling to protect the bastion of values, the university. He euphemistically refers to the strike as a "university situation," devaluing its status as an organized act of protest and disqualifying the students' attack as a political decision. Finally, he claims that "public opinion has unanimously repudiated these acts of violence." In a self-aggrandizing gesture, he writes:

> I tell you these unpleasant things because you should have a complete idea of the situation. It's a nihilist, suicidal group, and I am fighting against it for the soul of our youth. I think we have a chance at winning—that is, as long as we can give these youth real reasons to be enthusiastic and provide them the highest emotional, aesthetic, and spiritual rank.
>
> You and all the other guests would be, of course, separated from this entire struggle. You would determine what you wanted to say, when, where, and to whom. I am certain that an awareness of your presence among us would compel more generous and creative attitudes.[29]

Finally, on 7 May Benítez sent Mistral another telegram, informing her that the graduation ceremony was canceled and requesting that she send her speech instead. The speech was distributed to students who decided to cross the picket lines and graduate, and Benítez arranged for its publication in the press. The speech appeared on 14 June 1948 on the first page of the island's most important daily newspaper, *El Mundo*. It is now known as the major essay "Palabras a la Universidad de Puerto Rico" [Remarks for the University of Puerto Rico], reprinted by Roque Esteban Scarpa in his important anthology *Magisterio y niño* [Teaching and the child].

The published version, however, does not contain the first section of Mistral's speech. Additionally, it gives the date as November 1948 instead of the correct one, June 1948. In the missing section, Mistral sharply rebukes the dissident Nationalist students, praising Benítez as a true "man of letters," a visionary. This excised section exemplifies the deep irony and the crucial role of Americanism in Mistral's involvement.

Mistral's article, displayed across the front page of *El Mundo*, opens with the following proclamation:

> The first good news that alighted in my hands was a postcard depicting the image of the New University. From this novel image I knew that you had constructed from this architectural mass the heart of your civil life and your most vital entrail. . . . I believe in the visual more than the auditory. . . . I believe in the University, even as it traverses an unexpected crisis. Unexpected especially for those who know the sweet way of life that occurs in an island—the congenital tolerance of the Antillean who has a hard time hating us and an easy time wishing us well. Against the tide that has hit the beautiful House, and even though the dissidence expressed by one or another group of youngsters pains me, I still want to admire, alongside the child with his clean eyes, how much we can see that is strong and gay in what the Puerto Rican community built there.[30]

Mistral equates visual accessibility—the university as a literal image, a postcard at which she gazes—with the happiness of a people. She wants, she says, to "admire" the image of the (not so happy) university alongside "a child" with "clean eyes." Mistral contrasts the subject of primary education, the child, with its older counterpart, the university student, rendering the latter as potentially damaged goods, as someone who cannot really see beauty when it exists in front of him or her. Mistral encapsulates "beauty" in the clichéd idyllic image of the island of Puerto

Rico. Compare this to her markedly different tone in the letter to Alfonso Reyes about employment for Margot Arce, where the same island represents loss and decay and she is dismayed at the lack of nationalist sentiment among the university community.

The section of Mistral's speech later excised also includes an etymological discussion of the word *discipline*. Mistral concludes that the meaning of the word that springs to mind most often in the modern subject, "force" is not the most important meaning. The truer meaning of *discipline* is about an "organism's" need to defend itself from "physical and spiritual risk" (16). Implicitly, therefore, Mistral justifies the actions of the chancellor, because the dissidents threatened the health of the university as a body. Mistral also dictates that two subjects—politics and religion—should never enter the university and should be left out of all discussion in the name of "order," clearly indicating that when she wrote of the university as guardian of the spiritual life of the nation, she meant a secular spirit.

Without explicitly naming Albizu, Mistral writes of him: "This University, which had proven its liberalism, had to refuse to come under the sway of any political leader. She who writes this knows full well that this case concerned no less than a professional from Harvard, loved by an entire flank of the citizenship. Even though his background and the people's love are enormously important, they still cannot alter the institution's birth certificate, in which the word 'discipline' has iron determination and leaden verticality" (16). Mistral implicitly links the Nationalist Party to totalitarianism and anarchy. There is no mention of the violence unleashed by the state against the students in the supposedly "tranquil" house, referring to Benítez's characterization of the university as a "house of learning." In her typically hermetic allusion to the word *discipline*, she goes as far as to evoke the memory of Mahatma Gandhi and his nonviolent movement, describing the chancellor (and, by extension, the state) in those terms while depicting the students as violent instigators of social disorder. She expresses faith that the Nationalist youth (although she never names them as Nationalist or uses the word in the article) will "outgrow" their youthful impulsiveness and anger and will one day merely "laugh" at their childlike hotheadedness.[31]

In contrast, Mistral does refer to Jaime Benítez by name. Rather improbably, she states that she doesn't "know his religion or political affiliation" (16), suggesting, of course, that his actions are influenced by neither, especially not politics. Instead, Benítez operates in a hallowed university "tradition" that, as she claimed, excludes passions and interests from its interior. ("Among those fortified by tradition, I count Chancellor Benítez.") This rhetorical separation of the university, and more specifically the chancellor, from the political realm is at odds with Mistral's vision of the university as the double of the state in the essay "La unidad de la cultura."

Humanistic discourse authorizes this separation, and the democratic ideal of political opposition becomes "disturbances." In contrast to the repressive and violent actions of Benítez, Mistral's speech rescues the potential of university education to do the state's ideological work and to eliminate the need for bloody reprisals. Her own stated interest is to construct Puerto Rico as a "bridge" between the United States and Latin America, disregarding the issue of self-determination and the colonial exploitation of a people. To put it more accurately, she deploys Pan-Americanism precisely to annihilate the possibility of self-determination for Puerto Rico.[32] But there is more here than economic opportunism.

"Palabras a la Universidad de Puerto Rico" is firmly enunciated from the masculine position of the *magister,* the nineteenth-century "man of letters." Mistral speaks from a position of power to a cadre of social subjects in formation, the "generations," as she calls them. The students are evoked as the crew ("tripulación") of a ship, the professors as the ship's officers. Clearly, Mistral intends to steer the students away from the threat of "social unrest" symbolized by the strike. More than mere unrest, the strike symbolizes resistance to colonial power and an authoritarian university structure. Because the university is the double of the state, the strike also symbolizes a larger political rejection of the neocolonial Popular Democratic Party. Mistral never mentions the strike itself nor the exclusion of the students who were penalized by their participation, and she certainly doesn't discuss the different ideas on democracy and intellectual endeavors that some student strikers might have espoused. In brief, the essay cements Mistral's stance on the side of patriarchal humanism and, as such, patriarchal power.

The main figure that Mistral deploys is that of the "generation" of scholars and the transmission of knowledge through the generations. In this way, the thorny question of social change becomes an issue to manage and not an object of outright repression. Change is necessary, Mistral argues; sometimes the society created by the sons and daughters must be radically different from that created by their parents. The metaphor of nation as family naturalizes the changes that are, in fact, instituted in a fairly impersonal, bureaucratic way, and with ultimate recourse to force. But such outright demonstrations of state force and of policing must be avoided at all cost; the state benefits more from the concept of "social management" or of the nation as a kind of "household" (*casa* implies both house and household).[33] In this case, the nation becomes a body with parts that must function as a whole.

The existence of this university-body is apprehended through the primacy of the visual image. The state of affairs has to look good from the outside. Photographs of police in riot gear pummeling students or choking them with tear gas, like the ones that headlined the Puerto Rican newspapers, would simply not help as Puerto Rico became the showcase for development in Latin America.

Just as the events surrounding the 1948 strike were unfolding, and perhaps before Mistral had finished writing the speech-turned-article/essay, Benítez wrote Mistral a letter, dated 10 May 1948. Apparently there had been some confusion as to Mistral's true loyalties, which had unsettled Benítez. It's conceivable that Benítez, aside from whatever personal feelings he may have had for Mistral, was responding to the uncertainty about the speech itself. He writes: "Your letter of April 27 . . . has been the most important breath of encouragement in this mess. I don't know if you know that the radio, the press, and the loudspeakers had been announcing the cancellation of your trip as a result of your endorsement of the Nationalists, as an example of your repudiation of my attitude. I have limited myself to informing what appeared in today's newspaper."[34]

The hypervisibility of the university as image and of the "democratic" process in Puerto Rico takes on a different character when juxtaposed to Benítez's doubts about the "clarity" of Mistral's thoughts. This telling paragraph comprises the body of his letter:

> You have seen with great clarity the situation that we are up against. All the malice and the irresponsibility of which a hysterical mass hungry for destruction is capable has overflowed. They are agitated by professionals of terror, direct action and sabotage. Even in spite of how painful it is for me personally to see the University so divided—with our great work teetering on the verge of destruction—I think it's better that it came down this way. My hope is—as you said so well yourself—that this

upheaval will awaken and make militant the great majority of our
people who now take a siesta, comforted by the fantasy of our non-
existing normality. *In the same vein, the state's instruments of action have
to develop an imagination, understanding, readiness, agility, an intelligence
commensurate with, and appropriate for, dealing with the audacious
techniques of the opposition.* [También los instrumentos de acción del
estado tienen que desarrollar una imaginación, entendimiento, pre-
stancia, agilidad, inteligencia, conmensurables a, y adecuadas para la
brega con las audaces técnicas de la oposición.] This [the state] does not
have yet. I don't know if these three things—civic militancy, public efficaciousness, and a serene and diligent leadership—can be accomplished.
I have resolved—along with all the people who direct this University—
to do battle within the republican attitude (a better term for us than
liberal) and to win or lose in the line we have drawn in the sand.
(Emphasis added)

This personal correspondence gives insight into the avowed separation
between state and university that Mistral aggressively advocates in "Palabras a la Universidad de Puerto Rico." It seems clear that Mistral had
previously spoken to Benítez about the "techniques" that the state must
muster to face the "techniques" of the opposition. Benítez camouflages
the real subject of his analysis by speaking of a need to "awaken" the
people. What was really at stake in the events of 1948 was a turning
point in the state's "techniques" for handling a crisis, now called a "situation." The state's actions were extremely violent and antidemocratic
but were veiled by a skillful manipulation not only of rhetoric but of
images as well.

Mistral's image, however, remains ambivalent. As Benítez claims, many
in Puerto Rico speculated that she supported the Nationalists and that
her visit was canceled because of a clash of opinions with Benítez. Mistral probably fueled this uncertainty, but "Palabras a la Universidad de
Puerto Rico" unequivocally states her allegiances with state power. Her
ambivalence might be brushed off as mere personal tribulation, given
her affection for Albizu, but once more the explanation of disjuncture
between private and public fails to illuminate how the intentional manipulation of these boundaries functioned in the public sphere.

Mistral was a master at this blurring. Others weren't quite as successful as she. Almost comically, Benítez tries to imitate Mistral's stature by
positing himself as a sacrificial victim to the Nationalists:

I was talking to Millas [possibly a Chilean professor] two days ago and I was telling him that the best solution might be that one of those little beasts, or better, one of their professional instigators, accomplished through my person the threat that they mention so often. That way, they could end their present complex and kill the father. I don't think there is any great risk of it happening, but I am decided to give them their chance. I am on my way to Old San Juan to buy a doll for Clotidilita and a train for Jaimito [Benítez's children]—the two have behaved marvelously, and they deserve gifts.[35]

Benítez's analysis of the strikers' motives is purely psychoanalytical: they want to destroy the father, and he will provide them with that opportunity when he exercises one of his actual fatherly functions, buying gifts for his children—the good children, here rendered in the diminutive. Benítez, in his narcissistic paranoia, is convinced that he is the father figure for the student strikers, the primal father of "group psychology."

This chapter has surveyed areas of deep concern to Mistral as pedagogue: the elementary curriculum, the status of reading and the appeal to the image, and the university as the arena where the ambiguities and tensions of these proposals become played out. Mistral had a somewhat ambiguous relationship to state power, but she certainly identified with it. She also had an ambivalent relationship with written language, yet at the same time she was known as a "continental" or even "hemispheric" poet. This circuit of contradictions was particularly evident in her pedagogical treatises, for her projections for schooling extended beyond the circumscribed realm of the school and the limited purview of the schoolteacher, to model pedagogical conduct in the universities and possibly the global public sphere.

There is a close relationship, in Mistral's work, between pedagogy and systems of control—one where pedagogy is not simply the work done in the classroom but also work done outside it. In this way, Mistral blurs the scene of pedagogy—she extends its reach, amplifies it, and allows it to invade other sites of less self-evident control. Her collaboration with systems of power has been noted and explained in this chapter; how this collaboration relates to melancholia and loss will be the subject of the next.

CHAPTER SEVEN

Education and Loss

Mistral was a noted and respected figure in Puerto Rico, as in every Latin American nation at the time. Of course, against the backdrop of the rest of Latin America, Puerto Rico was an anomaly because of its queer political alliance to the United States. The story of its modern nationalism revolves around its perpetually postponed sovereignty. Contrary to the other Latin American nations after 1898, Puerto Rico remained a colony. After the Spanish-American War, it was "ceded" to the United States by Spain. This unleashed a series of complex identifications and cross-identifications with the ideal of "America" and with the "other" America—the United States—spawning narratives of national loss. Puerto Rico emerged as an exemplary case of melancholic nationalism. As will become clear through this chapter, this queer national status can be related to the cultural melancholia of Latin American female identity, for the two figures studied in this chapter—Inés Mendoza and Gabriela Mistral—provide the link between the cultural melancholia embedded in the colonial situation and the broader cultural melancholia already at work in the construction of the female Latin American subject.

Inés Mendoza was the wife of Luis Muñoz Marín, the first elected governor of Puerto Rico. As the architect of Puerto Rico's contemporary political institutions, Muñoz Marín was a towering political figure, immensely popular and enormously influential. Mendoza, in her own right, is probably the most fascinating of all the Puerto Rican women who were drawn to Mistral. Originally a schoolteacher during the tumultuous 1930s, Mendoza was considered one of Puerto Rico's leading feminists.

An outspoken member of the Nationalist Party, she was an aggressive defender of the use of the vernacular, Spanish, in primary, secondary, and higher education in Puerto Rico.[1] Interestingly, her nationalism was articulated from a very different space from that of her young husband-to-be,[2] and from a position of female authority. Hers was a militant nationalism, which was responsible for the loss of her job as a schoolteacher in 1937.[3] Once she met and married Muñoz, however, Mendoza's public persona and public image changed completely.

Mendoza met Mistral in the early 1930s, and they soon established a friendship with the Puerto Rican political situation as a backdrop to more intimate affective links played out in a curious, or "queer," correspondence. The letters, at this point, can be consulted only partially, as those Mistral wrote to Mendoza are unavailable for public consultation—a telling detail in itself, in terms of the construction of public and political images that are one of the themes of this correspondence, as we shall see. The letters can be said to recount the circuit of Mendoza's melancholia: they beckon Mistral to visit Puerto Rico in order to be "cured" of her ailments, but they also speak of the slow moving away from her years as a political fighter in order to focus on ministering to her husband's—and Mistral's—needs, couching these needs in a language of political action that turned Mendoza into the artificer and the nurse of a new political and personal situation.

Before examining Mendoza's letters to Mistral, it is useful to review two texts that correspond to the "older" and "younger" Inés Mendoza. "La mujer y Gabriela Mistral" [Woman and Gabriela Mistral], a newspaper article written by Mendoza many years after their early correspondence, opens by affirming that "being a woman today is a complex matter" and states: "Mistral is a revelation of femininity. . . . A daughter of a home without a father and with no brothers, men became for her the robust strength not accomplished, a peak of superiorities that she admires and loves."[4] How very ironic that the complexity of femininity is expected to be unraveled by the very butch Gabriela Mistral! And how uncoincidental, and productively blind, to constitute Mistral in terms of what she cannot have if the regulatory regime of gender is upheld: masculinity.

This heterosexualization dovetails with a racial understanding of pedagogy's aims: "When she was a young schoolteacher she expected all children sent by God to be blonde. She had to learn how to love the ugly children, those black-eyed, naked Mexicans burnt by the sun." Again, Mistral, according to Mendoza, must cope with a disjuncture between her desires and hopes—blond children for America—and the stark reality—brown-skinned Mexicans—that America perpetually has.

Most remarkable is Mendoza's observation on pedagogical issues: "[Mistral's] work shall become something akin to that of the glands of the human body, somewhat like stimulants or endocrine glands of society.... She hopes that this will be achieved through the advances of radio and cinema, which will transmit exact information to the students; information full of the authority of the researcher, the geographer, and the linguist, who will eliminate the Mr. Nobody Schoolteacher [Maestro Don Nadie]." Mendoza had certainly taken a page from Mistral. Mistral did not believe that the schoolteacher was at all essential to education, especially with the advent of mass culture. In a telling passage commenting on the works of H. G. Wells, she even goes as far as to argue that a voice is preferable to a body, which makes her uncannily prescient of the politics of what is now called "distance" learning:

> Wells has spoken of the future school based on radio and cinema—as if referring to the selected word and the beautiful image. The ordered thought of the best schoolteacher will speak with the best throat, and the child will follow the most carefully selected figures on the big screen. To those who read Wells' prophecies with sentimental horror, Wells would reply that it's better to have that speech without a body—but with order and sobriety—than the chit-chatter of vulgar schoolteachers. He would also deem preferable the forms that glide on the screen to the washed-out school murals.[5]

Mistral evinces class resentment in this scathing portrayal of her own profession. She singles herself out indirectly but no less forcefully, for clearly the selected, "best" schoolteacher is none other than herself. After all, whose image would be reproduced on the giant screen of cinema, and whose voice would blast through the speakers? It's important to note that, even if they sound preposterous or far-fetched, these thoughts were expressed in official essays printed in government serials. This fact is one of the reasons why Mendoza could publicly and openly call for the elimination of the "Mr. Nobody Schoolteacher."

Previously, the schoolteacher appeared as a transitional object, used by the state but without any loyalty from the state, an instrument to be left behind or destroyed. Here Mendoza, the former schoolteacher, fore-tells the aims of her husband's program for education in Puerto Rico: the substitution of reading materials by audio and visual materials, which ultimately entailed a slow erasure of individual relationships with the teacher and with her bodily presence through a sort of impersonal, bu-reaucratic relationship with a social body managed by "experts"; and the elimination, as she so chillingly says, of the "Maestro Don Nadie." Interestingly, the schoolteacher is not rendered in the feminine. (Although in Spanish the use of the male gender is regarded as a "universal"—sig-nifying both men and women—there is an interesting double sexism at work here. Possibly "Maestro Don Nadie" needed to be erased because he was from the lower classes, perhaps even ethnically inferior. In con-trast, female teachers were probably regarded as more compliant in, or more suited to, the innovative pedagogical system Mendoza and her husband sought for Puerto Rico. Male teachers could always create trou-ble in terms of their political program, in a way that "maternal" femi-nine schoolteachers or audio and visual aids presumably would not.) In this text, not only the schoolteacher but also the textbooks that are pre-pared for use in the classroom operate as transitional objects en route to mass culture. Reading material will be simplified and tailored to this goal, to orient people toward the auditory and visual (especially the latter).[6]

In this populist and positivistic thinking, as one can expect, women's role is to secure fulfillment, not to signify loss and destruction. Like the earth that industrial society dreams about but destroys, woman is equal to plenitude; she desires identification with this endless earth. Mendoza writes, in her capacity as symbolic wife and mother of Puerto Rico: "This love of the earth is the most saintly aspect of Gabriela Mistral. In truth, the land should be one of woman's loves; woman will till the earth, will plant it, will make of it her garden."[7]

In truth, the "earth" of the island of Puerto Rico, in the liberal project of modernization, is never enough; technology is never enough; and mothers and children never modernize quickly enough to fulfill devel-opmentalist projections. Moreover, Mendoza herself is never quite con-tent enough, despite her public image. Considering Mendoza's own level of activism in the 1930s before meeting Muñoz, this statement reads as intellectual and emotional suicide, pointing to a loss that must have been disavowed. Notably, this loss is poignantly evoked in her correspondence with Gabriela Mistral.

"You Gave Me Eyes"

In contrast to the impersonal and clichéd "La mujer y Gabriela Mistral," consider the extraordinarily different, clear, and defiant tone of the younger Mendoza in the 1930s, before meeting and marrying Muñoz—before becoming the persona that would forever be called Mrs. Muñoz or even, in a more populist vein, Doña Inés. An interview by Angela Negrón Muñoz in 1931, one in a series titled "Conversando con las principales feministas del país" [Conversations with the country's leading feminists], provides an example of Mendoza's radically different discursivity when she was a Nationalist schoolteacher, which sharply contrasts with her populist rhetoric in the newspaper articles and interviews of the 1940s and 1950s:

> "So, to what political party do you belong?"
> "I belong to the Nationalist Party of Puerto Rico."
> "And then, can you give us your opinion of our [the country's] status?"
> "Our natural right is to be free. I can't understand how one can think about it any other way."
> "In your opinion, can we support ourselves economically?"
> "It's been studied and proven that we would generate a budget which would double the one we have now. No intervention by a third party can possibly result in the good, or advance the interests of oppressed people.... The constitution of the Republic cannot be postponed any further."[8]

This image of the youthful and defiant Mendoza, the feminist political fighter, would be modified and restructured over time. Just as she fashioned herself for the interviewer as an independent woman, fully aware of her talents and deeply committed to a struggle seen in broad political terms, over time she reconstructed herself in a different image: the nurturing, maternal, but also melancholic subject that ultimately produced the populist construction of "Doña Inés." The process by which this swerve took place involved a triangulation in the relationship between Mendoza, her husband, and Gabriela Mistral. This is corroborated by a set of private letters written to Mistral by the schoolteacher–turned–first lady of Puerto Rico. This correspondence, which spans from the early 1940s to the mid-1950s,[9] is important to study in order to understand the links between the condition of the melancholic subject and the broader political condition of colonialism as a melancholic condition.

The first letter of this archive, dated 10 March, opens with a central discursive strategy Mendoza employs throughout the correspondence: the reference to a youthful foolishness replaced by a mature adulthood.[10] Mendoza's radical days are left behind as instances of reckless youth. She doesn't mention directly her past as a militant Nationalist, but that's exactly what she is referring to when she mentions "youth." "Juventud" [youth] was resemanticized over the years for Mendoza. In the 1930s, youth was Nationalist and spearheaded the awakening of the people and the defense of culture. In the 1940s, however, youth no longer signified nationalism; Nationalists had become murderous and evil. (The question of Nationalist youth became especially thorny; see chapter 6.) Mendoza lost her ideal, nationalism. Her ideal of love was turned into something loathsome, hateful, and harmful for *la patria* and *el pueblo*, the motherland and the people. There is talk of "action" in the political realm, always with a careful "we" in which her husband is included, establishing a three-way circuit of affection and action:

> We await your presence among us, and this time I do not see why we should be separated ever again. Having you has been like a dream. Now we need you more than ever. The burden of youth no longer hurts us and with you we can accomplish many things, many things which must be accomplished. You have no idea how much of what we have done we owe to you.

> You cleared my eyes of pedagogy, by merely touching me with your clarity. You made me see my landscape, my people, and my reality. We will stay together. Keep us company; be for us, be amongst us. This is a magnificent people, liberating itself without heroics of four centuries of peonage and exploitation, from Puerto Ricans, Spaniards, and Americans. Thanks to you, I learned to see the *jíbaro*. You gave me eyes. Do you think I owe you little? Stay here with us, in peace. Don't displace yourself anymore. You are well here.

In this beautiful and poignant section—in fact, one of many such moments in this extraordinary correspondence—Mendoza recalls the substance of her first meeting with Mistral and states that Mistral "cleared [her] eyes," or disabused her of pedagogy. It seems strange that one schoolteacher, entrusted with the mission of becoming a transmitter of state culture, is teaching another schoolteacher (who specifically trained in pedagogy at Teachers College) that a belief in pedagogy is the primary problem! "Pedagogy" is simply replaced with "sight." There is an urgent desire to remain attached to that object of sight, the object that bestowed sight; it is inscribed, in psychoanalytic terms, as a need.

Mendoza conflates her personal desire with the fate of the "people" she serves—the so-called *jíbaros*. She informs Mistral that she could not "see" the *jíbaro* before meeting her. Mistral "gave [her] eyes," altering Mendoza completely. If this is the case, why did the change take twenty years to surface? Perhaps this identity emerged only after the experience of deep loss. After twenty years, the distance from the object is finally cemented as loss, bringing about introjection in order to keep the object "close" in a way that can be satisfactory for the subject. Mendoza's contradictions need not be smoothed over, for she is, on the one hand, insisting on the fact that Mistral "disabused" her of the superfluous pedagogical presence of the teacher, while, on the other hand, longing for that very same presence.

Although Albizuist nationalism also wished to recover a motherland unjustly imprisoned and robbed of its essence, it considered that the object of its loss was never far away; indeed, the object—the nation—was always right within hand's reach. Concrete action was all that was needed to recuperate the object. In contrast, in the type of populism instigated by the Popular Democratic Party, loss became permanent, a defining feature of the subject and eventually of the nation.

One of the critical achievements of the Popular Democratic Party was the mass circulation of the image of the *jíbaro*. Arguably, the triumph of this image was detrimental to actual peasants and workers trapped in the changes that uneven industrialization brought.[11] Examples of how the elite "saw" this class of rural people and how the *jíbaros* literally became an experiment in the liberal fantasy of modernization are abundant. In this enactment, the ruling class formulated not only its political program but a Puerto Rican national subjectivity with a long afterlife. Undoubtedly, the class directing these developments was just as interested, according to critic María Elena Rodríguez Castro, in "preserving a style and cultural conduct."[12] In order to erect their class subjectivity, which must remain only their own and selectively accessible, the elite had to imagine a contrasting subjectivity that was social and had to circulate in accessible form.

In her letter of 10 March, Mendoza states, "What you gave us twenty years ago is still alive. Help us to do with others what you did with us." What is it that she wanted "to do with others"? First, Mendoza sought to import elements of Mistral's thought and presence to the island in the reform of educational business, which entailed the elimination of the schoolteacher as agent. Additionally, Mendoza wanted to reproduce herself—and reproduce that machinery of melancholic identification. This does not imply a conscious choice; in psychoanalysis, as is well known, what is unconscious is clearly as important as that which is conscious. The details that Mendoza writes to Mistral regarding the project of the Popular Democratic Party in terms of massified, remade culture are the conscious aspect of this reproduction. The letters indicate, however, that this social projection cannot be divorced from the psychic process unfolding in Mendoza, which directly relates to what she *truly* lost, not what she *thought* she lost.

Mendoza is certain that she has "lost" Mistral. In the first stages of her correspondence, the desire to regain Mistral's interest is the main topic. Notice that this desire is rendered passionately and insistently as a desire to live together and never to be separated:

How have I longed to live with you! Before, during my youth, I always wanted to follow you around. God gave me someone else to follow around and serve and in that I am happy because he has your essence in male form. Stop telling us you are sick. We have the best doctors and the best care here. Who's going to make demands on you, like professorships or papers to grade? Exist with our people! See them! See their nursing stations, their planting seed stations, their farms, their housing cooperatives. These things thrive, while "education" and "pedagogy" are worse than ever—horrible.

"Living together" is a static element in this correspondence; the "home" and the "house" suggest security, and yet they are permanently lost. By contrast, "youth" is a temporal marker that evokes a time of action and movement, a time of satisfcation, as in "andarle detrás" [follow you around]. This verb is immobilized when joined to the indefinition of "service" [andarle detrás y servirle], which is how Mendoza describes her life with Muñoz. Muñoz, the husband, emerges as a worthy second choice to Mistral, but a second (affective) choice nonetheless. Once again, Mistral is described as masculine by her identification with Muñoz, a public man ("tiene la esencia suya en varón" [he has your essence in male form]), but this time privately, without any reference to poetry or to the public sphere.

Whereas in the later correspondence the bureaucratic language and ideal take over, in this earlier letter bureaucratic changes are condensed into a few select units: nursing stations, social assistance for the needy, farms, and housing co-ops. All of these markers relate to fulfilling basic feeding, clothing, and sheltering needs, reminiscent of the anaclitic attachment that is structurally compatible in psychoanalysis with identification.[13] Identification is the type of attachment Mendoza ostensibly forges with Mistral, but after she sets up a cross-identification between Mistral and Muñoz, the status of her attachments to both is significantly clouded.

Mendoza requests, begs, even implores Mistral to come to Puerto Rico to see these governmental institutions. Mistral, as always, is depicted as being sick and infirm. Mendoza assures Mistral that the island is sufficiently advanced technologically to take care of her endless ailments. She promises to safeguard Mistral from the most detrimental element to her health—teaching—and ensures Mistral's total separation from correcting.

Mendoza fixates on the state of education and pedagogy in Puerto Rico as its worst ill—what needs to be "fixed" most urgently—in contrast with the rather unreal economic "bliss" that she claims has ensued from her husband's political endeavors. Even as she desperately seeks Mistral, she also identifies with Muñoz. Later in the same letter, Mendoza writes:

> In 1937 I met Muñoz. He had been expelled from the Liberal Party and I had been expelled from the Department of Education. After meeting you nobody had fascinated me—the saintly spirit of understanding, completely devoid of ambition and greed, had not appeared to me again. This time I had to surrender. I don't know if I did the right thing in surrendering things that maybe were not my own, that were with me, inseparably. I know he has given so much more to our people. He has a burden I wish I could free him of: politics.

Mendoza goes so far as to draw a parallel between Muñoz's exit from the Liberal Party and her exit from the Education Department, suggesting that they were both cases of expulsion (though only hers was) and therefore positing them both as victims of persecution. Her attachment to Muñoz is described in terms of a "fascination," of a desire to leave everything behind and surrender. This decision, of having surrendered to Muñoz, however, is met with ambivalence and experienced as an indeterminate loss. The surrender to Muñoz, Mendoza states, came after the opportunity to "surrender" to Mistral. Indeed, it reads as Mendoza's "second chance" at, as she writes, handing over "things that maybe were not my own." The clause "I don't know if I did the right thing" points to the true loss that transpired—the failure to "surrender" at the first opportunity, that is, to Mistral. But the failure to surrender what? This is left unstated in the correspondence but seems to be related to the loss of Mistral herself.

The narrative of Mendoza's life in her letters unfolds as an attempt to come to terms with the loss, to identify the source of the loss, and to initiate the process of mourning. Because she is incapable of identifying the loss, she is instead caught up in melancholia.

When Mendoza says "politics" is Muñoz's burden that she wishes to alleviate, she unconsciously identifies, as in dream-work, the source of her own loss: Mendoza lost her own politics. Both Mistral and Muñoz function as a screen for what is lost. Mistral, however, is more intimately introjected into Mendoza's ego—and not, it must be stressed, as the ideal of motherhood. In fact, Mendoza registers guilt in the correspondence for what she "took away" from her children. Mendoza's losses—that which she cannot properly mourn—are the political ideal of her militant years as a schoolteacher and affective alternatives now unavailable.

Of course, no loss is so totally complete as to be absent. Something of what is lost always remains, in some way, shape, or form. Mendoza's militant ideal—predating her encounters with Mistral and with Muñoz—survives in unrecognizable form, unsurprisingly enough, in her defense of the vernacular and of the Puerto Rican "culture" as a reified, abstract thing invested with the affect once apportioned to the (lost) ideal, the only trace that can be salvaged of her former identity. The image of loss and of inevitable death and destruction from here on haunts Puerto Rican public discourse, not because of the 1898 U.S. invasion—the event that "changed everything," as is popularly conceived—but because of the colonial state's creation of this melancholic discourse that we can see in Mendoza's letters to Mistral. The role of psychic processes cannot be underestimated in this analysis. Through the defense of the "language" and the "culture," Mendoza, and others like her, can come to terms with their loss, by disavowing it in the psychoanalytic sense. They become melancholics, and they set up melancholia as the defining political affect of the island. This melancholia allows Mendoza's letters to Mistral to be always something other than simply the private correspondence of a public figure. It turns those letters into invaluable documents that register the personal and the public creation of a Puerto Rican melancholic discourse—the melancholia that haunts all colonies and that creates never-ending cycles of loss in a temporal space of its own.

"And Knowing You Has Made My Life What It Is"

The issue of sexuality is clearly present here, somewhere—not merely in the space between the letters but all over the correspondence itself. Obviously Mistral, a masculine woman, exerted an enormous attraction on Mendoza, and this attraction lasted for at least thirty years. What was it in Mistral that provoked this level of love, this long identification, in Mendoza? Was this love desire as well? More information on their first meeting, and access to their early correspondence, is required to assess the matter, but excerpts from the correspondence that is available make plausible the idea that Mendoza also "lost" a sexual option, in the melancholic sense of "loss."[14]

Undoubtedly, this correspondence complicates the status of heterosexuality in places like Puerto Rico, especially the political image of heteronormative happiness, with marriage as its final frame. Additionally, the correspondence questions the reductive view of the psychic life of schoolteachers. Mendoza, the former schoolteacher, obviously experienced a rich fantasy life and a world of desire markedly different from that sanctioned by the colonial state—even as she authored many newspaper articles, columns, and pamphlets of proper national femininity.

The following letter, dated 28 September, probably written in 1943, clearly conveys Mistral's dominance in Mendoza's life:

> Since my soul is seeking company in you (as so many other times in these last six years), here then go the marks of my hands which seek to grasp your soul, which I know has an even greater pain and loneliness. . . . I have not written you in years, but I knew you. And knowing you has made my life what it is. I have given everything and even more and even that has been a sin against my first children. From you I obtained the courage to be generous and not dwell on loss, ever—and I have never lost. . . . For you, I lived my youth with spirit, honesty, and

love. Sometimes, only a few times, I started to be happy. I have two daughters: Victoria and Vivian. They resemble their father, Luis Muñoz Marín. I have loved this man as you would have loved him if you had encountered him in your path. He is the most perfect creature on earth, the best creature of God I have known. It doesn't mean that he does not consume and burn. Some years ago I offered you a house I owned and that I've since lost. I have nothing now, nothing, and I would like to have a home in which I can offer you a bit of peace, to you, in it, with my affection. I don't have it. Sometimes I go to a friend's house in the countryside and think of how nice it would be to have solitude in the countryside with you. Let me see, let's see if God gives us space and I put you in my lap, as in my soul, and I create some silences and truly accompany you. I want this so much! I lived my youth. When I started I met you. I would like to see you again. I would like my four children to hear you so that you can give them the courage they need in the life that awaits them.

Muñoz, Mendoza writes, is somebody Mistral could have loved. A complicated game, perhaps a code, is played out here, where the acceptable object—a man in a heterosexual marriage—effaces the unacceptable but fiercely desired object—a masculine woman. The masculine woman is figured as being able to love the heterosexual masculine man by virtue of identification. Mendoza suspends the issue of whether her love for Muñoz is identificatory as well. Muñoz is "perfect," but he "consume[s] and burn[s]," suggesting the polarity typical of characterizations of figures of plenitude. They give all, they take all; they are empty of sex, they have too much sex; they are mothers and fathers at once.

Being torn between Muñoz and Mistral might be interpreted as a classic example of what Marjorie Garber refers to as the bisexual plot, "a mode of erotic triangulation in which one person is torn between life with a man and life with a woman."[15] Garber's portrayal of bisexuality is appealing, to be sure, but applying it to Mendoza without reflection risks missing the important point that Muñoz and Mistral represent public figurations of "male masculinity" and "female masculinity" more so than they represent simply "man" and "woman" as discrete options. In other words, to reduce this complicated triangulation merely to the question of a "bisexual" option banalizes a very complex affective dynamic played out in the spheres where the public collides with the private and both at the same time effect concrete changes in the social polity of a nation. The two figures also represent different modalities of power, not just identitarian gender constructs. Mendoza had first operated from a feminized space but one that had female figures of authority. Possibly she associated Mistral with this sense of woman's power, which Mendoza herself had given up. Mistral was exalted as image, revered as group leader, and simultaneously made to signify as a nonthinking and nondesiring subject—the schoolteacher—for whom the group cared little. Mistral also represented the fantasy that every schoolteacher had to be a woman who created female homosocial worlds and facilitated alternative affective, and possibly sexual, attachments. This quandary might have resonated deeply for Mendoza.

The correspondence between Mendoza and Mistral evinces the uncanny reemergence of elements that belong to the public discourse, as seen in the examination of Mistral's person and as demonstrated in articles such as Mendoza's "La mujer y Gabriela Mistral." Populist rhetoric deploys the "home" and the "countryside" as providing inexhaustible satisfaction. They are static elements, devoid of any temporality or causality. For Mendoza, they are items of loss; she once possessed them and lost them. There is nothing left for her to offer Mistral, no place in which to minister to Mistral's needs and to ensure her happiness; no place for Mendoza to be "feminine" in contrast to Mistral's "masculine"; that is, no place except for the scenario of the island itself, pictured as the hearth, or home, where Mendoza's maternal and nurturing wishes can be supplemented by the technological advances Puerto Rico has been able to gain from the metropolis—all these at the service of Mistral's illness.

Especially telling is that, in Mendoza's letters, this evocation and longing for the lost "home" that Mendoza wishes to "give" to Mistral occurs after protestations of absolute admiration for Muñoz; he is the most perfect creature on earth. Loss may be a consequence of having "surrendered" to the (bureaucratic, impersonal, and male) ideal that Muñoz represented. Mistral also represented these ideals, but clearly in a different form. She provoked introjection and a deeply melancholic love, an attachment to a loss that could not be overcome. Mistral provoked a "long" identification.

Mendoza temporally relates the lost house and lost ownership to the loss of Mistral, whom she constructs as having been a viable partner. Again, the state symbols of national culture are circulating in this private discourse, constituting subjects at an intimate level as they attempt to convey through bureaucratized speech what they have trouble saying directly. This indirect speech, as I have previously shown, is part of the circuit of this correspondence, and in this sense the political situation—the bureaucratized speech—offers Mendoza a language that she can then use along with the language of affection.

It is impossible not to be swept away by the beauty of this language, by the heightened affect that it manifests and the affective impact it wants to cause on the reader. These are "literary" letters in the broadest sense: they point to their own language as a performance, not in the inauthentic sense of the term but in the literary sense. Readers well versed in Puerto Rican political history and in the living image of the public figure of Inés Mendoza cannot help but be taken aback by how different this language is from the bureaucratized pose of the public political figure. Even if Mendoza is revered by generations of Puerto Ricans for the maternal imagery she sustained as first lady, there is nothing in the public archives of this figure that closely resembles the intimate sense of longing these letters manifest. It's as though Mistral has been completely introjected into Mendoza; when Mendoza is lonely, she seeks company through her imagination in Mistral. She confesses to Mistral that, "knowing you has made my life what it is," that this "knowing," left unexplained in the correspondence, has altered her life. This change entails an oscillation between the sense of having gained and having lost.

As if to convince herself, Mendoza tells Mistral that she has no regrets, that she never "lost." What she refers to is unclear, as the verb is rendered intransitively, without an object. The contrast between Mendoza's visions of Mistral and of Muñoz is striking. Mendoza writes to Mistral, "For you, I lived my youth with spirit, honesty, and love." When describing Muñoz, Mendoza writes that she loves him "as you [Mistral] would have loved him if you had encountered him in your path." The Spanish "su camino de encontrarle" almost sounds like Mendoza's was a compulsory and duty-laden love. And although she notes that Muñoz is "the best creature of God" that she has known, she inmediately follows with a reference to the demands he placed on her: "It doesn't mean that he does not consume and burn" [consuma y queme].

Additionally, Mendoza refers to something that constitutes a "sin against" her infant children. She speaks of her "youth" as a time of action and decision. She then goes on to describe the two daughters she had with Muñoz, marveling at how much Victoria and Vivian resemble their father. The intimation is not that they do not resemble her, their mother, but that she does not resemble them. There is little, if any, identification with her female children detectable in this excerpt.

In the same letter, Mendoza refers to the deplorable state of the schools:

> I remember you when I visit the schools, which are in the same or worse
> state as before. No learning goes on there. No writing. No talking. The
> only communication that has been implemented is that of Luis Muñoz
> with the *jíbaros*. He taught them not to sell their vote and in that way to
> vanquish the large, absenteeist sugar corporations.... Muñoz's Party, I
> can tell you this, we created it, he and I, along with the peasants. Nobody
> knows this. I tell you this—keep it secret. Our triumph is assured and
> it's wrenching to see how the career politicians, the ambitious ones,
> assault the false homeland. If you were to return to our University it
> would be without any teaching obligations. Only to speak when you
> want, on whatever subject you want, and wherever you want....
> Gabriela, you can always come to wherever I am. There's always room
> for you. If I could, I would go to you.

Several aspects of this passage are notable. Mendoza considers the Popular Democratic Party to be her creation as well as Muñoz's; she places herself on equal footing with him and exudes confidence that "they" will win the election. All the others who participated in the creation of the party are excluded. Mendoza has constructed a triangle consisting of Muñoz, the *jíbaros*, and herself. Both Mistral and the *jíbaros* represent something necessary in this triangle. The nation needs an image of telluric purity, to erase the lived experience of the countryside and to live on after the period of rapid industrialization. Mistral brings affectivity that is apparently absent. Like the *jíbaro*, Mistral could occupy a privileged place in Puerto Rico; an institutional place that nevertheless preserves, nostalgically, the love fostered in another home: the private home of nonpublic affection.

It is understood that Muñoz won the *jíbaros* over through his image, because, as Mendoza says, they are intellectually null and void. She claims they can't write, read, or learn anything ("No se aprende todavía. No se escribe. No se habla"), because the school is a dead space. Moreover, those responsible for the ignorance of the countryfolk are the "sugar corporations," never the U.S. government or the exploitative native elites. In other words, the fact that the school is a space devoid of learning is not a consequence of anything; it just is.

Mendoza must have recognized, consciously or unconsciously, the attraction that universities and university education held for Mistral.

Again she offers Mistral a professorship in the university without any teaching duties, so Mistral can "speak when [she wants], on whatever subject [she wants], and wherever [she wants]"; in brief, Mendoza promises that Mistral will have a life that is lived entirely on her own terms. She will feel at home, except that Mendoza can offer Mistral only a "queer" home—the nation-as-home—instead of a "real" one. What sense would it make for the government to extend such a generous offer to Mistral, if not to display her image? When Mendoza urges Mistral to come and "school" Muñoz, can she be referring to Mistral's success as image maker? Mistral's attractiveness as an image works in both a public and a private way. Muñoz can learn a lot about "publicity" from Mistral and, from Mendoza's personal point of view, her call is for company. One is not sure if Mendoza introjected Mistral herself, or the image of Mistral. Furthermore, was this image that of the successful icon, or of its abject reverse, of the schoolteacher cut off from teaching and the school? On a local scale, Mendoza occupied both positions.

"At Least You Are with Us in Our Dreams"

Some of Mendoza's letters to Mistral contain extremely cryptic associations. For instance, in a letter dated 15 July (perhaps 1948), Mendoza writes: "I had taken to dreaming about conversation and company, really for my husband more than for myself. Even though he has seen many people, he has never seen anybody like you. And since he has a few hard years ahead, you would stir in him the hidden resources of beauty and creativity that you are able to 'detect,' as if your mere presence were a radar."

Mistral's presence inspires Mendoza, and this presence is located at the threshold between reality and imagination. The conversation that she will "dream about" in order to pass on to her husband occurs either in dreams or in daydreams, epitomizing Freud's notion of wish fulfillment. In Mendoza's fantasy, Mistral's presence is justified because it will "stir" Muñoz's sense of beauty and creation. In other words, Mistral is the purveyor of the "aesthetic effect," the importance of which Muñoz has not yet grasped. The "schooling" takes place, according to Mendoza, fundamentally at the level of the aesthetic, because Muñoz is yet unschooled in the laborious task of image construction. This is where Mistral's talent lies, according to Mendoza, and her setting up the situation allows her brief access to a kind of authorial function. She wants to fashion Muñoz's image in terms of Mistral, by teaching Mistral, in turn, how to teach Muñoz and allow him to understand how important image construction is, in terms of the aesthetic effects of power.

Muñoz, Mendoza explains, has never seen anyone even remotely like Mistral, and Mendoza's heartfelt wish is that Mistral's presence will inspire the same sort of catalytic change in Muñoz as it has inspired in her:

> It was hard to cry, yet again, over your absence, and since I am very selfish, I did it with a little bit of anger, not directed at you, but at the circumstances we were faced with. But I haven't given up. I want to have more of you, for me and Muñoz—a little bit more. Margot had so much. For years I was jealous of the fact that she could enjoy your presence in the world. What I had from you, the little snippets of time I had, I've stretched to fill my life, the part of my life that you supported without knowing it—in the beauty, in the generosity and that immense creative humbleness that you have and that's contagious.

In this instance, Mendoza's loss of Mistral is made tangible—through tears, as well as by her jealousy of Professor Margot Arce de Vázquez. Mendoza probably knew that Mistral regarded Arce as the fulfillment of her own promise.[16] As opposed to Arce, the university professor, who "had so much" of Mistral, Mendoza had only "snippets of time" and pleads to have "a little bit more" [un poco más]. Notably, Mendoza is unable to state her desire to "have" Mistral apart from a reference to Muñoz. Mendoza never represents herself as a discrete individual through the correspondence, and when she tries, loss and grief inevitably arise.

Without any pause, Mendoza confidently asserts the "gains" that her "loss" does give her: a triumph in the elections of 1948; and the chance to create a national subject, the *jíbaro*, which she hopes will bring Mistral closer to her:

> We are going to win the elections of November 2. Their vote of confidence will force us to give our very best to our *jíbaros*. You have to come then, so we can commune together for a while. . . . And we will get together after they have returned from voting, in that show of force that the docile ones will enact in the electoral process—which, since 1940, is the most pure, and occurs without selling or buying of votes. . . . They constitute a quiet, silent group, the most impressive one you will ever imagine. . . . I wish you could be here with us when they come down the mountains to vote. Hanging their machetes on a nail in the wall, they bring their hands—resistant to any gift that day—free. Free to express through voting their desire for the program that they wanted in 1940,

that they will want again in 1948, that they want now as a way to live permanently in justice and in peace. You will come and you will eventually stay with us. I have hope.

The promise of seeing the *jíbaros*—represented as childlike, docile, and pure—will influence Mistral to come and, more importantly, to stay. Remarkably, the election is presented as an opportunity for Mendoza, Mistral, and Muñoz to witness the thing of beauty that, in Mendoza's view, the three of them created: the Puerto Rican peasant against the backdrop of the island's first elections for governor. Nevertheless, there is a threat: "And all this can end one day, on or before November 2, when a few madmen shoot us." Melancholics are preoccupied with their own extinction, as are narcissists. In the case of Mendoza, the lost ideal, nationalism—more specifically, the Nationalist Party—emerges as a real threat to her life.

After Muñoz was in power, Mendoza concretely requested Mistral's collaboration in preparing "selections for simple readers" in order to "clear up the tropical embroilment, lack of attention, and general weakness of thought that we suffer." In a letter of 21 February, probably written in 1949, she writes: "We have to produce our own, simple readings and create cheap publishing houses. We are waiting for you. Jaime wrote to you already." The Jaime in this letter is, of course, Jaime Benítez, who emerged as a key figure in chapter 6. It is important to notice how this seductive game of longing and want involves a broader cast of characters, an intellectual cohort responsible for the task of nation building by means of image and affect.

Mendoza's letters to Mistral when Muñoz was in power concentrate on such practical requests for help and advice in educational reform. These are, however, entwined with a depressed affect:

> I write to you today because I've been feeling a little sad. I have always sought you in my moments of loneliness or worry, throughout all these years. So there can be water in the countryside, in order to build the rural aqueduct, washing-stations for the peasants so that we may stop contaminating the rivers—in short, for the rural extension of pure waters, we have to raise the price of water for the middle class of the towns. Not that this bothers me, it's that I know that our honeymoon with the middle class is over, once they have to start paying for things they can't see, that they have never seen. And I got to thinking about how to make them see. After all, I am of the middle class myself and I

understand. And I think there must be a way, maybe a poetic or
educational way to make them definitively side with us.

This letter is undated, but its content clearly indicates that Muñoz had
just won the election in 1948 and that Mendoza was grappling with social issues from the seat of power. Mendoza discusses the quandary of
losing middle-class support, specifically the middle classes' refusal to
see or, more accurately, to finance what they cannot see. Clearly, the
middle classes did not wish to "see" the *jíbaro* in this sense. For them
the *jíbaro* mattered solely as a populist image. For their part, however,
the *jíbaros* expected Muñoz to make good on his promises of uplift, because they had given him electoral support.

Naturally, education is one arena in which to showcase the "success"
of liberal modernization. The government, however, was not about to
institute truly democratic resource sharing in Puerto Rico. Instead, the
matter of education and its institutions followed the stratification typical of liberal projects based on a shock-injection economy. Education
became a type of wish fulfillment; it would prove that the political party
that had been chosen electorally had the best formula for Puerto Rican
improvement—the Commonwealth—and that the United States was
indeed a beneficent superpower that would help its adopted "child,"
Puerto Rico, to take its first "baby steps" toward adulthood. During this
time of despair and incipient failure, Mendoza turned to Mistral, as is
clear in the postelection letter:

> I despair then and I think of you. Why are you not near me? Sometimes
> all we need is one look, a presence with which to sit in silence. I know
> you are sick. There are doctors here. We're not going to ask you for a
> single word, not spoken, not written. Be with us. Whenever you want.
> Soon. Jaime will take care of the details. You will live wherever you want
> in this island. I will never allow you to make any effort in our struggles.
> It's just about being here. You know how God is above us—well, just
> like that.

The "communing" promised in the previous letter is here rendered as
meditation—as the possibility to sit and share and partake of silence,
while the national and political struggles take place in the background,
almost as an afterthought. Mistral is invoked as some sort of talisman,
possessing magical or godlike characteristics. She does not have to emit
a single word—"not spoken, not written"—she just has to "be" among
them, "look" at them. In brief, Mistral doesn't need to participate in any

of their political endeavors. Curiously, this time Mendoza does not tell Mistral to "stop" her references to illness. Instead, she embraces Mistral's narcissistic image as infirm and in need of constant care. This change is significant, for it implies that Mendoza is now a true melancholic subject, no longer mourning the losses of her youth. This change results from the fact that Mendoza now conceives of herself as a maternal figure to the ailing Mistral. Motherhood, in this sense, allows Mendoza to push aside the offer for care given by an impersonalized technological progress, and to substitute for it her own vision of herself caring for Mistral as a patient. Motherhood, with all of its nurturing connotations, not only implies acceptance of Mistral's own self-description but also remotivates Mendoza's vision of herself. She becomes again the schoolteacher, the educator, the caring advocate for melancholic and ailing figures that she also renders as beings consumed by loss:

> We set immediately to implement a new way of educating people. We
> don't want to lose the quality of our peasant, his magnificent social
> virtues, his peaceful habits, as we modernize his life. We don't know how
> to educate this generation quickly, so we do it without knowing. I go
> back to what you told me years ago: obtain exemplary teachers for the
> deepest learning, person to person, with love—and use cinema, visual
> and mechanical aids, books and newspapers accessible to all—we'll do it
> immediately.

Mendoza's later letters still include requests for Mistral to visit, but they contain a less hopeful and passionate tone. Mendoza's passion now appears to revolve around schooling, and its target is taken for granted: the *jíbaro*. Mendoza's melancholic subjectivity is displaced into the image. Fully aware of the social changes her husband's political project is effecting, she understands the *jíbaros* as the melancholic figure itself, social beings consumed by a loss whose object they themselves may be unable to name. The *jíbaros* will not be taught the traditional skills through reading and other such pursuits. The emphasis on the program and its efficiency revolves squarely around the technology that the Popular Democratic Party imports from the United States: visual and auditory materials, a condensed, image-oriented education. As Mendoza explains in a letter dated 21 April 1949:

> We have a Publications Department in which we make simple books,
> records, movies, posters. We intend to enlarge this department markedly
> in the next four years. With respect to education, we plan to not only

educate children, but to put the whole community into action. We want to set a chain reaction into motion, including everyone from the children to the elderly in all the neighborhoods and towns. The schools will stay open and we will try to modernize them as quickly as possible, but personally, I am a bit pessimistic about our chances of advancing all that we need to in the area of collective wisdom, by relying on these empty shells that we call our schools. . . . We will never have enough money to provide them with traditional schools and with the books that we have had in the past.

Those familiar with Puerto Rican history will see the birth of the División de Educación a la Comunidad [Division of Community Education] in this reference; they will also know that the payroll of this institution included some respected visual artists, as well as a fair number of American "experts" and foreign-born economists.[17] The plan was to bypass both the school as embryonic national space and the schoolteacher as supreme symbolic object of identification. Mendoza treats the community as the "child"—collapsing ages and experiences, homogenizing cultural expression, and rendering it normative and state-sponsored.[18]

Certain realities are expressed here: there exists a shortage of teachers and money; the infrastructure is bad; an overhaul of the school system is simply too costly. The road to industrialization demands that rural peasants be quickly transformed into skilled laborers with minimum skills in literacy. Mendoza's private or personal discourse does not uphold, as is readily noticeable, childhood and motherhood: "There simply aren't enough schoolteachers for the task. We have to mechanize it as much as possible. Records, recordings, movies, simple books, group discussion, collective actions, to turn the profane ones into teachers-in-action within the community. We already have a location where we are going to produce these, and the team to begin the production."

The mechanization of schoolteaching clearly required the disinheritance of schoolteachers—and the majority of these, in Puerto Rico, happened to be women. Additionally, many of the schoolteachers were Nationalist or pro-independence, as Mendoza herself had once been.

The notion of displaying Puerto Rico as a "success story" depended on the literal crafting of images. Part of the substitution of images for critical thinking entailed the transformation of primary, secondary, and higher education. Instead of investing in education for all, the colonial government took advantage of the potential of image-based education to

secure a fragile simulacrum of inclusion. Viewership became the medium
of citizenship. (This turn toward the visual was discussed in full in chapter 6.) Recalling previous discussions of motherhood in its various guises,
it is important to zero in on the interesting—and alarming—role that
mothers played in this educational project, as can be ascertained in Mendoza's letter to Mistral. In the letter of 21 April 1949, Mendoza continues:

> We don't have enough money for all the nurseries we need. But we do
> have enough money for the diet of all the children who should be
> enrolled in these schools. So we'll use the money to provide the diet, and
> everything else we need for the nurseries we'll get from the community.
> We will organize the mothers. The workers will work for free when they
> build the school, and the painters will paint the school for free. They'll
> have an income, not in terms of a salary to be paid for their day's work,
> but in terms of what they will gain in the health of their children, in
> their care, in their education. We won't hire specialized teachers to take
> care of the children. That much is clear; it'll be really good, and much
> quicker than one would expect.

Mothers and, it seems, workers will labor "for free," or will consider
themselves "paid" through the "health" that their children will obtain in
an abbreviated school that collapses nursery and primary school in a
project that can be called "escuelas maternales," or "maternal schools,"
where children are entrusted to "mothers" who watch over their education in exchange for nutritional health. The proof of the success will be
an improvement in "diet." "Diet," it appears, dispenses with the problem
of wages. The state fantasizes taking over the care of the child, fulfilling
its anaclitic needs, and believes it will do a better job than mothers. The
entire program will require few schoolteachers, because the "problem"
of the home as origin of disease and poor habits—not to mention im-
pure children—will be eliminated.

Taking advantage of Mistral's proclamations of illness, Mendoza renders teaching as being inimical to health. In the more social sweep of
the correspondence, teaching is inimical to the nation's health. Mendoza
decries the shortage of teachers, yet she populates the sociocultural scenario with technological experts, especially experts in mass culture. Apparently, *that* personnel is not in short supply. No more need, then, for
the schoolteacher, especially since the "technicians" are plentiful:

> We have all the technicians we need. What we need the most is the
> enthusiasm coming from the part of the educational leaders with whom

we begin implementing the program. I think some recordings of yours would help us greatly in the initial conferences that we hold. I don't know up to what point you could simplify the laws of learning so that any one person can feel secure in teaching what they know. . . . That's what I would like you to record for me in a simple talk. . . . It would also be good to cover the topic for our "portfolio" of simple instructions for leaders.

It is striking that Mendoza requests Mistral to condense into one recording the tools needed to teach; previously, this would have constituted a full training program in a normal school, such as the one that Mendoza attended herself. Also apparent is that it's the quality of Mistral's voice and the enormous weight of her prestige as a leader that will seal the completeness of this training. It is evident that Mendoza wants everything related to education to be simplified to an absurd degree, while specialists take over the question of diet, using it to showcase the Popular Democratic Party's success. While foods are imported from the United States, transforming the much cheaper Puerto Rican diet, the workers are urged toward their "patriotic" duty to till the fields. Of course, these fields are rapidly disappearing because of accelerated industrialization. Obviously, there is a colossal gap between image and reality:

> We have to create enthusiasm in the peasant with his crops, with the idea of growing his crops. You could also create a recording explaining in simple language this subject—the land and tilling of the land.
>
> Then we need simple books, simple readers with the topics we have already discussed, which I've copied over at the end of this letter. You could dictate these readers and we would buy them from you and publish them. With your poetic force of synthesis and emotion, you would bequeath a treasure to all the American countries. This treasure would be destined to the simple folk forgotten by the great libraries, bequeathed to those for whom no one writes, addressed to whom no one divulges human thought. You could give them methods to clarify the difficulties inherent in the pursuit of justice and communal living.

The peasant is a complex category in this passage. Certainly, the *jíbaros* were peasants, and their identification with the land and its ways was the crux of their identity. Faced with problems of hunger and desperate poverty—real social problems—the government infantilized the peasants and reduced the totality of their existence to the fulfillment of basic survival needs. By contradistinction, the middle class was constructed as having something more than a needy body, consequently demanding more of the government. Although agriculture was being dealt a severe blow, Mistral's readers would magically restore the land as a hallowed and protected space in the social imaginary. As far as I know, Mistral did not respond to Mendoza's request to record her voice for mass use, but the plea is significant. Instead of addressing literacy through critical reading and writing, Mendoza requests auditory materials to stand in for national education, in its explicit goal of forming citizens.

The issues of introjection and melancholia reappear in the opening paragraph of an 18 May 1950 letter. The excerpt here includes a reference to a dream, but its content is absent from the letter, replaced by a long discussion on adult education and community education (only partially reproduced here):

> Some nights ago, I spent the entire night dreaming about you. Yesterday, I dreamt about you again. Since I never dream, I thought it was a sign that you wanted to communicate with me, so I'm writing you this letter.
>
> I have one big worry and that's why I dreamt of you. It concerns adult education. I'm also concerned with continuing education. We have eight hundred thousand dollars budgeted for this program annually. There's a magnificent, modern production center which will provide visual aids, posters, movies, records, simple books, and all the material that we might need. This is a dream that I never thought would come true, and now that I see it with my own eyes, I ask myself this all-important question: what are our objectives? What do we want to teach our communities? So, two questions for you: I need and ask you to help me clarify our educational objectives right now, immediately, so we don't waste any more time, since we have a strong disposition and such a great opportunity. Write them down on a piece of paper as the ideas flow from your great mind and your great soul and your beautiful life. My second question: which people should we choose to become the teachers and leaders of their communities—for the Morovis Plan and for continuing education? How does one go about the selection of teachers? I await your answer very soon.
>
> Don't go to Italy. Receive our affection. At least you are with us in our dreams.

Mendoza continues to enumerate for Mistral the advances of technologically and mass-produced materials for a classroom that appears less and less like a classroom. The schoolteacher, formerly the central object of the state's manipulation, is now difficult to define. The schoolteacher seems to be slipping away, often replaced in the correspondence by the rubric of the "leader"; the child is similarly left behind.

Mendoza considers that her dreams about Mistral carry an all-important message about public life. The clause "I never dream" is Mendoza's clue to reestablish contact with Mistral, but this contact ostensibly no longer contains any personal feelings. Rather, she asks Mistral for guidance, and the dream to be deciphered concerns the deployment of mass culture. The former schoolteacher, it seems, has "forgotten" or repressed her ability to judge by herself what constitutes education and who are fit to educate.

The replacement of the schoolteacher with the leader is evident once more in a letter dated 9 June 1950. It discusses the various "scientific" programs implemented in nutrition, hygiene, and industry, and contains another request for Mistral's recorded voice. The didactic potential of her voice resides in its massified quality. Her voice, big, weighty, and expansive, is equal to the expansion and growth of industry in Puerto Rico: "You don't know how useful the calls for cooperation would be if you just made a record for us. Don't forget to make a few recordings for us when you can. Our variety of industries is ever expanding and multiplying, which fills us with optimism."

But now, melancholia explicitly reappears. Mendoza realizes with resignation that Mistral will never come to live with her in Puerto Rico. She draws a parallel between the company that Mistral could provide Muñoz and the company that Mistral did provide Mendoza, still unspecified. The "leader"—the burdened, overworked, and lonely Muñoz—has supplanted the "schoolteacher"—Mendoza's dead life, her desire to be with Mistral: "You don't know how sad it makes me that you have never been able to come keep my husband that magnificent company you are capable of. The company you gave me nineteen years ago is still with me, in spite of the little time we spent together. The leadership role, as you know, is one of great loneliness. I spend the better part of my day keeping my husband company."

Finally, in the last letter available in this archive, dated 21 October, probably 1953, the introjected object—the lost object—resurfaces in clear allusion to Pedro Albizu Campos, the staunch Puerto Rican defender of independence. Against autonomy, he became Muñoz's nemesis in the political arena, arguing always for a more radical solution to the Puerto Rican status vis-à-vis the United States than Muñoz's compromising—and perhaps acquiescing—position. Mendoza's allusion to the

militancy of the Nationalist Party is a reference to the disturbing image
of Albizu:

> I cannot forget you and I always remember you as the mother you once
> were to my youth. I hadn't written you before because I was burdened by
> a prisoner, although he wasn't in prison because he opposes us—he has
> a right—nor for being a revolutionary—he also has a right—but rather
> because he undertook to terrorize the masses who went to the voting
> booths peacefully, and he, who knows they want what he does not,
> machine-gunned and fired upon them so he could terrorize them and
> inhibit their free expression. Even so, I felt bad about the prisoner be-
> cause he's sick, he's old, he's sincere and he spent many years [imprisoned]
> in Atlanta. Any day now he'll order us killed again, but let history judge
> him then—not us.[19]

Mendoza's invocation of youth and her address to Mistral as "mother"
attest to the poignancy of the many losses recorded in this correspondence. Mendoza includes an unfounded charge against Albizu: having
ordered shootings and killings in order to terrorize the people into not
voting. At the same time, she expresses regret over her husband's jailing
of Albizu and the fact that Albizu is ill and in need of care—care that
she knows he will not receive.[20] Mendoza alleviates her sense of guilt
and loss by stating that someday Albizu, or the nationalism that he represented, will be responsible for her and her family's death. Not only is
her guilt individual, it also represents the social. Albizu should not have
been treated inhumanly, and political opposition should have been allowed to thrive in Puerto Rico. Likewise, Mendoza's melancholia, expressed as a loss of a very singular object (Mistral), is not purely individual either. Instead, Mendoza's letters register the confluence of personal
and public discourse; the intrusion in the public sphere of unresolved
private feelings; and the transformation of social activity into personal-
ized rights and wrongs.

"I cannot forget you and I always remember you as the mother you
once were to my youth," Mendoza writes. Regardless of whether this
was truly the last letter she wrote to Gabriela Mistral, there is a sense of
finality to it, sealed by the three words *forget, remember,* and *mother.*
Mendoza's mention of Mistral as the "mother" of her youth confirms
the melancholic reading of her correspondence. If dreams are instances
of wish fulfillment, as Freud claimed, then Mendoza's dreams about

Mistral succeeded in partially restoring the lost object to her, even if only through memory.

If dreams are also about displacement, then Mistral's recurrent appearance in Mendoza's dreams allowed Mendoza to displace the pressing realities confronting her husband, the party, and herself. As we read on, it's sometimes not quite clear when issues of education are actually part of a dream's content, blurring the line between the social and the individual. What we have seen in the letters is a tour de force of melancholia where the individual's yearning meshes with social yearnings for objects that dreams cannot restore. Though the indivdual can restore the loss to an extent in her dreams, in the social, the losses are much more difficult to cope with.

Puerto Rico as a nation lost a number of important things. First, it lost a militant schoolteacher and nascent feminist activist in Inés Mendoza. It also lost the vibrant political culture of the 1930s, when several political constituencies, including many workers' movements, vied for Puerto Rico's politics, offering concrete and distinct political solutions to some of the island's social, cultural, and economic problems. Puerto Rico lost Pedro Albizu Campos, Muñoz's formidable political opponent. This left Puerto Ricans with virtually a single option in the autocratic Muñoz. Puerto Ricans lost the independence that the majority clearly sought when they elected Muñoz to power in 1948 and that Muñoz promised to obtain from the United States. Puerto Rican politics slid to a level of low accountability and populist abstractions.

To return to the level of personal loss, Inés Mendoza, as she says, lost "things that maybe were not my own." She lost her profession and she let her profession die, providing very little support for schoolteachers after becoming Muñoz's wife and supporting the transformation of Puerto Rican education into a laboratory for technology (as well as an enormous profit-ground for mostly U.S. capital). Mendoza lost her most cherished ideal, nationalism. And she lost Mistral.

EPILOGUE

The "National Minority Stereotype"

> When the national hieroglyph is an object, its capacity to condense
> and displace cultural stress is made possible by its muteness as a
> thing. But when the national stereotype represents a "minority"
> person, the ambivalences of the culture that circulates the form are
> brought to the fore, for the national minority stereotype makes
> exceptional the very person whose marginality, whose individual
> experience of collective cultural discrimination or difference, is the
> motive for his/her circulation as an honorary icon in the first place.
> —Lauren Berlant, *The Queen of America Goes to Washington City*

In exploring Inés Mendoza's private and public quandaries regarding
Puerto Rico's rapid industrialization period, I am not trying to be banal, ascribing this watershed moment in Puerto Rican politics solely or
even primarily to Gabriela Mistral's hold on Mendoza's psychology. Of
course, the process was very complex. The preceding chapters discuss
Mistral's specific involvement with far-reaching issues, such as race
(chapter 1), schooling (chapter 2), maternal discourse in public and private (chapters 3 and 4), visual culture (chapter 5), pedagogy (chapter 6),
colonialism (chapter 7), and, most important, women and nationalism.
In none of them have I meant to suggest that Mistral was single-hand-
edly or directly responsible for massive social changes in the first half of
the twentieth century in nations as diverse as Chile, Mexico, Brazil, and
Puerto Rico. My point regarding Mistral is that she was a fundamental
actor and a leader in transnational politics during her time.

As Mexico refined its idea of the "Mexican" for the world's stage; as Brazil's difference with respect to "Latin America" continued to be a thorn in the side of Latin Americanism; as Mistral exported and refined the practice of "Chileanizing" to make the locals strangely more national by stripping them of their particularity; and as Puerto Rico navigated colonialism in part by upholding cultural nationalism, so today we see in globalization the often maddening intensification of the "local," with one result being to homogenize both cultural politics and political behavior across the hemisphere. Historical approaches, like the one I have undertaken, help us to contextualize many of our present-day debates. They have a genealogy; many issues are not really new. Our postmodernity is still very "modern," in the early-twentieth-century sense of the term. Mistral's politics traveled widely and helped transform the idea of the local in each country, prefiguring many of our own debates today.

Although she is often thought of as archaic, no figure strikes me as more modern than Gabriela Mistral. In her approach to pedagogical issues; in her astute manipulation of her image; in her racial politics and her conflicted intimate sphere, Mistral shows how modernity's perturbing aspects do not merely stand on an "outside" to its progress but are central to its development and implementation. More work remains to be done, certainly, but I hope this book will motivate studies revisiting, among other things, Mistral's poetry and its reception then and today; her complicated use of religions both dominant and alternative; and her international career, especially her career at the League of Nations and the United Nations.

Scholars today sometimes are skeptical about Mistral's fame, but she was truly a celebrity in her time, and her impact was enormous. The book has tried to answer the question, Why would the state champion a queer mother? State-sanctioned national motherhood brought us to the issue of national desire. The mythic mother conjoins, in her figure, both the nation and desire as universal modes, contributing to the impression of equality among the nation's members and also transnationally, across nations. The articulation also creates the illusion that the state cares for all its members equally, notwithstanding what it actually does or helps other entities (such as the market in our present day) to do. Not only should our theories not universalize desire as if it were a constant around the globe, but we should also attend carefully to this mobilizing of desire as universal and equalizing. I have argued that Mistral spoke directly to the deployment of desire by the supposedly neutral and nondesiring liberal state. I have also seen this mobilization of desire in terms of what cannot be fulfilled but should remain implanted in the psyche; hence the usefulness of melancholia to discuss this thwarted desire and its introjection in the national ego.

I did not want to embark on an exercise of myth exploding for its own sake, although obviously the book proceeds along the narrative lines offered by myth: Mistral the schoolteacher, the mother, the champion of racial minorities, women, and children. My interest in the myths has been to discover what they say about a national culture in the profound sense of the term, as the epigraph suggests. Unfortunately, too many people still think of "queering" as the defense of a particular sexuality, or as the desire to see homosexuality and lesbianism everywhere. It was not my project to "out" Mistral or deliver some truth about her sexuality. I wanted to explore what lies beneath the fixation on the mythical, national, and queer mother. What cultural work does this figure, of hyperbolic and simultaneous attraction and repulsion, perform?

Lauren Berlant's expansion of an idea set forth by Homi Bhabha (the "national stereotype") suits Mistral perfectly. Reframing Bhabha's question as one of iconicity, Berlant suggests that the "national minority stereotype" is an image of superpersonhood experienced in social life primarily through affect, and that this affect "overorganizes" the public sphere.[1] Not only does this approach frustrate a political response to structural inequalities, it also forces us to imagine ways of political intervention into this familial public sphere that take into account our own subjectivation to both the politics of affect and the consensus-generating spectacle of feeling. Just as Mistral could not remain in a pure space to protect herself from her decision to represent the state as its image of the queer mother, we cannot imagine ourselves to be in a space above or separated from public life as spectacle and feeling, where we regard not only entertainment but a series of mirrors and masks that, we're supposed to believe, contain the national truth.

In his essay on speech genres, Mikhail Bakhtin proposed that one's own voice always stands in relation to the perspectives expressed in others' speech, in relationships such as opposition, contradiction, overlap, and simulation. "Authoring" oneself is about how the speaker uses these perspectives and also how the speaker, to a certain extent, is shaped by others' speech.[2] This idea dispenses with the attempt (bound to fail, in my opinion) to ascertain whether Mistral was totally instrumental in her public life, or whether there were levels at which she was being "sincere" (meaning sincerity as preserved and protected mostly in her private existence).

Mistral's public voice, expressed in writings and speeches, is difficult to track, because it spoke to different audiences, using them to different ends. Her private feelings, although at times very jumbled, were less hard to categorize and often went against views she expressed publicly—as private expression often does. In fact, the focus on the private/public relationship has helped to clarify many elements that would otherwise be mysterious and muddled and to approach contradictions that seem untenable. I have analyzed some Mistral materials that are not as familiar or as popular as others. Her interaction with mass and popular culture has been reviewed systematically in this book, from newspapers to folklore, photography, and sound. Employing correspondence at critical junctures has revealed that this genre doesn't necessarily function as private in all instances, not only because letters were opened and were probably self-censored but also because ideas circulated among a group that was not always defined in terms of liberal privacy, occurring in a two-way circuit.

Many of Mistral's positions were naturalized in private and public. Schoolbooks and public policy had to do with this, but also gossip and celebrity culture. I do not mean that this deployment was always successful. Ideas of protest were especially relevant to my discussion of university students (chapter 6), and policy was explicitly discussed as a potential failure, reflected in the letters written by Inés Mendoza (chapter 7). In sum, I have tried to make clear that Mistral's was an active and conflicted historical moment, with diverse actors and outcomes. Mythology immobilizes the period, erases conflict, or turns it into something merely banal. Exploding myth here has been about restoring the heterogeneity of the process, not replacing old myths with new ones or resignifying a heroic narrative to suit another constituency, be it women, queers, or lesbians.

The main points of this study concern Mistral's individual quandaries but also deal with social practices, specifically Latin American cultural politics and, to an extent, hemispheric politics. Gabriela Mistral was a true cultural machine, generating and refracting multiple social meanings, even beyond her death. Some of her cultural work occurred rather self-consciously. By now, it is hard to dispute that she took the school-teacher persona to heights it had not known before, and in this way she elevated the metaphors of education and schooling to a degree resembling those of her nineteenth-century predecessors who championed republican motherhood. Other aspects of her success as icon occurred without her explicit direction and responded, to be sure, to many of her psychic dilemmas. I think that in her case, queerness is best located in this liminal space where personal and social contradictions become played out, and it includes both the violence Gabriela Mistral suffered and the violence she wreaked on others. There is a complex interplay, at times virtually impossible to unravel, between her conscious and unconscious impulses, and between her and the state that she wholeheartedly came to represent. My intent has been not to judge her but to provoke readings that consider the complexity, the unpredictability, and, above all, the historicity of her figure and work.

I do want to judge and impugn the liberal state Mistral vigorously aided. On the one hand, the state may not have been conscious of its deployment of Mistral's ambivalences and ambiguities to the degree that it consciously deployed her straightforward maternal presence, the way she seemed to be a "secular nun," celibate without vows. On the other hand, I do not find completely implausible the possibility that the state mobilized queerness consciously, and I would encourage more critical reflection along these lines. As I showed in chapter 2, at times the state barred certain subjects, such as women schoolteachers, from normative sexuality. At others, it circulated the "national minority stereotype." However, my intent in this book has not been to understand queer sexuality as completely persecuted and suffocated. I have wanted to show how queer subjects, like any other sexual subjects, are susceptible to desires for the normative ideal and sometimes work quite diligently toward achieving membership in the norm.

Recently theorists such as José Muñoz and David Eng have attempted to construe melancholia as something other than a completely negative project.[3] Although I do not discount this possibility, the melancholic nationalism arrived at toward the end of the book—the melancholic citizenship predicated on "feminine" loss (chapter 2), which is a running theme throughout—produced few positives. In the case of Mistral and her time period, melancholia was also accompanied by paranoid tendencies and a pronounced narcissistic strain (chapter 4). Infantilization characterized national discourse. It even haunted Mistral's poetic oeuvre, a mostly disturbing body which itself became a sort of "dead" object, extolled by critics but virtually unread for decades and not part of the curriculum. I am not saying that Mistral perpetually suffered, experiencing no pleasure in life, as she sometimes presented. By enlisting psychoanalytic concepts, I am interested in joining in the critique of oedipal relations as mechanisms of subjugation that are especially harsh for the cast of less fortunate characters in psychoanalysis: women, mothers, racially marked individuals, and queers—subjects critical to the state's deployment of the psychic aspects of power, to paraphrase Judith Butler.[4] Children, too, deserve new kinds of studies in this regard.

In the case of exceptional figures like Mistral, I would urge great caution in making them "gay saints" or heroic precursors.[5] And I certainly reject all nationalist notions of family and education, as should be evident in this book. Instead of seeing Mistral in binaries (good/bad, instrumental/sincere, public/private, social/individual, prose/poetry, and so forth), I have employed a Foucauldian approach to break down the clean opposition between such binaries, attending at every point Foucault's injunction not to see the world as simplistically divided between the dominant power, along with its discourse, and the dominated, with their resistance strategies. Instead, the picture presented here is complex, shifting, and unstable.

The stories we tell about our important historical figures are revealing. They tell us about ourselves—about what, how, and why we remember. Competing stories swirl around Gabriela Mistral, coming from multiple locations and points in time. In its simplest formulation, the task of this book has been to examine the dominant story and to explore sources from a feminist, queer, antiracist, antihomophobic, and progressive perspective. Creating a queer mother for the nation was, paradoxically enough, a way of trying to engage all citizens in an impass that queers often know too well: being consigned to dead space, often feeling like living ghosts in society. Gabriela Mistral herself probably had, at times, an inkling of these feelings. Personally, I do not agree with the ways she dealt with her quandaries and the path that she chose: to represent the national mother. My impression is that Mistral was not an easy person to understand in real life, and she is definitely not an easy subject to write about. However, I have found that studying Mistral carries enormous rewards. I believe she is fundamental to twentieth-century history and culture, and certainly meaningful to the present. While resisting nostalgic appreciations and reappropriations of the past, *A Queer Mother for the Nation* has attempted to give a sense of her exceptional life and extraordinary importance, then and today.

Notes

All translations of correspondence, poetry, interviews, and prose works of Gabriela Mistral are my own.

Introduction

1. Fernando Alegría, quoted in Elizabeth Rosa Horan, *Gabriela Mistral: An Artist and Her People* (Washington, D.C.: Organization of American States, 1994), 58.

2. Juan Andrés Piña, "Diamela Eltit: Escritos sobre un cuerpo. Entrevista con Diamela Eltit," in *Conversaciones con la narrativa chilena* (Santiago: Editorial Los Andes, 1991), 252.

3. For a concise yet insightful exploration of the treatment of Mistral's sexuality, see Elizabeth Rosa Horan, "Gabriela Mistral," in *Latin American Writers on Gay and Lesbian Themes: A Bio-critical Sourcebook,* ed. David William Foster (Westport, Conn.: Greenwood, 1994), 221–35. The interested reader will also find in Horan an introductory bibliography to Mistral's works and to criticism on her works.

4. In a funny yet pointed passage, Lila Zemborain recounts a telling experience during a recent trip to Chile. She had the opportunity to visit Montegrande, where Mistral is buried. This is her impression of the official narrative regarding Mistral: "I witnessed one of the visits by a group of schoolchildren to Gabriela Mistral's home-school. The story recounted by the guide to those young boys and girls constructed an image of Mistral's personal life which, seen from an adult perspective, might appear tragic; but seen from the schoolchildren's perspective must have struck them as a true horror story. The guide told of a life marked by the suicides of those closest to her; by loneliness; by the turmoil of too much travel and professional success. The morbidity of the details proffered about Mistral's life is worthy of note. When she was a child, Mistral's father abandoned the family because he liked to 'drink.' She maintained a spiritual, non-carnal relationship with Romelio Ureta, her beloved, who committed suicide because he robbed a friend's money. Her adopted son, Juan Miguel Godoy, also committed suicide because a 'Frenchwoman' rejected

him. Juan Miguel had been born deformed because he had been extracted with forceps from his mother's womb. His biological mother died in the process. This dubious information appears as the prelude to Mistral's professional success as a teacher, diplomat and writer, whose corollary is the Nobel Prize which she received in Sweden in 1945. The kids looked at each other in astonishment. What does suicide mean? What are forceps? It's possible that they retained the image of the horribly deformed child, instead of the desire to read Mistral's poetry. Even if it is based on real-life events in Mistral's life, the distortion of biographical details shows an image of a rural schoolteacher, lonely and single, who, in spite of the many sufferings she had to confront, was able to triumph professionally." "Modalidades de representación del sujeto lírico en la poesía de Gabriela Mistral" [Modalities of the lyrical subject in Gabriela Mistral's poetry] (Ph.D. diss., New York University, 1997), 6–7.

5. The most important postings were Antofagasta in 1911, Los Andes in 1912, Punta Arenas in 1918, Temuco in 1920, and finally Santiago in 1921.

6. For useful and accessible background on the time period and its specific influence on Mistral's choices, see Horan, "Gabriela Mistral and Women in Chile, 1800–1920," in *Gabriela Mistral*, 11–42. For a general introduction to the history of feminism in Chile, see Julieta Kirkwood, *Ser política en Chile: Los nudos de la sabiduría feminista* [To be a political woman in Chile: Knots of feminist knowledge] (Santiago: Editorial Cuarto Propio, 1990), especially 91–175. An account of the relationship between intellectuals and the state in Latin America is found in Nicola Miller, *In the Shadow of the State: Intellectuals and the Quest for National Identity in Twentieth-Century Spanish America* (London: Verso, 1999).

7. There are many, many theories of nationalism, and it is impossible to cite all the works that have influenced me. With respect to nationalist education, perhaps the best-known studies are those of Benedict Anderson, *Imagined Communities: Reflections on the Origin and Spread of Nationalism* (London: Verso, 1991); and Ernest Gellner, *Nations and Nationalism* (Ithaca, N.Y.: Cornell University Press, 1983). A recent study that I found useful is David Lloyd and Paul Thomas, *Culture and the State* (New York: Routledge, 1998). Indeed, Lloyd and Thomas employ a Gramscian idea of the relationship between the state and education, arguing that the ethical state's reach extends beyond the Althusserian notion of the "ideological state apparatus" (although, of course, Althusser's formulation is clarifying). Additionally, this book shares the Gramscian understanding of the state and civil society as distinct, but not necessarily opposed, entities, especially within liberal-capitalist orders. Lloyd and Thomas summarize it thus: "Gramsci's conception that the institutions of civil society that are usually conceived of as private are actually part of a general conception of the state turns on his understanding of the 'educative and formative role of the state,' on the state as *educator*" (21). See also Antonio Gramsci, *Selections from the Prison Notebooks* (New York: International Publishers, 1971), 242, 247, 263.

Feminist, postcolonial, and queer works on nationalism have decisively influenced this study, among them (in no particular order of importance) George Mosse, *Nationalism and Sexuality* (Madison: University of Wisconsin Press, 1984); Andrew Parker, Mary Russo, Doris Sommer, and Patricia Yaeger, eds., *Nationalisms and Sexualities* (New York: Routledge, 1992); Doris Sommer, *Foundational Fictions: The National Romances of Latin America* (Berkeley and Los Angeles: University of California Press, 1991); Jean Franco, *Plotting Women: Gender and Representation in Mexico* (New York: Columbia University Press, 1989); Anne McClintock, *Imperial Leather:*

Race, Gender, and Sexuality in the Postcolonial Contest (New York: Routledge, 1995); Ann Laura Stoler, *Race and the Education of Desire: Foucault's "History of Sexuality" and the Colonial Order of Things* (Durham, N.C.: Duke University Press, 1995); Lauren Berlant, *The Queen of America Goes to Washington City: Essays on Sex and Citizenship* (Durham, N.C.: Duke University Press, 1997); Lisa Duggan, *Sapphic Slashers: Sex, Violence, and Modernity in America* (Durham, N.C.: Duke University Press, 2000); Homi K. Bhabha, *The Location of Culture* (New York: Routledge, 1994); Lisa Lowe and David Lloyd, eds., *The Politics of Culture in the Shadow of Capital* (Durham, N.C.: Duke University Press, 1997); Lora Romero, *Home Fronts: Domesticity and Its Critics in the Antebellum United States* (Durham, N.C.: Duke University Press, 1997); Partha Chatterjee, *The Nation and Its Fragments: Colonial and Postcolonial Histories* (Princeton, N.J.: Princeton University Press, 1993); Julio Ramos, *Desencuentros de la modernidad en América Latina: Literatura y política en el siglo XIX* (Mexico City: Fondo de Cultura Económica, 1989), translated into English by John D. Blanco and published as *Divergent Modernities: Culture and Politics in Nineteenth-Century Latin America* (Durham, N.C.: Duke University Press, 2001); and Francine Masiello, *Between Civilization and Barbarism: Woman, Nation, and Literary Culture in Modern Argentina* (Lincoln: University of Nebraska Press, 1992).

For explorations of the position of women in nationalism, see Floya Anthias and Nira Yuval-Davis, introduction to *Woman-Nation-State*, ed. Floya Anthias and Nira Yuval-Davis (London: Macmillan, 1989), 1–15; M. Jacqui Alexander and Chandra Talpade Mohanty, eds., *Feminist Genealogies, Colonial Legacies, Democratic Futures* (New York: Routledge, 1997); and Caren Kaplan, Norma Alarcón, and Minoo Moallem, *Between Woman and Nation: Nationalisms, Transnational Feminisms, and the State* (Durham, N.C.: Duke University Press, 1999).

8. She adopted "Gabriela" either from the archangel Gabriel or from Gabriele d'Annunzio, an early favorite writer. "Mistral" she took either from the Provençal poet Fréderic Mistral or from the French word for a northerly wind that blows cold, dry air into the French Mediterranean region.

9. Mistral, "Sonetos de la muerte" [Sonnets of death], in *Desolación, Ternura, Tala, Lagar* [Desolation, Tenderness, Felling, Wine press], with an introduction by Palma Guillén de Nicolau (Mexico City: Porrúa, 1986), 28.

10. Enrique González Martínez issued the formal invitation, on behalf of Vasconcelos.

11. See Rubén Gallo, "Technology as Metaphor: Representations of Modernity in Mexican Art and Literature, 1920–1940" (Ph.D. diss., Columbia University, 2001).

12. Approximately twenty years after its initial publication, Mistral summed up the success of her pedagogical volume: "The 'Anthology,' in any case, had much more success than it had originally intended. Not only did the official first edition of seventy-five thousand copies, printed by the Mexican government, run out; the Spanish edition published by Calleja is out of print too." "Palabras de la recolectora" [Words of the compiler] (1941), in Mistral, *Recados para hoy y mañana: Textos inéditos de Gabriela Mistral*, comp. Luis Vargas Saavedra (Santiago: Editorial Sudamericana, 1999), 1:147.

13. The date of Mistral's receiving this title is given variously as 1931, 1932, and 1933.

14. I have used the dates given by the Mistral Museum of Vicuña, Chile. Dates are approximate and vary in other accounts.

15. Patricia Rubio, *Gabriela Mistral ante la crítica: Bibliografía anotada* [Criticism of Gabriela Mistral: An annotated bibliography] (Santiago: Direccion de Bibliotecas, Archivos y Museos, Centro de Investigaciones Diego Barros Arana, 1995), 1.

16. Horan, "Gabriela Mistral," 222.

17. Judith Halberstam, *Female Masculinity* (Durham, N.C.: Duke University Press, 1998).

18. David Halperin, *Saint Foucault: Towards a Gay Hagiography* (New York: Oxford University Press, 1995). Simultaneously playful and serious, Halperin uses the phrase "gay hagiography" ironically to discuss critically Michel Foucault's gay identity and politics. I, of course, am not replicating Halperin's gesture with Mistral, but I am referencing his gesture in order to provoke reflection on the general topics of exemplarity and self-making in the case of figures in recent history widely suspected to be queer. I wish to interrogate the bases upon which to construct a "queer life" and "queer politics." A more straightforward critique of hagiography in Mistral and women's studies is Elizabeth Rosa Horan, "Sor Juana and Gabriela Mistral: Locations and Locutions of the Saintly Woman," *Chasqui: Revista de literatura latinoamericana* 25, no. 2 (November 1996): 89–103.

19. See Lisa Duggan, "Queering the State," in Lisa Duggan and Nan D. Hunter, *Sex Wars: Sexual Dissent and Political Culture* (New York: Routledge, 1995), 179–93.

20. Anna Marie Jagose's *Queer Theory: An Introduction* (New York: New York University Press, 1996), which provides a concise overview of the various developments of this contested concept and field, including a comprehensive bibliography, hardly touches, however, on issues of race, unwittingly showing queer theory's presumptive whiteness and Eurocentrism. For queer Latin American studies, see Emilie L. Bergmann and Paul Julian Smith, eds., *¿Entiendes? Queer Readings, Hispanic Writings* (Durham, N.C.: Duke University Press, 1995); Daniel Balderston and Donna J. Guy, eds., *Sex and Sexuality in Latin America* (New York: New York University Press, 1997); and Sylvia Molloy and Robert McKee Irwin, eds., *Hispanisms and Homosexualities* (Durham, N.C.: Duke University Press, 1998). I also acknowledge my debt to Eve Kosofsky Sedgwick's groundbreaking work in queer studies. See, for instance, her *Epistemology of the Closet* (Berkeley and Los Angeles: University of California Press, 1990).

1. Race Woman

1. "Race woman," a phrase borrowed from African American studies, refers to a militant woman who upholds or defends the race. Often her actions and writings adapt to the normative standards that define the race, presupposing a conservative and heterosexualized gender discourse. At other times the race woman may be more critical of the sexism of her male coleaders.

2. Licia Fiol-Matta, "The 'Schoolteacher of America': Gender, Sexuality, and Nation in Gabriela Mistral," in *¿Entiendes? Queer Readings, Hispanic Writings,* ed. Emilie L. Bergmann and Paul Julian Smith (Durham, N.C.: Duke University Press, 1995), 201–29.

3. Elizabeth Rosa Horan discusses the conflation of Mistral's body and the nation in "Santa Maestra Muerta: Body and Nation in Portraits of Gabriela Mistral," *Taller*

de letras 25 (1997): 21–43. Horan addresses the monumentalization of Mistral's figure after her death through public sculpture, currency, and the like.

4. Sylvia Molloy, "The Politics of Posing," in *Hispanisms and Homosexualities,* ed. Sylvia Molloy and Robert McKee Irwin (Durham, N.C.: Duke University Press, 1998), 142.

5. This is an idea that is found in many of Foucault's writings but is perhaps most succinctly and accessibly expressed in *The History of Sexuality,* vol. 1, *An Introduction,* trans. Robert Hurley (New York: Vintage, 1980). See also "The Subject and Power," in *Essential Works of Foucault, 1954–1984,* ed. Paul Rabinow, vol. 3, *Power,* ed. Colin Gordon, trans. Robert Hurley et al. (New York: New Press, 2000), 326–48.

6. Molloy, "Politics of Posing," 150, 151.

7. Mistral to Pedro Aguirre Cerda, Mexico City, 10 January 1923, *Antología mayor* [Comprehensive anthology], vol. 3 *Cartas* [Letters], ed. Luis Vargas Saavedra (Santiago: Cochrane, 1992), 100 (emphasis added).

8. Mistral, prologue to Roque Esteban Scarpa, *La desterrada en su patria: Gabriela Mistral en Magallanes, 1918–1920* [Exiled in her homeland: Gabriela Mistral in Magallanes, 1918–1920] (Santiago: Nascimento, 1977), 1:18. On *chilenizar,* see also Volodia Teitelboim, *Gabriela Mistral pública y secreta: Truenos y silencios en la vida del primer Nobel latinoamericano* [The public and secret Gabriela Mistral: Thunder and silence in the life of Latin America's first Nobel Prize winner] (Santiago: Ediciones BAT, 1991), 87.

9. Acts of organized protest included the worker revolts in Puerto Natales and Punta Arenas in 1919 and 1921, respectively. The state violently suppressed both, massacring workers and indigenous peoples alike. Mistral was stationed in Punta Arenas during the former revolt and had already left the region by the time of the latter. See Teitelboim, *Gabriela Mistral pública y secreta,* 87–91.

10. See Mistral's prologue to Scarpa, *La desterrada en su patria,* 1: 11–25. This prologue was written almost three decades after Mistral had left Magallanes. It is possible that Mistral, on hearing of her friend's intention to compile a book about her early years in Chile, wanted to influence its reception and to shape the public perception of her stay in Magallanes. She insisted on writing the prologue.

11. For varied accounts of the pervasive preoccupation with "right" and "wrong" racial mixing, see Nancy Leys Stepan, *The "Hour of Eugenics": Race, Gender, and Nation in Latin America* (Ithaca, N.Y.: Cornell University Press, 1991); Richard Graham, ed., *The Idea of Race in Latin America, 1870–1940* (Austin: University of Texas Press, 1990); and Thomas E. Skidmore, *Black into White: Race and Nationality in Brazilian Thought* (Durham, N.C.: Duke University Press, 1993).

12. Michel Foucault, *Genealogía del racismo: De la guerra de las razas al racismo de estado* [A genealogy of racism: From the war between races to state racism] (Madrid: Ediciones de la Piqueta, n.d.). See also Ann Laura Stoler's brilliant analysis of Foucault's lectures in *Race and the Education of Desire: Foucault's "History of Sexuality" and the Colonial Order of Things* (Durham, N.C.: Duke University Press, 1995).

13. Mistral, quoted in Ana Pizarro, "Mistral, ¿qué modernidad?" in *Re-leer hoy a Gabriela Mistral: Mujer, historia, y sociedad en América Latina* [Rereading Gabriela Mistral today: Woman, history, and society in Latin America], ed. Gastón Lillo and J. Guillermo Renart (Ottawa: University of Ottawa Press; Santiago: Editorial de la Universidad de Santiago, 1997), 49.

14. Pizarro also notes that Mistral changed her supremacist stance after her visit to Mexico in 1922, but at this point our views diverge. Pizarro writes: "Mistral's gaze changes, of course, in Mexico, and this new gaze reaffirms itself in Brazil, in a period when Gilberto Freyre and Sergio Buarque de Holanda had undertaken the fundamental reconsideration of black culture" (ibid., 49). Freyre and Buarque de Holanda were part of the trend toward normalization and contributed to what Foucault labeled "governmentality." With respect to black people, Mistral's racist views remained unchanged. If anything, they became more murderous. Her references to Brazil precisely crystallized this dangerous racism.

15. Quezada also attributes Mistral's decision to defend the indigenous peoples to her tenure in Mexico, but, he insists, "this approach to the Indian truths would have originally begun in 1919, in her exile in Magallanes." Jaime Quezada, prologue to Gabriela Mistral, *Escritos políticos* (Santiago: Fondo de Cultura Económica, 1994), 12.

16. Jorge Salessi, "Prevención de los males de un adentro" [Preventing a disease from within], in *Médicos, maleantes, y maricas: Higiene, criminología, y homosexualidad en la construcción de la nación argentina (Buenos Aires, 1871–1914)* [Doctors, thugs, and fags: Hygiene, criminology, and homosexuality in the construction of the Argentine nation (Buenos Aires, 1871–1914] (Rosario, Argentina: Beatriz Viterbo Editora, 1995), 213–58. On "fetishism" and "uranism," see Víctor Mercante, "Fetichismo y uranismo femenino en los internados educativos" [Fetishism and uranism in boarding school], *Archivos de psiquiatría y criminología* [Archives of psychiatry and criminology] (Buenos Aires) 4 (1905): 22–30.

17. Mistral to Radomiro Tomic, Rapallo, Italy, 1951, *Vuestra Gabriela: Cartas inéditas de Gabriela Mistral a los Errázuriz Echenique y Tomic Errázuriz* [Your Gabriela: Unpublished letters of Gabriela Mistral to the Errázuriz Echenique and Tomic Errázuriz], ed. Luis Vargas Saavedra (Santiago: Zig-Zag, 1995), 162.

18. Molloy, "Politics of Posing," 154.

19. I am not suggesting that Vasconcelos intentionally hired queers or that he was conscious of this deployment. Indeed, he railed against "the deadly effects of women's and gay emancipation," as Jean Franco writes in *Plotting Women: Gender and Representation in Mexico* (New York: Columbia University Press, 1989), 127. Even if it is counterintuitive, his attraction for Mistral can be understood as an identification with her masculinity. In the same way that his treatment of the indigenous peoples and race in Mexico perpetually vacillates between identification and repulsion, there is room to question whether Vasconcelos could have been oblivious to Mistral's sexual and gender difference.

20. Mistral wrote this letter to Aguirre on 2 October 1918, from Punta Arenas, Chile (see Scarpa, *La desterrada en su patria,* 2:333).

21. Juan Villegas Morales, "El estado como mecenas: El caso de Gabriela Mistral" [The state as patron: The case of Gabriela Mistral], in *Estudios sobre la poesía chilena* [Studies in Chilean poetry] (Santiago: Nascimento, 1980).

22. When Mistral was twenty-five, for example, she described herself as "this good old lady who writes verse" [esta buena vieja que hace versos]. See Isauro Santelices, *Mi encuentro con Gabriela Mistral, 1912–1957* [My encounter with Gabriela Mistral, 1912–1957] (Santiago: Editorial del Pacífico, 1972), 73.

23. For a lucid explanation of these psychoanalytic terms from a queer perspective, see Diana Fuss, *Identification Papers* (New York: Routledge, 1995).

24. Michael Omi and Howard Winant, *Racial Formation in the United States: From the 1960s to the 1990s* (New York: Routledge, 1994), 67.

25. Mistral, "El tipo del indio americano" [The type of the Indian of the Americas], in *Gabriela anda por el mundo* [Gabriela wanders around the world], ed. Roque Esteban Scarpa (Santiago: Andrés Bello, 1978), 179.

26. Amy Kaminsky, "Essay, Gender, and *Mestizaje:* Victoria Ocampo and Gabriela Mistral," in *The Politics of the Essay: Feminist Perspectives*, ed. Ruth-Ellen Boetcher Joeres and Elizabeth Mittman (Bloomington: Indiana University Press, 1993), 121.

27. Though I single out Vasconcelos, he was not the only adherent to the ideology of *mestizaje*, much less its formulator. For an introduction to the genealogy of this model in Mexico, see Alan Knight, "Racism, Revolution, and *Indigenismo:* Mexico, 1910–1940," in Graham, *Idea of Race*, 71–113.

28. "We define *racial formation* as the sociohistorical process by which racial categories are created, inhabited, transformed, and destroyed"; "we argue that racial formation is a process of historically situated *projects* in which human bodies and social structures are represented and organized"; "*racial projects* do the ideological 'work' of making these links. A *racial project is simultaneously an interpretation, representation, or explanation of racial dynamics, and an effort to redistribute resources along particular racial lines.*" Omi and Winant, *Racial Formation*, 55–56.

29. José Vasconcelos, *La raza cósmica* [The cosmic race] (Mexico City: Espasa-Calpe, 1996), 42–43; emphasis added. I thank Julio Ramos for calling this passage to my attention.

30. Asunción Lavrin, *Women, Feminism, and Social Change in Argentina, Chile, and Uruguay, 1890–1940* (Lincoln: University of Nebraska Press, 1995), 164.

31. On Mistral's admiration for Argentina's racial project, see "La pampa argentina" [The Argentinean pampa], in *Gabriela anda por el mundo*, 51–53; "Recado sobre una maestra argentina" [Message about an Argentinean schoolteacher], in *Magisterio y niño* [Teaching and the child], ed. Roque Esteban Scarpa (Santiago: Andrés Bello, 1979), 124–35; and "Madrinas de lectura" [Godmothers of reading], in *Magisterio y niño*, 98–100.

32. Mistral, "El folklore argentino" [Argentinean folklore], in *Magisterio y niño*, 58–59.

33. Stepan, *"Hour of Eugenics,"* 105.

34. See, e.g., Patricio Marchant, "Desolación" [Desolation], in *Una palabra cómplice* [A complicitous word], 2d ed., ed. Raquel Olea and Soledad Fariña (Santiago: Cuarto Propio, 1997), 60–61.

35. Mistral, "A la mujer mexicana" [To the Mexican woman], in *Lecturas para mujeres: Destinadas a la enseñanza del lenguaje* [Readings for women: Intended for language teaching] (Madrid: Godoy, 1924), 173.

36. Marchant, "Desolación," 67.

37. Alberto Sandoval Sánchez, "Hacia una lectura del cuerpo de mujer" [Toward a reading of the woman's body], in Olea and Fariña, *Una palabra cómplice*, 139–51.

38. Mistral, "Primer recuerdo de Isadora Duncan" [First recollection of Isadora Duncan], in *Gabriela anda por el mundo*, 118.

39. Mistral, "El folklore argentino," 62–63.

40. Sandoval Sánchez, "Hacia una lectura," 145.

41. Mistral to Alfonso Reyes, written aboard a Grace Liner ship, 1933, *Tan de usted: Epistolario de Gabriela Mistral con Alfonso Reyes* [Always yours: Correspon-

dence from Gabriela Mistral to Alfonso Reyes], comp. Luis Vargas Saavedra (Santiago: Hachette/Editorial de la Universidad Católica de Chile, 1991), 84.

42. The most famous proponent of the "racial harmony" theory is the influential Gilberto Freyre. See Michael George Hanchard, "Racial Democracy: Hegemony, Brazilian Style," in *Orpheus and Power: The Movimento Negro of Rio de Janeiro and São Paulo, Brazil, 1945–1988* (Princeton, N.J.: Princeton University Press, 1994), 43–74.

43. Mistral to Lydia Cabrera, Nice, probably 1938, *Cartas a Lydia Cabrera: Correspondencia inédita de Gabriela Mistral y Teresa de la Parra* [Letters to Lydia Cabrera: Unpublished correspondence of Gabriela Mistral and Teresa de la Parra], ed. Rosario Hiriart (Madrid: Torremozas, 1988), 77.

44. Sylvia Molloy, "Disappearing Acts: Reading Lesbian in Teresa de la Parra," in *¿Entiendes?* 230–56.

45. Mistral may not have simply invented this commonality. Cabrera and Parra may indeed have shared this imaginary of fetishized and subservient black people, which may have had something to do with the gestation of Cabrera's works, especially *Cuentos negros de Cuba* [Black tales of Cuba].

46. Some of the most important of Cabrera's works are *El Monte, Yemayá y Ochún,* and *La sociedad secreta abacuá.*

47. Mistral to Cabrera, Lisbon or Nice, 17 October 1938 or 1939, *Cartas a Lydia Cabrera,* 73. All the letters to Cabrera quoted here are found in Hiriart's edition (and are subsequently cited in the text).

48. Apparently Cabrera did not respond to this letter. In a subsequent undated letter from Nice, Mistral wrote: "I did not receive any response to a long letter I sent you. Don't take it the wrong way. You know how brusque we Chileans are." *Cartas a Lydia Cabrera,* 77.

49. Mistral, quoted in E. Fernández Arredondo, "Al margen del 'incidente' con Gabriela Mistral" [Notes on the margin: The Gabriela Mistral "incident"], *Diario de la Marina* (Havana), 13 April 1930, 1.

50. Mistral, "Recado de las voces infantiles" [Message about children's voices] (n.d.), in *Magisterio y niño,* 61.

51. Mistral to Reyes, 21 April 1947, *Tan de usted,* 160; Mistral to Tomic, 18 January 1948, *Vuestra Gabriela,* 131; Mistral to Tomic, Rapallo, Italy, 18 February 1951, *Vuestra Gabriela,* 150; Mistral to Reyes, Roslyn Harbor, New York, July 1954, *Tan de usted,* 220.

52. "'Sobrino' de Gabriela Mistral era en realidad su hijo" [Gabriela Mistral's "nephew" was in reality her child], *El Mercurio* (Santiago), 6 November 1999; "Polémica genera supuesta maternidad de Mistral" [Supposed maternity of Mistral generates polemic], *El Mercurio,* 7 November 1999. Doris Dana was interviewed by the Chilean network TVN, in the United States. Teitelboim mentions earlier speculations regarding the subject (*Gabriela Mistral pública y secreta,* 213).

53. Mistral to Reyes, Roslyn Harbor, New York, n.d., 1954?, *Tan de usted,* 218.

54. See Thomas E. Skidmore, "Racial Ideas and Social Policy in Brazil, 1870–1940," and Aline Helg, "Race in Argentina and Cuba, 1880–1930: Theory, Policy, and Popular Reaction," in Graham, *Idea of Race,* 7–36 and 37–69 respectively.

55. Mistral, quoted in Teitelboim, *Gabriela Mistral pública y secreta,* 214.

56. Mistral, "Imagen y palabra en la educación" [Image and word in education], in *Magisterio y niño,* 195–96.

57. On Mistral's ambivalent reception in Chile, see Santelices, *Mi encuentro con Gabriela Mistral*; and Teitelboim, *Gabriela Mistral pública y secreta*.

58. Elizabeth Rosa Horan records one of the rare direct allusions in print to Mistral's masculinity, Arévalo Martínez's story "La signatura de la esfinge" [The Mark of the sphinx], which, "with its cover of fiction, is unique in recording what Mistral's contemporaries thought and spoke about, but kept from print." Horan, "Gabriela Mistral," in *Latin American Writers on Gay and Lesbian Themes: A Bio-critical Sourcebook*, ed. David William Foster (Westport, Conn.: Greenwood, 1994), 222.

59. Mistral, "Sobre la mujer chilena" [About the Chilean woman], in *Escritos políticos*, 61–65.

60. Important references for the case of Chile include Néstor Palacios, *Raza chilena* [Chilean race] (1990; reprint, Santiago: Antiyal, 1986); Vicente Pérez Rosales, *Recuerdos del pasado (1814–1860)* [Memories of the past, 1814–1860] (1882; reprint, Buenos Aires: Francisco de Aguirre, 1970); and Francisco Antonio Encina, *Nuestra inferioridad económica: Sus causas, sus consecuencias* [Our economic inferiority: Its causes, its consequences] (1911; reprint, Santiago: Editorial Universitaria, 1978).

61. I thank Marcial Godoy for referring me to Palacios's text. Sonia Montecinos has rescued his formulation in her interesting book *Madres y huachos: Alegorías del mestizaje chileno* [Mothers and *huachos*: Allegories of Chilean miscegenation] (Santiago: Sudamericana, 1996).

62. Mistral, "Sobre la mujer chilena," 61.

63. Salvador Novo, "Ventana: Con Gabriela Mistral I" [Window: With Gabriela Mistral I] in *Novedades* (Mexico City: Stylo, 1948), 4.

64. Luis Mario Schneider, *Gabriela Mistral: Itinerario veracruzano* [Gabriela Mistral: Her itinerary in Veracruz] (Jalapa, Mexico: Biblioteca de la Universidad Veracruzana, 1991), 10.

65. Sagrario Cruz Carretero, "The Afro-Mexican Presence in the Twentieth Century," lecture given at Columbia University, 15 February 2000. It is generally agreed that Gonzalo Aguirre Beltrán is the founder of Afro-Mexican studies: see his *La población negra de México: Estudio etnohistórico* [Mexico's black populations: An ethnohistorical study] (Mexico City: Fondo de Cultura Económica, 1946).

66. Salvador Novo, *La estatua de sal* [The salt statue], ed. Carlos Monsiváis (Mexico City: Consejo Nacional para la Cultura y las Artes, 1998).

67. Novo, "Ventana," 4.

68. Mistral to Reyes, Veracruz or Santa Barbara, California, 1950, *Tan de usted*, 193–94; Reyes to Mistral, Mexico City, 25 February 1950, *Tan de usted*, 195.

69. It's not possible to ascertain whether the phrase "ugly, of the worst species" was actually Mistral's or whether those are Novo's words. Given the virulence with which Mistral attacks Brazil, the repetition of her opinion about Mexican immigration in personal correspondence, and her comments about Josephine Baker's body, it's quite likely that the words are hers. Of course, Novo seems to have wholeheartedly shared this opinion. In his book *La vida en México durante el periodo presidencial de Miguel Alemán* [Life in Mexico during the presidential period of Miguel Alemán] (Mexico City: Consejo Nacional para la Cultura y las Artes/Instituto Nacional de Antropología e Historia, 1994), he wrote that Mistral "spoke at length about her travels, books, friends we had in common, and how happy she was in Yucatán; about how she wanted to tell President Alemán, whom she did not know

personally even though she was in Mexico thanks to his invitation, that the Mexican workers that emigrate to California have all access to white women prohibited, they become entangled with disgusting black women and as the years go by that coast starts to become overrun with mestizos descended from black women and Mexican men, really deplorable children. 'Why, in God's name, do they not let the Mexicans take their women with them?'" (241). Thanks to Robert Irwin for the latter citation.

70. See Kobena Mercer's and John Ellis's very useful formulation of the disavowal that founds the Freudian theory of fetishism: "I know...but..." Kobena Mercer, *Welcome to the Jungle: New Positions in Black Cultural Studies* (New York: Routledge, 1994), 184; John Ellis, "Photography/Pornography/Art/Pornography," *Screen* 21, no. 1 (spring 1980): 100.

71. I thank Janet Jakobsen for the phrasing of this point in my work.

2. Schooling and Sexuality

1. Julia Varela and Fernando Alvarez-Uria, citing the case of Spain, judgmentally state that "the schoolteacher does not possess knowledge so much as techniques of domestication, methods to condition and maintain order; s/he does not transmit knowledge, but morals acquired through her own experience of discipline when she herself was enrolled in normal school." *Arqueología de la escuela* [Archaeology of schooling] (Madrid: Ediciones de la Piqueta, n.d.), 37. In their view, schoolteachers want to assume bourgeois culture, blind to the fact that they are not part of the bourgeoisie and will not be integrated into it.

2. *Normal*, in this sense, is from the French *école normale*, or model school; in the United States, a teachers' college. Normal schools were created to train primary schoolteachers. For their development in Latin America, see Francesca Miller, "Women and Education in Latin America," in *Latin American Women and the Search for Social Justice* (Hanover, N.H.: University Press of New England, 1991), 35–67. They did not emerge at the same time across the Latin American countries; neither was the curriculum consistent. Miller makes the case that normal schools were overwhelmingly attended by women; data for the Southern Cone countries suggest that this was indeed the case. Other countries, such as Mexico, problematize this assumption. What is common to all countries is the fact that a normal-school certificate was not considered equal to a secondary-school degree; therefore, normal graduates were effectively barred from attending universities. See also Beatriz Sarlo's introduction to part 3 of *Women's Writing in Latin America*, ed. Sara Castro-Klarén, Sylvia Molloy, and Beatriz Sarlo (Boulder, Colo.: Westview, 1991), 231–48.

A ludic approach to the subject of normal schools is Marjorie Garber's, "Normal Schools," in *Bisexuality and the Eroticism of Everyday Life* (New York: Routledge, 2000), 297–316. Garber provides an entertaining overview of same-sex schools' reputation as hotbeds of homosexuality and lesbianism. Doris Sommer suggested to me that one way to regard Mistral is, in fact, through Garber's analysis of the "bisexuality" of celebrity.

3. See Sonia Montecino, *Madres y huachos: Alegorías del mestizaje chileno* [Mothers and *huachos*: Allegories of Chilean miscegenation] (Santiago: Sudamericana, 1996), for an overview of this figure in Chile. Montecino offers a summary of prominent Chilean historiography on the subject in pp. 125–31. As she details, the republic

saw it necessary to correct the "dire" familial situation of the Chilean nation (of unwed indigenous mothers with mestizo children), with the "healthy" national, nuclear family. The *roto* was probably repudiated by Mistral at first, as there are no writings defending the indigenous people of Chile, or exalting the *roto,* in all the years she spent in Chile prior to her departure in 1922.

4. Beatriz Sarlo, *La máquina cultural: Maestras, traductores, y vanguardistas* [The cultural machine: Female teachers, translators, and vanguardists] (Buenos Aires: Ariel, 1998).

5. See, e.g., Mistral, "El oficio lateral" [The lateral profession], in *Magisterio y niño* [Teaching and the child], ed. Roque Esteban Scarpa (Santiago: Andrés Bello, 1979), 43–51. This essay was written in 1949, and it contrasts sharply in tone with the early essays, written when Mistral was a schoolteacher in Chile.

6. In part Mistral admired the Mexican model because it reached out to the countryside, which she felt Chile did not do. In 1926 she wrote, "I am moved by everything done in Mexico and Argentina to take the breath of urban culture to the countryside. I compare this situation to that of the forgotten schoolteacher in a corner of the countryside somewhere in the penal colonies of Ushuaia and Punta Arenas (Patagonia). They are forgotten as if they were in a labor camp." "La reforma educacional de México" [Mexico's educational reform], in *Magisterio y niño,* 150. In fact, these provinces had been penal colonies before they were targeted for the "civilizing mission." Mistral is careful not to privilege one model over the other, as these were her two prospective employers. Significantly, Mistral's reference is autobiographical; she spent two years directing a girls' school in Punta Arenas and clearly resented the government of Chile for this assignment.

7. See Mistral, "Comento a *Ternura*" [A comment on *Ternura*], in *Recados para hoy y mañana: Textos inéditos de Gabriela Mistral,* comp. Luis Vargas Saavedra (Santiago: Editorial Sudamericana, 1999), 1:174, 175–76. I have consulted the draft version of this text in the Library of Congress; in the index to the microfilmed papers of Gabriela Mistral in the Manuscript Division, it is titled "Colofón con cara de excusa," which indicates that "Comento a *Ternura*" is a draft version of the final essay discussed in chapter 3. The two versions are strikingly different.

8. Here I am echoing Anne McClintock when she writes, in *Imperial Leather: Race, Gender, and Sexuality in the Colonial Contest* (New York: Routledge, 1995), "Every child rehearses in organic miniature the ancestral progress of the race" (50).

9. Mistral, "Colofón con cara de excusa" [Colophon to offer an apology], in *Desolación, Ternura, Tala, Lagar* [Desolation, Tenderness, Felling, Wine press], with an introduction by Palma Guillén de Nicolau (Mexico City: Porrúa, 1986), 106–10. See my discussion of this essay in chapter 3.

10. Ibid., 110.

11. On industrial society and education, see Ernest Gellner, "Industrial Society," in *Nations and Nationalism* (Ithaca, N.Y.: Cornell University Press, 1983), 19–38.

12. Miller, *Latin American Women,* 48. Chile conferred its first-ever bachelor's degree to a woman student in 1881, becoming the first Latin American country to do so.

13. Sarlo, *La máquina cultural,* 75–76.

14. Foucault wrote of "a double assertion that practically all children indulge or are prone to indulge in sexual activity; and that, being unwarranted, at the same time 'natural' and 'contrary to nature,' this sexual activity posed moral, individual and collective dangers; children were defined as 'preliminary' sexual beings, on this

side of sex, yet within it, astride a dangerous dividing line." "Pedagogization" refers to the army of specialists that "take charge . . . of this precious and perilous, dangerous and endangered sexual potential." Michel Foucault, *The History of Sexuality*, Vol. 1, *An Introduction*, trans. Robert Hurley (New York: Vintage, 1980), 104.

15. See Ann Laura Stoler's discussion "Toward a Genealogy of Racisms: The 1976 Lectures at the Collège de France," in *Race and the Education of Desire: Foucault's "History of Sexuality" and the Colonial Order of Things* (Durham, N.C.: Duke University Press, 1995), 55–94.

16. Ibid., 143.

17. Ibid.

18. "If the task of the state is, as Gramsci defined it, to 'educate consent,' then it should be no surprise that childrearing practices also would have been directed at extracting consensus." Ibid.

19. Ibid., 144.

20. This appears to be the conclusion reached by Jacques Donzelot in *The Policing of Families* (Baltimore: Johns Hopkins University Press, 1979) as well.

21. Foucault, *History of Sexuality*, 1:97.

22. Asunción Lavrin, "*Puericultura*, Public Health, and Motherhood," in *Women, Feminism, and Social Change in Argentina, Chile, and Uruguay, 1890–1940* (Lincoln: University of Nebraska Press, 1995), 97–124.

23. Mistral, "La escuela nueva en nuestra América" [The new school in our America], *Magisterio y niño*, 183; emphasis added. Significantly, this text was written as a prologue to Julio R. Barcos, *Cómo educa el estado a tu hijo* [How the state educates your child] (Buenos Aires: Editorial Acción, 1928).

24. Stoler, *Race and the Education of Desire*, 144.

25. George Mosse offers a good discussion of these types, and of the deployment of masculinity and femininity in nationalist contexts, in his *Nationalism and Sexuality* (Madison: University of Wisconsin Press, 1985). See also Andrew Parker, Mary Russo, Doris Sommer, and Patricia Yaeger, eds., *Nationalisms and Sexualities* (New York: Routledge, 1992), which sets out, in part, to broaden Mosse's initial discussions.

26. It could be said that even within British and American studies, studies of men are more abundant than studies of women. For an example having to do with women, see Diana Fuss, "Sexual Contagion: Dorothy Strachey's *Olivia*," in *Identification Papers* (New York: Routledge, 1995), 107–34.

27. See Jorge Salessi, "La educación nacionalista como profilaxis contra el mal de las lesbianas profesionales" [Nationalist education as a prophylactic measure to curb the disease of lesbian professionals], in *Médicos, maleantes, y maricas: Higiene, criminología, y homosexualidad en la construcción de la nación argentina. (Buenos Aires, 1871–1914).* [Doctors, thugs, and fags: Hygiene, criminology, and homosexuality in the construction of the Argentine nation (Buenos Aires, 1871–1914)] (Rosario, Argentina: Beatriz Viterbo Editora, 1995), 216–25.

28. Fuss, *Identification Papers*, 36–40.

29. Homi K. Bhabha, "The Other Question: Stereotype, Discrimination, and the Discourse of Colonialism," in *The Location of Culture* (New York: Routledge, 1994), 66.

30. In *Identification Papers*, Fuss lucidly explains the false opposition of identification and desire, and shows Freud's own inconsistent treatment of the subject; see chapter 1, "Identification Papers," 21–56. Generally speaking, specialists agree that

Freud considered heterosexuality as something that the child had to acquire through some version of oedipal loss.

31. Judith Butler, *The Psychic Life of Power: Theories in Subjection* (Stanford, Calif.: Stanford University Press, 1997), 135; Butler's emphasis.

32. Fuss, *Identification Papers*, 6.

33. Judith Halberstam, *Female Masculinity* (Durham, N.C.: Duke University Press, 1998).

34. Fernando Alegría, "Notes toward a Definition of Gabriela Mistral's Ideology," in *Women in Hispanic Literature: Icons and Fallen Idols*, ed. Beth Miller (Berkeley and Los Angeles: University of California Press, 1983), 216, 217.

35. Pablo Neruda, *Confieso que he vivido: Memorias* [Memoirs] (Buenos Aires: Losada, 1974), 31.

36. Cintio Vitier, "La voz de Gabriela Mistral" [The voice of Gabriela Mistral], in *Crítica sucesiva* [Successive criticism] (Havana: UNEAC, 1971), 147–78.

37. Given the pronounced tendency to read Mistral's poetry as a function of her biography and her mythology, it's unlikely that Vitier was exempt from this interpretation. Patricia Rubio has verified the tendency to read the poetry in light of the life in her monumental bibliographical study *Gabriela Mistral y la crítica: Bibliografía anotada* [Gabriela Mistral and criticism: An annotated bibliography] (Santiago: Dirección de Bibliotecas, Archivos y Museos, Centro de Investigaciones Diego Barros Arana, 1995).

38. Volodia Teitelboim, *Gabriela Mistral pública y secreta: Truenos y silencios en la vida del primer Nobel latinoamericano* [The public and secret Gabriela Mistral: Thunder and silence in the life of Latin America's first Nobel Prize winner] (Santiago: Ediciones BAT, 1991), 28.

39. Neruda, by contrast, having taken a page from Mistral's pedagogization of the Indian's "beauty," describes Mistral's face as "a beautiful Indian pitcher," adding to her gender ambiguity. *Confieso que he vivido*, 25.

40. Most of the pulp volumes are sensationalist in their depictions and not worth examining in detail here. Some examples include Virgilio Figueroa, *La divina Gabriela* [Divine Gabriela] (Santiago: Imprenta El Esfuerzo, 1933); Gladys Rodríguez Valdés, *Invitación a Gabriela Mistral (1889–1989)* [An invitation to Gabriela Mistral (1889–1989)] (Mexico City: Fondo de Cultura Económica, 1992); and Marta E. Samatán, *Los días y los años de Gabriela Mistral* (Puebla, Mexico: Editorial José M. Cajica Jr., 1973). Other testimonies are more interesting, though nearly all have their problems. See the recollections of two of her friends: the Peruvian writer Ciro Alegría, who writes, in *Gabriela Mistral íntima* (Lima: Editorial Universo, 1968), "It's true that she liked to give orders, but what woman doesn't? . . . She had the complexity of a great spirit and of a mestizaje that had not yet accomplished harmony" (14–15); and the Spaniard Francisco Ayala, *Recuerdos y olvidos* (Madrid: Alianza, 1998), 332–40. The latter is interesting because Ayala describes Mistral as quite a party goer and because he provides his own interpretation of Mistral's racial narrative of Brazil (discussed in chapter 1 and chapter 4).

41. Teitelboim, *Gabriela Mistral pública y secreta*, 23–24. Teitelboim recreates the episode dramatically. According to him, Mistral happened upon a funeral in Vicuña, where she was born, during one of her few return visits to Chile. Mistral was mesmerized by the funeral procession, and only when the funeral was over did she inquire about the deceased. The deceased turned out to be a schoolteacher, Adelaida

Olivares, who had overseen an alleged stoning when Mistral was seven. Teitelboim suggests that Mistral was forever traumatized by the stoning.

42. Matilde Ladrón de Guevara, *Gabriela Mistral, rebelde magnífica* [Gabriela Mistral, the magnificent rebel] (Santiago, 1957; Buenos Aires: Losada, 1962), quoting Mistral in an interview: "'It was a young man who visited the house often. Apparently they [the ones in my house] thought of him as family and since I had matured as a woman by then, his bestial instincts were unleashed the one day that he found me alone.... Do I know what that is or was? Matilde, everything at that point seemed over for me, life itself, everything.' (She did not want to continue)" (98–99).

43. Mistral denied that "Sonetos de la muerte" was written in grief over a male lover, much less over Romelio Ureta, but this statement from the supposed "source" herself did not change the story that the public wanted to create around her. Teitelboim writes: "She herself reacted later, wishing to clarify the truth: 'Those verses are based on a real story, but Romelio Ureta did not kill himself over me. That's just gossip.'" *Gabriela Mistral pública y secreta,* 26. Unfortunately, Teitelboim rarely cites his sources; this was probably taken from an interview. Critic Elizabeth Rosa Horan reminds us that Mistral was complicit in setting this mythography into motion, in her bio-bibliographical essay on Gabriela Mistral in *Latin American Writers on Gay and Lesbian Themes: a Bio-critical Sourcebook,* ed. David William Foster (Westport, Conn.: Greenwood, 1994), 221–35.

44. See, e.g., Ladrón de Guevara, *Gabriela Mistral, rebelde magnífica* and *La rebelde Gabriela* [Gabriela, the rebel], 2 vols. (Santiago, 1924); and the biography by Teitelboim, *Gabriela Mistral pública y secreta.*

45. Sigmund Freud, *Group Psychology and the Analysis of the Ego* (New York: Norton, 1959), 13. He also compares the group mind to that of children and primitives. Naturally, my study does not subscribe to his assignment of childlike qualities to so-called primitives. Mistral, though, manipulated the connection between these registers to perfection.

46. Jaime Concha, *Gabriela Mistral* (Madrid: Júcar, 1987), 19.

47. Isauro Santelices, *Mi encuentro con Gabriela Mistral, 1912–1957* [My encounter with Gabriela Mistral, 1912–1957] (Santiago: Editorial del Pacífico, 1972).

48. Mistral to Isauro Santelices, La Serena, Chile, 30 June 1925, in ibid., 80.

49. Ibid., 81: "Que mi conducta es mala. *No he cuidado mis versos como mi vida,* Isauro; he sido i soi limpia. Si no me he casado, es que cuando he querido, no me han querido, i cuando dicen que me han querido, no he querido yo. Historia vulgar que casi es estúpida por repetida en el mundo."

50. Santelices, *Mi encuentro con Gabriela Mistral,* 85.

51. Laura Rodig to Mistral, Chile, 1954. The Gabriela Mistral Papers, Manuscript Division, Library of Congress, Washington, D.C.

52. As this book went into production, Elizabeth Rosa Horan published an excellent article on these early writings: "Alternative Identities of Gabriel(a) Mistral, 1906–1920," in *Reading and Writing the Ambiente: Queer Sexualities in Latino, Latin American, and Spanish Culture,* ed. Susana Chávez-Silverman and Librada Hernández. (Madison: University of Wisconsin Press, 2000). 147–77. Horan analyzes Mistral's early work in *La Voz de Elqui* and in *El Mercurio de Antofagasta,* considering, among other things, issues of gender bending among theosophical and bohemian circles in Santiago and provincial Chile as spaces for alternative gender embodiment.

53. Abel Madera, letter to the editor, *La Voz de Elqui*, November 1905, in *Proyecto no. 13565: Recopliación de la obra mistraliana, 1905–1922*, comp. Pedro Pablo Zegers B. (Santiago: Consejo Nacional del Libro y la Lectura, 1998).

54. Julio Martínez Núñez and Juan Agustín Araya, quoted in Zegers, introduction to *Proyecto no. 13565*, n.p.

55. Lucila Godoy Alcayaga, "Carta íntima" [Intimate letter], *El Coquimbo*, 16 January 1908. A very interesting sketch of the biographical problem is found in Ángel Rama, "La oscura formación de un poeta," *Revista iberoamericana de literatura* (Montevideo), 2d ser., 1, no. 1 (1966): 109–18. The distinguished Uruguayan critic noticed the intense tone of "Carta íntima," which he had consulted in the manuscript original of one of Mistral's youthful notebooks. He commented: "Unlike her references to the rail worker, Ureta, this notebook testifies to the ways in which a passionate friendship, real or imagined, is expressed against a background of communication difficulties, so that they are experienced as doubly difficult during the solitary years of youth. Even though literature should not be confused with an intimate journal, and neither should the sentimental style appropriate to the period be confused with true feelings, these materials are far removed indeed from the typical pedagogical sketch of the time. Manuel Rojas [author of *A Brief History of Chilean Literature* (1964)] wrote: 'There is a mystery in Mistral's life, both in her lover's legend and in her personal life,' and traditional literary criticism in Chile, which has gone to great lengths to establish life-work relationships, has nevertheless not treated the topic with any depth" (117).

56. Alma, "A ella, la única" [To her, the only one], *El Coquimbo*, 10 October 1907; reprinted in Zegers, *Proyecto no. 13565*.

57. Lucila Godoy Alcayaga, "Adiós a Laura" [Goodbye to Laura], *La Voz de Elqui*, 5 July 1906; reprinted in Zegers, *Proyecto no. 13565*.

58. Halberstam, *Female Masculinity*, 13. In a related vein, Martha Vicinus discusses the discontinuities and the hardships entailed in trying to assemble "lesbian history," in "'They Wonder to Which Sex I Belong': The Historical Roots of the Modern Lesbian Identity," in *Feminist Studies* 18, no. 3 (fall 1992): 470. Although I, like Halberstam, do not subscribe to the paradigm of "lesbian history," it's important to acknowledge methodological problems identified by previous researchers.

59. Manuel Magallanes Moure was a minor Chilean poet with whom Mistral was acquainted. He was one of three judges who awarded Mistral the Flor Natural in the 1914 Juegos Florales, for "Sonetos de la muerte" [Sonnets of death]. He was also a member of the Chilean literary group informally referred to as Los Diez, to which Mistral also belonged. Mistral's correspondence to Magallanes Moure is published as *Cartas de amor de Gabriela Mistral* [Love letters from Gabriela Mistral], ed. Sergio Fernández Larraín (Santiago: Editorial Andrés Bello, 1978). Luis Vargas Saavedra expects to bring to light some letters that were left out of the original publication, apparently by the Magallanes family. See Horan's dicussion of this correspondence in "Alternative Identities of Gabriel(a) Mistral," where she makes clear that these letters were subject to surveillance, as they were routinely opened and read, and perhaps more importantly that Mistral's engagement with "lover's discourse" was part of a self-making by the young Mistral, affording her not only protection but also writerly pleasure to the extent that she was "trying on" a literary genre.

3. Citizen Mother

1. For a discussion of "separate spheres," see the excellent special issue "No More Separate Spheres!" *American Literature* 70, no. 3 (September 1998), ed. Cathy N. Davidson.

2. Certainly the most lucid example is Elizabeth Rosa Horan, *Gabriela Mistral: An Artist and Her People* (Washington, D.C.: Organization of American States, 1994).

3. The centennial of Mistral's birth, in 1989, renewed interest about her, provoking a surge of studies on various facets of her work and life. Many of these readings, as might be expected, merely recycled commonplaces and clichés, drawing heavily on Mistral's prestige as a Nobel Prize winner and as a significant figure in the continental discourse of America. There were, however, important manifestations of truly subversive readings, some of which aspired to transcend the chiefly academic domain of discourse that enveloped Mistral's figure and safeguarded her status as national icon (particularly in Chile). In that vein, a new feminist vision of Mistral emerged. This feminist revaluation served as a much-needed corrective to the hegemonic version. Unfortunately, it, too, was largely silent on the question of Mistral's sexuality—still an explosive subject.

Reexamining Mistral in 1989 and emphasizing the feminine as a way to escape the "official" occurred in a climate of protest over the censure and ideological control exercised by the dictatorship of General Augusto Pinochet. Resistance to Pinochet's dictatorship was carried out largely by women and other gender- and sexually marginalized members of Chilean society; they forged a temporary alliance with nongovernmental organizations that were primarily financed by northern European governments as prodemocracy, antidictatorship efforts. One such institution, the Casa de la Mujer la Morada, sponsored a groundbreaking conference on Mistral in 1989, titled "Una palabra cómplice: Encuentro con Gabriela Mistral" [A complicitous word: An encounter with Gabriela Mistral]. La Morada arranged for the publication of the conference proceedings in book form, under the same title and edited by Raquel Rodríguez (Santiago: Isis Internacional, 1990). In the book, influential Chilean critics like Raquel Olea, Soledad Bianchi, and Eliana Ortega, among others, read against the grain of official discourse, sometimes borrowing heavily from a male-centered revisionist tradition exemplified by texts like *Diferencias latinoamericanas* [Latin American difference], by Jorge Guzmán (Santiago: Centro de Estudios Humanísticos de La Universidad de Chile, 1984), and *Sobre árboles y madres* [About trees and women], by Patricio Marchant (Santiago: Sociedad Editora Lead, 1984).

Motherhood had been a hallmark of the official, Catholic-inflected discourse of gender and nation in Chile. The new feminist readings deployed national motherhood once again—although it was certainly a more palatable essentialism, in the name of social justice. In the hands of Mistral's new, feminist, and mostly female critics, women's writing emerged as a field marked by pleasure as well as power; the female body became a zone independent from dominant, male-oriented reason. Mistral's textual strategies were considered as lessons for younger women writers, and Mistral was proclaimed as an important, perhaps supreme, Chilean "foremother." Her position was reinterpreted but still remained oddly ahistorical. Mistral remained firmly ensconced in a halo of "glory," but now for another, presumably new, constituency. Critics missed the point that the female world was already cordoned off from male hegemony in official discourse. They also did not consider that Mistral herself might have regarded this discourse as an imposition and might have privately railed against it.

Significantly, Mistral's thornier aspects surfaced, albeit in muted fashion, from some of *Una palabra cómplice*'s explicitly queer-oriented contributions. Diana Bellessi, an openly lesbian Argentinean poet, for example, wrote that she was not at all interested in Mistral's role as schoolteacher and mother but was more attuned to the "other," "truer" Mistral—the trickster who left the traps of the social world behind in her poetry ("La aprendiz" [The apprentice]). In one of the more incisive arguments of the collection, Eliana Ortega, a Chilean critic, questioned the need to see Mistral only from the viewpoint of heterosexuality. She suggested the importance of envisioning Mistral's relationships with women as primary, and possibly lesbian, relationships. Ortega, however, retained the idea of the nurturing and universal feminine world—the world of motherhood as being benign and all-giving ("Amada amante: Discurso femenil en Gabriela Mistral" [Beloved lover: Female discourse in Gabriela Mistral]). Alberto Sandoval, a United States–based critic and playwright, was the only contributor in the original volume who studied Mistral's prose, taking issue with her racial constructions and the racism she directed at black people. Sandoval correctly insisted on the interconnectedness of woman-to-woman desire and the desire for whiteness in Mistral's work. However, he echoed previous masculinist constructions of her as sexually repressed ("Hacia una lectura del cuerpo de mujer" [Toward a reading of the female body]).

Other contributors to the original volume wittingly or unwittingly redeployed the ambiguous constructions of Mistral. Raquel Olea, for instance, wrote of reclaiming Mistral in the name of the mestiza woman, which is what all Chilean women are ("El lugar de Gabriela Mistral" [The place of Gabriela Mistral]). Lilliana Trevizán downplayed the importance of Mistral's most "maternal" poems—those written "for children"—curiously reaffirming the dominant construction of these poems as unworthy or inferior, almost embarrassing ("Deshilando el mito de la maternidad" [Unraveling the myth of maternity]). Adriana Valdés examined *Tala* [Felling], Mistral's third and groundbreaking book, but, taking Mistral at face value, she repeated Mistral's construction of *Tala* as being primarily concerned with "the root of Indoamericanism" ("Identidades tránsfugas" [Defecting identities]).

The revised second edition, published in 1997 and edited by Raquel Olea and Soledad Fariña (Santiago: Editorial Cuarto Propio), corrected the celebratory tone of the first edition by adding critical pieces by Ana Pizarro, Diamela Eltit, and Patricio Marchant. Unfortunately, the second edition omitted the many beautiful photographs of Mistral that the first edition had included. Still, the book *Una palabra cómplice* remained mostly concerned with restoring the true literary greatness of Mistral's texts—a commendable endeavor. But it disregarded the thornier issue of the relationship between culture and power—especially state power—that is unavoidable in Mistral's complete oeuvre and in her life. In short, the new feminism still offered a mythical Mistral instead of a thoroughly historicized figure.

Newer readings of Mistral have not, as of yet, broken with this tendency, although many are very sophisticated. See, e.g., Grínor Rojo, *Dirán que está en la gloria (Mistral)* [They claim she is in heaven (Mistral)] (Mexico City: Fondo de Cultura Económica, 1997); and the dossier in *Nomadías* 3 (January–June 1998), especially the contributions by Kemy Oyarzún, Raquel Olea, and Eliana Ortega. An excellent volume is Gastón Lillo and J. Guillermo Renart, eds., *Releer hoy a Gabriela Mistral:*

Mujer, historia, y sociedad en América latina [Rereading Gabriela Mistral today: Woman, history, and society in Latin America] (Ottawa: University of Ottawa Press; Santiago: Editorial de la Universidad de Santiago, 1997).

4. Gabriella de Beer, "Pedagogía y feminismo en una olvidada obra de Gabriela Mistral, *Lecturas para mujeres*" [Pedagogy and feminism in a forgotten work by Gabriela Mistral, *Readings for women*], *Monographic Review/Revista monográfica* 6 (1990): 211–20; María Luisa Ibacache, "Gabriela Mistral y el México de Vasconcelos" [Gabriela Mistral and Vasconcelos's Mexico] *Atenea: Ciencia, arte, literatura* 459–60 (1989): 141–55; Ivette Malverde Disselkoen, "Gabriela Mistral quiere educar mujeres: Relectura de 'Introducción a estas *Lecturas para mujeres*'" [Gabriela Mistral wants to educate women: "Introduction to *Readings for women*"], *Acta Literaria* 14 (1989): 11–24; and Regina Cortina, "La maestra en México: Asimetrías de poder en la educación pública" [The schoolteacher in Mexico: Power asymmetrics in public education], unpublished.

5. Elizabeth Rosa Horan, "Gabriela Mistral," in *Latin American Writers on Gay and Lesbian Themes: A Bio-critical Sourcebook*, ed. David William Foster (Westport, Conn.: Greenwood, 1994), 221–35. Claudia Lanzarotti, "Sospechosa para todos" [Suspicious in everyone's eyes], *Apsi* 418 (1992): 30–33; Sylvia Molloy, "Female Textual Identities: The Strategies of Self-Figuration," in *Women's Writing in Latin America*, ed. Sara Castro-Klarén, Sylvia Molloy, and Beatriz Sarlo (Boulder, Colo.: Westview, 1991), 113; and Ortega, "Amada amante."

6. Elizabeth Rosa Horan, "Matrilineage, Matrilanguage: Gabriela Mistral's Intimate Audience of Women," *Revista canadiense de estudios hispánicos* 14, no. 3 (spring 1990): 447–57.

7. Mistral, "Introducción a *Lecturas para mujeres*" [Introduction to *Readings for women*] (Mexico City: Porrúa, 1974); and "Colofón con cara de excusa" [Colophon to offer an apology], in *Desolación, Ternura, Tala, Lagar* [Desolation, Tenderness, Felling, Wine press], with an introduction by Palma Guillén de Nicolau (Mexico City: Porrúa, 1986), 106–10. Henceforth these pieces will be cited in the text as "Palabras" and "Colofón," respectively, with page numbers. I use the title "Palabras a la extranjera" [Remarks of the foreigner], because it is the essay's first heading and it gives the reader a sense of the essay; most scholars refer to it as "Introducción a *Lecturas para mujeres*." This enormously successful book featured a curious cover on its first edition: a "lady" stands in an unmarked, barren landscape wearing a parasol, corset, and hat, and holding a very small book in her left hand. Naturally, she doesn't resemble Mistral at all, but more importantly, her image also hardly coincides with that of the working students of the Gabriela Mistral School.

8. Gabriela Cano, "The *Porfiriato* and the Mexican Revolution," in *Nation, Empire, Colony: Historicizing Gender and Race,* ed. Ruth Roach Pierson and Nupur Chaudhuri (Bloomington: Indiana University Press, 1998), 106–20.

9. José Vasconcelos, *El desastre: Tercera parte del Ulises criollo* [The disaster: Third part of *Creole Ulysses*] (Mexico City: Ediciones Botas, 1938), 26–27; 61. Vasconcelos is also famous for the following statement: "What this country needs is to start reading the *Iliad.* I am going to distribute a thousand Homers, in the national schools and in the Libraries that we are going to found" (63).

10. Vasconcelos mentions the inauguration of the Gabriela Mistral School in ibid., 330–31. According to him, Mistral herself was not present at the unveiling of

her statue symbolizing "the teacher." See also "Homenaje a Gabriela Mistral" [Tribute to Gabriela Mistral], in *Discursos, 1920–1950* [Speeches, 1920–1950] (Mexico City: Ediciones Botas, 1950), 22–29, a text Vasconcelos wrote in 1945 upon Mistral's award of the Nobel Prize in literature. The Gabriela Mistral School was part of a larger program combining architecture and nationalism; see Enrique X. de Anda Alanis, *La arquitectura de la Revolución mexicana: Corrientes y estilos en la década de los veinte* [Architecture of the Mexican Revolution: Currents and styles during the 1920s] (Mexico City: UNAM, 1990). Thanks to Rubén Gallo for the reference.

11. Claude Fell, *José Vasconcelos: Los años del águila (1920–1925): Educación, cultura, e iberoamericanismo en el México postrevolucionario* [José Vasconcelos: The years of the eagle, 1920–1925: Education, culture, and Iberoamericanism in postrevolutionary Mexico] (Mexico City: UNAM, 1989). Fell's study is a monumental contribution. Thanks to Rubén Gallo for bringing it to my attention. For background into primary-school education in Mexico, see Alberto Arnaut Salgado, *Historia de una profesión: Los maestros de educación primaria en México, 1887–1994* [A history of a profession: Primary schoolteachers in Mexico, 1887–1994] (Mexico City: CIDE, 1996).

12. According to Fell, "The defenders of the 'Indian school' do not attempt to re-suscitate ancient native civilizations. Rather, they promote national cohesion by making the Indian accede to a standard of life comparable to other national inhabitants. In first place, they try to remove him from the vice-ridden, sordid context in which he lives. The solution is to create 'obligatory intern schools' in the regions of greatest Indian concentration. It's necessary to separate the young Indians from their family environment." He continues: "José María Bonilla symbolically labels these institutions 'escuelas-hogar,' where teachers, whom he describes as married men of unquestionable probity, will serve as 'fathers' to the pupils. The schools were to be essentially rural; their pedagogy, even more practical than those in the urban institutions; they should be 'prevocational schools.' They will, of course, be engaged in a literacy campaign, but essentially they will provide the educational bases necessary to agriculture, mining, industrial activities, and so forth. In truth, they will be slightly more active rudimentary schools where bilingualism won't exist, autonomous techniques won't be improved, and communitarian spirit won't be fortified *a fortiori*. Their objective—which some proclaim openly and others more implicitly—is distancing the children from their place of origin. These Indian schools, when examined more closely, are no more than internment camps for in-digenous children, providing them with an embryonic professional education. The school is not in a symbiotic relationship to the community; by definition its access is prohibited to adults, and it turns its back quite deliberately on local traditions, symbols of 'degeneracy,' 'vice,' and 'abjection'" (*José Vasconcelos,* 208).

13. Ibid., 209–10.

14. Cortina, "La maestra en México."

15. Fell, *José Vasconcelos,* 208.

16. For example, in her excellent study on education in Latin America, "Women and Education in Latin America," in *Latin American Women and the Search for Social Justice* (Hanover, N.H.: University Press of New England, 1991), 48, historian Francesca Miller leaves untheorized the case of countries with a majority of black or in-digenous people, claiming simply that normal schools succeeded in countries with "relatively homogeneous populations," those that underwent immigrations but not,

she implies, racial heterogeneity as such. Unwittingly, she correlates whiteness with the success of normal schooling in Argentina, Uruguay, and Chile, versus its failure in Brazil, Cuba, and Mexico, among others.

17. Fell, *José Vasconcelos*, 198. He also gives information as to the prerequisites for enrollment in vocational and trade schools: a student had to have completed primary education and received a medical exam, needed to be at least thirteen years of age, and had to have a certificate of good conduct (199). The objective was training and channeling into distinct trades, with an eye to homogenizing age groups and, therefore, productivity cycles of workers. The Gabriela Mistral School was a home-economics school; other schools for women existed. Enrollment included day and night students.

18. Ibid., 218; see also Vasconcelos, *Desastre*, e.g., 26–27.

19. Contract between the Ministry of Education of Mexico and Gabriela Mistral, 2 January 1922, quoted in Ibacache, "Gabriela Mistral y el México," 144.

20. Elizabeth Horan explains this target audience extremely well in her *Gabriela Mistral*. Juan Villegas Morales also expounds on the emergence of the middle class in "El estado como mecenas: El caso de Gabriela Mistral" [The state as patron: The case of Gabriela Mistral], in *Estudios sobre la poesía chilena* (Santiago: Nascimento, 1980).

21. See Julio Ramos for an excellent overview and analysis of the changing conceptions of "letters" and the function of "literature" in Latin America. *Desencuentros de la modernidad en América Latina: Literatura y política en el siglo XIX* (Mexico City: Fondo de Cultura Económica, 1989); translated into English by John D. Blanco and published as *Divergent Modernities: Culture and Politics in Nineteenth-Century Latin America* (Durham, N.C.: Duke University Press, 2001).

22. Asunción Lavrin, "*Puericultura*, Public Health, and Motherhood," in *Women, Feminism, and Social Change in Argentina, Chile, and Uruguay, 1890–1940* (Lincoln: University of Nebraska Press, 1995), 124.

23. Donna J. Guy, "Mothers Alive and Dead: Multiple Concepts of Mothering in Buenos Aires," in *Sex and Sexuality in Latin America*, ed. Daniel Balderston (New York: New York University Press, 1997), 170.

24. *Primer congreso americano del niño* [First American child congress] (Buenos Aires: Escoffier, Caracciolo, 1916); quoted in Lavrin, "*Puericultura*," 108.

25. Lavrin, "*Puericultura*," 112.

26. Guy, "Mothers Alive and Dead," 170.

27. Cortina, "La maestra en México."

28. Nancy Leys Stepan, *The "Hour of Eugenics": Race, Gender, and Nation in Latin America* (Ithaca, N.Y.: Cornell University Press, 1991), 105, 106.

29. Carroll Smith-Rosenberg, "The Female World of Love and Ritual: Relations between Women in Nineteenth-Century America," in *Disorderly Conduct: Visions of Gender in Victorian America* (New York: Knopf, 1985), 53–76.

30. Some examples are, in prose, "Recuerdos de la madre ausente" [Recollections of the absent mother] and, among her early poems, "El suplicio" [The torment], [The Supplice] "Poema del hijo" [The child's poem], and "Sonetos de la muerte" [Sonnets of death].

31. Guillén, introduction to Mistral, *Desolación, Ternura, Tala, Lagar*, xiii.

32. Lauren Berlant, *The Queen of America Goes to Washington City: Essays on Sex and Citizenship* (Durham, N.C.: Duke University Press, 1997). Berlant refers continuously to emotions and affect experienced as national sentimentality (especially

through pain) in her book-length study. I am indebted to her analysis for the re-
mainder of this section.

33. Ibid.

34. Ibid.; see also "Poor Eliza!" in Davidson, "No More Separate Spheres!" 636.

35. Mistral, "Feminismo" [Feminism], in *La tierra tiene la actitud de una mujer*
[The earth has a woman's attitude], comp. Pedro Pablo Zegers Blanchet (Santiago:
Red Internacional del Libro, 1998), 46; Mistral's emphasis.

36. "De Gabriela Mistral a Juan Orts González" [From Gabriela Mistral to Juan
Orts González], in *Antología mayor* [Comprehensive anthology], vol. 2, *Prosa* [Prose],
comp. Fernando Alegría et al. (Santiago: Cochrane, 1992), 261–63. Originally this
was an open letter to Orts González, director of the newspaper *La Nueva Democracia*
[New Democracy] (New York City), written in August 1927 and published in November with the title (given by the editor) "Gabriela Mistral, feminista de derechas"
[Gabriela Mistral, a right-wing feminist]. Despite Mistral's protestations of sympathy
for feminism, hers is a difficult position to gauge. In the same essay, she wrote:
"Through my observations of the women's struggle, I have always known that women
are the worst enemies of women."

37. Mistral, "El voto femenino" [The female vote], in *La tierra*, 56–60.

38. See Mistral, "La palabra maldita" [The cursed word] (1951), reprinted in Diamela Eltit, *Crónica del sufragio femenino en Chile* (Santiago: SERNAM, 1994), 90–93.

39. Mistral, "Cómo escribo" [How I write], *Revista de crítica cultural* 15 (November 1997): 12–15.

40. Gayatri Chakravorty Spivak, *Outside in the Teaching Machine* (New York:
Routledge, 1993), 3–6.

41. Mistral, "Cómo escribo," 12; "I am very afraid that Minister Aedo's beautiful
attempt to submit us to a verbal poll, a clear confession, a testimony, will fail" (12).

4. Intimate Nationalism

1. Mistral, "Sobre sus *Canciones de cuna*" [Regarding her *Lullabies*], in *Recados
para hoy y mañana: Textos inéditos de Gabriela Mistral*, comp. Luis Vargas Saavedra
(Santiago: Editorial Sudamericana, 1999), 1:130–31. It's not necessary, of course, always to take Mistral at her word. Cultural critic Jean Franco reminds us that Hum-
berto Díaz Casanueva was a close friend of Mistral and that his work, subsequently
collected in *Selección de poemas para niños* (1928), might have been used as a reference for Mistral's own lullabies. Jean Franco, "Loca y no loca: La cultura popular en
Gabriela Mistral" [Crazy and not crazy: Popular culture in Gabriela Mistral], in
Re-leer hoy a Gabriela Mistral: Mujer, historia, y sociedad en América Latina [Rere
ing Gabriela Mistral today: Woman, history, and society in Latin America], ed.
Gastón Lillo and J. Guillermo Renart (Ottawa: University of Ottawa Press; Santiago:
Editorial de la Universidad de Santiago, 1997), 31.

2. My paraphrases of Mistral, "Meciendo" [Rocking] and "Piececitos" [Little
feet], in *Desolación, Ternura, Tala, Lagar* [Desolation, Tenderness, Felling, Wine
press], with an introduction by Palma Guillén (Mexico City: Porrúa, 1986), 55 and
90 respectively.

3. Gramsci's discussion of the "national-popular" is relevant here. See *Prison
Notebooks* (New York: International, 1991), 130–33.

4. Judith Butler's exegesis of Klein in *The Psychic Life of Power: Theories in Sub-jection* (Stanford, Calif.: Stanford University Press, 1997) is helpful: "In the work of Melanie Klein, guilt appears to emerge, not in consequence of internalizing an external prohibition, but as a way of preserving the object of love from one's own potentially obliterating violence. Guilt serves the function of preserving the object of love and, hence, of preserving love itself. What might it mean to understand guilt, then, as a way in which love preserves the object it might otherwise destroy?" (25); "In order to preserve the object from one's own aggression, an aggression that always accompanies love (as conflict), guilt enters the psychic scene as a necessity" (26); "Following Freud, Klein situates such a desire to vanquish within the problematic of melancholia, thus making the point that the desire to vanquish characterizes a relation to an object already lost: already lost and thus eligible for a certain kind of vanquishing" (26). See also Eve Kosofsky Sedgwick, "Paranoid Reading or Reparative Reading, or You're So Paranoid, You Probably Think This Introduction Is about You," in *Novel Gazing: Queer Readings in Fiction,* ed. Eve Kosofsky Sedgwick (Durham, N.C.: Duke University Press, 1997), 1–37.

5. Mistral, "Poema del hijo" [The child's poem], in *Desolación, Ternura, Tala, Lagar,* 36 (my paraphrase).

6. For the Freudian position on narcissism, melancholia, and paranoia, respectively, see *The Standard Edition of the Complete Psychological Works of Sigmund Freud,* ed. James Strachey, vol. 14 (New York: Norton, 1959), "On Narcissism: An Introduction" (73–102); "Mourning and Melancholia" (243–58); and "A Case of Paranoia Running Counter to the Psycho-analytic Theory of the Disease" (263–72).

7. See, for instance, Eve Kosofsky Sedgwick, *Epistemology of the Closet* (Berkeley and Los Angeles: University of California Press, 1990); Butler, *Psychic Life of Power*; and Diana Fuss, *Identification Papers* (New York: Routledge, 1996).

8. Examples include (from *Desolación, Ternura, Tala, Lagar*) "Hallazgo" [Discovery] (55); "Yo no tengo soledad" [I am not alone] (57); "Dormida" [Asleep] (58); "Encantamiento" [Bewitched] (56); the beautiful "Canción de la sangre" [Song of blood] (64); "Niño chiquito" [Small child] (62); and "¡Que no crezca!" [May he never grow up!] (76). All feature the child liberated from the oppressive marks of the national, but mired in the struggle with the classic Kleinian good/bad object: the breast. All include a struggle between envy and gratitude, to reference another Kleinian formulation. See Melanie Klein, "A Study of Envy and Gratitude," in *The Selected Melanie Klein,* ed. Juliet Mitchell (New York: Free Press, 1987), 211–29.

9. Freud, "On Narcissism": "The first auto-erotic sexual satisfactions are experienced in connection with vital functions which serve the purpose of self-preservation. The sexual instincts are at the outset attached to the satisfaction of the ego-instincts; only later do they become independent of these, and even then we have an indication of that original attachment in the fact that persons who are concerned with a child's feeding, care, and protection become his earlier sexual objects: that is to say, in the first instance his mother or a substitute for her. Side by side, however, with this type and source of object-choice, which may be called the 'anaclitic' or 'attachment' type, psycho-analytic research has revealed a second type, which we were not prepared for finding. We have discovered, especially clearly in people whose libidinal development has suffered some disturbance, such as perverts and homosexuals, that in their later choice of love-objects they have taken as a model not their mother but their own selves. They are plainly seeking *themselves* as a love-object,

and are exhibiting a type of object-choice which must be termed 'narcissism'" (87–88).

10. Freud linked narcissism to identification, group psychology, and homosexuality. Identification ran the risk of regression, substituting for object-choice and hovering dangerously close to narcissism. Group psychology was a kind of regression enacted by a group of people who identified with the ego-ideal, embodied by the leader, but with the same end result of taking oneself as an object-choice. Homosexuals were prone to both identification and narcissism, providing the model for the behavior of people in groups. See Sigmund Freud, *Group Psychology and the Analysis of the Ego*, ed. James Strachey (New York: Norton, 1959). Naturally, I do not share in Freud's assumption, but I believe that his descriptions allow us to see the destructive effects of heteronormativity as they get played out in the psychic realm, shedding light on the creation of individuality within normative society.

11. On popular culture and nationalism, see William Rowe and Vivian Schelling, *Memory and Modernity: Popular Culture in Latin America* (London: Verso, 1991); and Jean Franco, "Loca y no loca," 30–42. For a comparison to José Martí, see Arcadio Díaz-Quiñones, "Martí: Las guerras del alma" [Martí: The wars of the soul], *Apuntes postmodernos/Postmodern Notes* 5, no. 2 (spring 1995): 4–13. An essay concentrating solely on the lullabies is Bernardo Subercaseaux, "Gabriela Mistral: Espiritualismo y canciones de cuna" [Gabriela Mistral: Spiritualism and lullabies], *Cuadernos americanos* (Mexico City) 205 (1976): 208–25. Subercaseaux offers a fairly restricted view of the lullabies as literal substitutes for children and of their spirit as that of religious sacrifice. For a comparison between Mistral and other practitioners of the children's genre in Spanish, such as Nicolás Guillén and Federico García Lorca, see Elizabeth Rosa Horan, "Redeploying the Spanish Lullaby in Latin America," *Paradoxa*, 2, nos. 3–4 (1996): 411–19. For a recent survey and interpretation of Mistral's maternal poetic voice, see Lila Zemborain, "El sujeto maternal" [The maternal subject], in "Modalidades de representación del sujeto lírico en la poesía de Gabriela Mistral" [Modalities of representation of the lyrical subject in Gabriela Mistral] (Ph.D. diss., New York University, 1997). For an illuminating inquiry into the children's genre and women's position in it, see Marina Warner, *From the Beast to the Blonde: On Fairy Tales and Their Tellers* (New York: Farrar, Straus, & Giroux, 1995).

12. Such rejection also involves rejecting, as it were, entry into the Lacanian Symbolic, but refusing Kristeva's Semiotic as well.

13. See, e.g., Melanie Klein, "A Contribution to the Psychogenesis of Manic-Depressive States," in *Selected Melanie Klein*, 116–45.

14. Marina Warner, *Alone of All Her Sex: The Myth and the Cult of the Virgin Mary* (New York: Knopf, 1976).

15. Eve Kosofsky Sedgwick, "Tales of the Avunculate: Queer Tutelage in *The Importance of Being Earnest*," in *Tendencies* (Durham, N.C.: Duke University Press, 1993), 52–72.

16. Luis Vargas Saavedra, *El otro suicida de Gabriela Mistral* [The suicidal other of Gabriela Mistral] (Santiago: Ediciones Universidad Católica de Chile, 1985). Quotations from this volume will be cited parenthetically in the text.

17. I tried to ascertain some of these details by contacting Gabriela Cano, a Mexican researcher who is currently at work on a biography of Palma Guillén. She, however, also does not know anything about the letters.

Palma Guillén was a university professor who, upon Mistral's first arrival in Mexico, in 1922, was assigned to be Mistral's companion as Mistral fulfilled her obligation to the government of Mexico to assist in educational reform. Guillén was Mistral's companion for years, and her lifelong friend. At points she was also a member of the diplomatic corps. Reputedly quite beautiful, she posed as a model for Diego Rivera and frequented the bohemian gatherings held at Rivera and Frida Kahlo's Casa Azul in Coyoacán, a suburb of Mexico City. Cano believes Mistral and Guillén had an intense relationship, but she isn't certain it necessarily unfolded along the lines dictated by today's sexual categories. Possibly, Guillén identified as a femme and was attracted to masculine figures. Certainly, more information about Mistral's closest companions will help to fill in the gaps in what we know about gender, sexuality, and embodiment in the period.

18. Mistral wrote to Alfonso Reyes that she never "understood" Guillén's obstinate refusal to give up Mexicanism in favor of a (presumably more reasonable) Latin Americanism: "You know, my failure with her has been to never be able to instill in her sympathy for our own [Latin American] countries. She regards them . . . as not Mexican, and therefore as having nothing to do with her." Mistral to Alfonso Reyes, Lisbon?, 14 July 1936, in *Antología mayor* [Comprehensive anthology], vol. 3, *Cartas* [Letters], ed. Luis Vargas Saavedra (Santiago: Cochrane, 1992), 255.

19. This letter appears in Vargas Saavedra, *El otro suicida*, 51.

20. Mistral's words, quoted in ibid.

21. Mistral, Consular Report of 1950; quoted in ibid., 52.

22. Mistral, from an interview for the Cuban journal *Carteles*, conducted in Italy in 1951 by Osvaldo Valdés; quoted in Vargas Saavedra, *El otro suicida*, 53.

23. Palma Guillén, quoted in Volodia Teitelboim, *Gabriela Mistral pública y secreta: Truenos y silencios en la vida del primer Nobel latinoamericano* [The public and secret Gabriela Mistral: Thunder and silence in the life of Latin America's first Nobel prizewinner] (Santiago: Ediciones BAT, 1991), 211.

24. Palma Guillén, quoted in Vargas Saavedra, *El otro suicida*, 54.

25. Mistral, collective letter to various friends, Petrópolis, Brazil, probably late 1943, quoted in ibid., 47.

26. Juan Miguel Godoy, suicide note; quoted in Teitelboim, *Gabriela Mistal pública y secreta*, 213.

27. Mistral, quoted in Vargas Saavedra, *El otro suicida*, 49.

28. Julia Kristeva, "The Semiotic and the Symbolic," in *The Portable Julia Kristeva*, ed. Kelly Oliver (New York: Columbia University Press, 1998), 32–70.

29. Butler, "Melancholy Gender/Refused Identification," in *Psychic Life of Power*, 132–50.

30. As a routine alternative in the interpretation of Mistral's gender, critics frequently emphasize her Christian beliefs. For this group, the narrative of salvation in regard to Mistral directly relates to her father's abandonment when she was a child and is transparently taken to be the underlying theme of her first book of poetry, *Desolación* [Desolation]. All the events of Mistral's life are then understood as offshoots of this early, presumably tragic event. Moreover, her quandary in this scheme metonymically represents the problems of the national family: Where is the Chilean male? What became of the source of Chilean (and Latin American) virility?

In this scheme Mistral suffers because she is searching for this lost father figure in a Christological suffering: Mistral imitates the Passion of Christ and poetically searches for the meaning and possible routes of salvation. The landscape of Latin

America becomes a pantheistic universe in this approach. Mistral's loss of her son, Juan Miguel Godoy, is equal to Christ's sacrifice on the cross and is the definitive proof of her suffering on this earth. This is a narrative of loss and threat with both private and public implications.

31. In *Diferencias latinoamericanas* [Latin American difference] (Santiago: Centro de Estudios Humanísticos, Facultad de Ciencias Físicas y Matemáticas, Universidad de Chile, 1984), the Chilean critic Jorge Guzmán attempts to separate himself from the traditional narratives of long-suffering femininity in Mistral. He proposes that women in Chile were the ones who "took charge" of the nation in the face of the pathetic figure of the Chilean father, who was merely "a mirroring," "a referential ghost" (67). Guzmán sees in Mistral's poetry a sentimentalist narrative that sounds somewhat like this: love gives way to jealousy; death gives way to the child as poetry. Therefore, Guzmán understands Mistral's emphasis on motherhood as creation, as the birthing of poems. He alternately perceives her as virgin and demon, both resulting in extinction, because, on the one hand, she is a saint and, on the other, a kind of executioner.

It is in this exaggerated, hyperbolic femininity, understood merely in terms of fulfilling childlike needs—a male fantasy if ever there was one—that Mistral the poet rebels. She rebels against woman's destiny, "to be fertile" (72). In this gynocentric world, according to Guzmán, God is feminine and the mother divine. The poetic "I" is simultaneously the creator of the universe and the end of the race. She does not experience frustrated love, because speaking of the male as lover in this separatist world, Guzmán posits, is pointless.

Although Guzmán believes, probably, that his is a feminist vision of Mistral and a centering of woman in a Latin Americanist tradition, his is a heteronormative vision. He does not account for the disappearance of the male. The implication is that Latin America is deformed by this patriarchal absence. Poetry in this system is appropriately perverse, a symptom of trauma. Mistral's separatism is also a symptom and is explained psychologically as a deviation from what happens to "most" women.

Guzmán does not consider a world where there may be a lover other than the male one. Neither does he stop to ponder that sexuality need not be understood strictly in reproductive terms (if there is no child, then there is no sexuality). Additionally, his attempt to feminize Mistral by imposing this normative experience belies an anxiety about her lack of femininity—what might be conceived as her decidedly "queer" experience of motherhood.

32. See Patricio Marchant, *Sobre árboles y madres* [About trees and women] (Santiago: Sociedad Editora Lead, 1984), and Grínor Rojo, *Dirán que está en la gloria (Mistral)* [They claim she is in heaven (Mistral)] (Mexico City: Fondo de Cultura Económica, 1997), for updated versions of Mistral's suffering as a stubborn attachment to a phantasmatic femininity.

33. Fuss, *Identification Papers,* 14, 38.

34. Guzmán, *Diferencias latinoamericanas.*

35. Michel Foucault, "The Subject and Power," in *Essential Works of Foucault, 1954–1984,* ed. Paul Rabinow, vol. 3, *Power,* ed. Colin Gordon, trans. Robert Hurley et al. (New York: New Press, 2000), 332–36.

36. Franco, "Loca y no loca," 33, 41.

37. Mistral, "La dichosa" [The happy woman], in *Desolación, Ternura, Tala, Lagar,* 189.

38. Elizabeth A. Marchant, "The Professional Outsider: Gabriela Mistral on Motherhood and Nation," *Latin American Literary Review* 27, no. 53 (January–June 1999): 49–63.

39. Fuss, *Identification Papers,* 38.

40. Mistral, "País de la ausencia" [Land of absence], in *Desolación, Ternura, Tala, Lagar,* 151. See also Mary Louise Pratt, "Women, Literature, and the National Brotherhood," in Seminar on Feminism and Culture in Latin America (Emilie Bergmann et al.), *Women, Culture, and Politics in Latin America* (Berkeley and Los Angeles: University of California Press, 1990), 48–73, for a study of related themes in Mistral's posthumous *Poema de Chile* [Poem of Chile]. Pratt recognizes the "escapist vision" (71) of Mistral's unfinished poem and its relevance to discussions of female citizenship, republican motherhood, and Mistral's own grappling with the mother and child figures.

5. Image Is Everything

1. The only other critical examination of Mistral as image that I'm aware of is Elizabeth Rosa Horan's excellent article "Santa Maestra Muerta: Body and Nation in Portraits of Gabriela Mistral," *Taller de letras* 25 (1997): 21–43. Horan explores the monumentalization and memorialization of the dead Mistral in currency, statues, and monuments, critiquing this heroic narrative. I focus on the image of Mistral while she was alive, and on the creation of an extreme form of desire that was functional and productive in state terms.

2. Jacques Lacan, "Of the Gaze as *objet petit a*," in *The Four Fundamental Concepts of Psychoanalysis* (New York: Norton, 1981), 74. See also Laura Mulvey's classic "Visual Pleasure and Narrative Cinema," *Screen* 16, no. 3 (autumn 1975): 6–18, for a more feminist psychoanalytic analysis of the gaze, femininity, and sexual difference. There are dozens of testimonies of how Mistral's physicality did not correspond to the period's visual conventions of femininity; for one typical example, see Gladys Rodríguez Valdés, *Invitación a Gabriela Mistral (1889–1989)* [An invitation to Gabriela Mistral (1889–1989)] (Mexico City: Fondo de Cultura Económica, 1990), 12.

3. Throughout this discussion, I have employed the dates given by the National Library in Santiago, Chile, with additional context from the Gabriela Mistral Museum in Vicuña, Chile. However, the reader should know that more research into and curation of the photographic archive might yield different dates and places for some of these pictures. I believe that the information is essentially accurate but that there may be a margin of error. Luckily, this archive is now receiving the attention it deserves, thanks to the efforts of Pedro Pablo Zegers, director of the Archivo del Escritor, National Library of Chile, and Ilonka Csillag Pimstein, director of the Patrimonio Iconográfico Nacional de Chile.

4. Hernán Rodríguez Villegas, "Historia de la fotografía en Chile: Registro de daguerrotipistas, fotógrafos, reporteros gráficos, y camarógrafos" [A history of photography in Chile: A register of daguerreotypists, photographers, graphic reporters, and cameramen], *Boletín de la Academia Chilena de la Historia* 52, no. 96 (1985): 189–340. See also Eugenio Pereira Salas, "El centenario de la fotografía en Chile, 1840–1940" [Photography's centennial in Chile, 1840–1940], *Boletín de la Academia Chilena de la Historia* 20 (1942).

5. Rodríguez Villegas, "Historia," 190.

6. Ilonka Csillag Pimstein, personal communication with author, 25 September 2000; Pedro Pablo Zegers, interview with author in Santiago, Chile, August 2000; and Luis Vargas Saavedra, interview with author in Santiago, Chile, August 2000.

7. For the case of Latin America, see, e.g., Jorge Salessi, "The Argentinean Dissemination of Homosexuality, 1890–1914," and Oscar Montero, "Julián del Casal and the Queers of Havana," in ¿Entiendes? Queer Readings, Hispanic Writings, ed. Emilie L. Bergmann and Paul Julian Smith (Durham, N.C.: Duke University Press, 1995), 49–91 and 92–112 respectively; Rob Buffington, "Los Jotos: Contested Visions of Homosexuality in Modern Mexico," in Sex and Sexuality in Latin America, ed. Daniel Balderston and Donna J. Guy (New York: New York University Press, 1997), 118–32; Daniel Bao, "Invertidos Sexuales, Tortilleras, y Maricas Machos: The Construction of Homosexuality in Buenos Aires, Argentina, 1900–1950," Journal of Homosexuality 24, nos. 3–4 (1993): 183–219; and Robert McKee Irwin, "The Famous 41: The Scandalous Birth of Modern Mexican Homosexuality," GLQ 6, no. 3 (fall 2000): 353–76.

8. See Jorge Salessi, Médicos, maleantes, y maricas: Higiene, criminología, y homosexualidad en la construcción de la nación argentina (Buenos Aires, 1871–1914) [Doctors, thugs, and fags: Hygiene, criminology, and homosexuality in the construction of the Argentine nation (Buenos Aires, 1871–1914)] (Rosario, Argentina: Beatriz Viterbo Editora, 1995).

9. In a related vein, see Sylvia Molloy, "The Politics of Posing," where she demonstrates the visibility of, and preoccupation with, these raros. Molloy persuasively shows that the preoccupation with queerness was linked to the homosexual and other sexually "deviant" types. In Hispanisms and Homosexualities, ed. Sylvia Molloy and Robert McKee Irwin (Durham, N.C.: Duke University Press, 1998), 141–60.

10. The Juegos Florales was the name given to an annual combination poetry competition–beauty pageant held in the capital city of Santiago. Mistral won the Flor Natural, the festival's highest honor for poetic achievement, in 1914. She won for "Sonetos de la muerte" [Sonnets of death], a cycle of three sonnets mourning the death of a child-lover. The elegiac tone of the sonnets obviously contrasted sharply with the pageant's frivolous tone. Additionally, Mistral was nearly the opposite of the feminine image extolled at the pageant: she was not conventionally feminine, nor did she belong to the upper classes.

11. Mistral to Rubén Darío, 1912, Antología mayor [Comprehensive anthology], vol. 3, Cartas [Letters], ed. Luis Vargas Saavedra (Santiago: Cochrane, 1992), 9.

12. Mistral, "Comento a Ternura" [A comment on Ternura], in Recados para hoy y mañana: Textos inéditos de Gabriela Mistral, comp. Luis Vargas Saavedra (Santiago: Editorial Sudamericana, 1999), 1:176.

13. Mistral, "Pensamientos pedagógicos" [Pedagogical thoughts], in Magisterio y niño [Teaching and the child], ed. Roque Esteban Scarpa (Santiago: Andrés Bello, 1979), 40. See also Freud's description of the girls' school as a psychologically infectious breeding ground for hysteria, in Group Psychology and the Analysis of the Ego (New York: Norton, 1959), 49.

14. Mistral, "Pensamientos pedagógicos," 39.

15. Ibid., 40.

16. Photographers certainly recorded the "native" peoples of Chile, but the conventions were strikingly different. Condemned to a sort of dead time, as ghosts belonging to the past and living, as it were, only to achieve final extinction, these people

were photographed as the racial "other" in an attempt to give information about them before they no longer existed. They occupy the frame as oddities left behind in the Chilean positivistic and racist march toward progress. For examples, see the survey article by Theodoro Elssaca "La fotografía como arte en Chile" [Photography as art in Chile], *Mapocho: Revista de humanidades y ciencias sociales* 46 (July–December 1999): 84, 86, 88, 92. Note specifically the difference between the conventions governing the photography of middle-to-upper-class "ladies of society" and those ruling the portraits or snapshots of the Mapuche people. See also Vicente Rafael, "The Undead," in *White Love* (Durham, N.C.: Duke University Press, 2000).

17. I am certainly not stating that we can divine Mistral's feelings throughout the photographic corpus; merely that there are certain modalities of posing and portraiture that are constructed on expression of feeling and that, as such, they can enlist mass affect when circulated massively, particularly in newspapers at this time.

18. Roland Barthes, *Camera Lucida: Reflections on Photography* (New York: Hill & Wang, 1981), 26–27 and passim.

19. Mistral can also be thought of as occupying the point of the *objet petit a,* if we follow Lacan's visual terminology, at the moment when she begins to appear "Indian." There is a tremendous disjuncture between the idealized image of Mistral as mestiza and the documented conditions of indigenous peoples.

20. Leandro Urbina, "Memoria de lectura" [A memoir of reading], in *Re-leer hoy a Gabriela Mistral: Mujer, historia, y sociedad en América Latina* [Rereading Gabriela Mistral today: Woman, history, and society in Latin America], ed. Gastón Lillo and J. Guillermo Renart (Ottawa: University of Ottawa Press; Santiago: Editorial de la Universidad de Santiago, 1997), 183.

21. *Melancholia* is a complex term; see Sigmund Freud's classic "Mourning and Melancholia" for an introduction to the discussion of identification, introjection, and the afterlife of the lost object within the ego. *The Standard Edition of the Complete Psychological Works of Sigmund Freud,* ed. James Strachey (New York: Norton, 1959), 14:243–58.

6. Pedagogy, Humanities, Social Unrest

1. Michel Foucault, *Discipline and Punish: The Birth of the Prison,* trans. Alan Sheridan (New York: Vintage, 1979), 200.

2. This is a development admirably studied by Julio Ramos, in *Desencuentros de al modernidad en América Latina: Literatura y política en el siglo XIX* (Mexico City: Fondo de Cultura Económica, 1989), translated into English by John D. Blanco and published as *Divergent Modernities: Culture and Politics in Nineteenth-Century Latin America* (Durham, N.C.: Duke University Press, 2001).

3. Mistral, "Introducción a *Lecturas para mujeres*" [Introduction to *Readings for Women*], in *Magisterio y niño* [Teaching and the child], ed. Roque Esteban Scarpa (Santiago: Andrés Bello, 1979), 105.

4. Antonio Gramsci, *Prison Notebooks* (New York: International, 1991), 259.

5. Michel Foucault, *The History of Sexuality,* vol. 1, *An Introduction,* trans. Robert Hurley (New York: Vintage, 1980), 140.

6. Mistral, "Poesía infantil y folklore" [Children's poetry and folklore], in *Magisterio y niño,* 277.

7. Mistral, "La geografía humana: Libros que faltan para la América nuestra" [Human geography: Books that are missing in our America], in *Magisterio y niño*, 136.

8. Mistral, "Niño y libro" [The child and the book], in *Magisterio y niño*, 90.

9. Mistral, "Contar" [Storytelling], in *Magisterio y niño*, 95.

10. Mistral, "Pasión de leer" [A passion for reading], in *Magisterio y niño*, 101–4.

11. Mistral, "Recado sobre una maestra argentina" [Message about an Argentinean schoolteacher], in *Magisterio y niño*, 130; Mistral's emphasis.

12. Mistral, "Biblioteca y escuela" [The library and the school], in *Magisterio y niño*, 85.

13. Recall the "biological civil wars" in Foucault's *Genealogy of Racism*, and the penchant to corporealize the social body; that is, to regard it literally as an organism whose health is a cleansing prerogative.

14. Mistral, "Una mujer escribe una geografía" [A woman writes a geography book], in *Magisterio y niño*, 120.

15. Mistral, "Imagen y palabra en la educación" [Image and word in education], in *Magisterio y niño*, 199. In this same essay, Mistral expresses faith in the capacity of images to bind people across classes—especially binding the middle classes to a subaltern class, the indigenous peoples. Although not discussed here, the passage is reminiscent of the cult of the image practiced in fascist states.

16. Although, from a modern vantage point, Mistral might have exaggerated the triumph of cinema and television over books, her somewhat hallucinatory musings bear a concrete relationship to contemporary discussions.

17. Mistral to Alfonso Reyes, Madrid, 6 and 10 April 1934, *Tan de usted: Epistolario de Gabriela Mistral con Alfonso Reyes* [Always yours: Correspondence from Gabriela Mistral to Alfonso Reyes], comp. Luis Vargas Saavedra (Santiago: Hachette/Editorial de la Universidad Católica de Chile, 1991), 98–99.

18. Mistral, "La unidad de la cultura" [The unity of culture], in *Gabriela anda por el mundo* [Gabriela wanders around the world], ed. Roque Esteban Scarpa (Santiago: Andrés Bello, 1978), 191–97.

19. Sometimes she did not do so. The essay "Palabras a la Universidad de Puerto Rico" [Remarks for the University of Puerto Rico], discussed shortly, is one example.

20. Mistral: "Madre se llamaría con razón entonces a la Universidad." "La unidad de la cultura," 193.

21. "Dualidades no aceptaremos sino la fundamental de cuerpo y alma, de Estado y de Universidad"; "Unidad fortalecedora, unidad teológica, sea la frase de orden de nuestra empresa de cultura. Nada grande viviendo su grandeza puertas afuera de la Universidad. Nada que sea nacional viviendo desgajado de su tronco." Ibid., 195, 196.

22. Jaime Benítez, quoted in Isabel Picó, "Albizu Campos y la lucha estudiantil," in *Pedro Albizu Campos: Reflexiones sobre su vida y obra: Ensayos de Margot Arce de Vázquez et al. y una selección de reseñas periodísticas sobre su muerte y entierro* [Pedro Albizu Campos: Reflections on his life and work: Essays by Margot Arce de Vazquez et al. and a selection of newspaper articles about his death and funeral] (Río Piedras, Puerto Rico: Editorial Marién, 1991), 85.

23. Eve Kosofsky Sedgwick, *Between Men: English Literature and Male Homosocial Desire* (New York: Columbia University Press, 1985).

24. Jaime Benítez to Mistral, Río Piedras, Puerto Rico, 30 April 1948, from the Gabriela Mistral Papers, Manuscript Division of the Library of Congress, Washington, D.C.

25. Albizu's wife, Laura Meneses, mentions Mistral's efforts in a letter to her that is dated 6 September 1941, from the Gabriela Mistral Papers.

26. Jaime Benítez, *La casa de estudios* [The house of learning] (San Juan: Biblioteca de Autores Puertorriqueños, 1985).

27. Telegram from Jaime Benítez to Mistral, 21 April 1948, from the Gabriela Mistral Papers. Not only Benítez but also Muñoz perfected a discourse on "democracy" that masked the often brutal maneuvering that happened in Puerto Rico, sometimes in visible fashion, as in the repression of the students in 1948.

28. Jaime Benítez to Mistral, 27 April 1948, from the Gabriela Mistral Papers.

29. Ibid.

30. "Gabriela Mistral alaba el espíritu creador del pueblo puertorriqueño" [Gabriela Mistral praises the creative spirit of the Puerto Rican people], *El Mundo,* 13 June 1948, p. 1; reprinted as "Palabras a la Universidad de Puerto Rico" [Remarks for the University of Puerto Rico], in *Magisterio y niño.* I consulted a copy of the pamphlet distributed to the graduating class of 1948, which is available in the Library of Congress: *Palabras a la Universidad de Puerto Rico: Trabajo para ser leído en la cuadragésima cuarta colación de grados de la Universidad de Puerto Rico* [Remarks for the University of Puerto Rico, to be read at the forty-fourth commencement exercises of the University of Puerto Rico] (Río Piedras: Universidad de Puerto Rico, 1948). Of course, Mistral never read the speech to the graduating class, as there was no actual graduation. Thanks to Julio Ramos, who noticed the date of the essay in Scarpa's compilation *Magisterio y niño* and wondered out loud to me how Mistral could have read it, given the strike of 1948. I then searched for more information about the piece and found the original newspaper article as well as the pamphlet.

The salutation in the pamphlet reads: "For the second time, I have the honor of saying goodbye to the graduates of the beloved University, who, upon this occasion, leave this House to enter Life fully, life with a capital *L,* going from the refuge to the crude wind." This seems fairly ironic, given that the chancellor had canceled the graduation, expelled students, and repressed all demonstrators. With the exception of the salutation, the pamphlet speech is identical to its reprinting in the daily newspaper, *El Mundo.* For unknown reasons, Scarpa excised about a third of the speech's original text when he reprinted it. I have no idea whether he was working from another source or whether he cut the text intentionally. My analysis will focus mostly on this expunged section.

31. The repression of students who showed any affiliation with independence struggles dated from decades before 1948. In other words, it was a systematic operation with a degree of continuity. As Isabel Picó writes of the 1920s, "The decade was characterized by a substantial repression; pro-independence students were summarily expelled or suspended" ("Albizu Campos," 59). Although Benítez presented the 1948 strike as an extraordinary move by a minority to intimidate the majority, in actuality he was only exercising the typical prerogative of all those who had headed the university before him. This violence against students and this invocation of the violent meaning of the word *discipline* are constitutive of the University of Puerto Rico and central to our understanding of its psychic dimension. It is worth noting that, after the strike of 1948, the "Ley de la Mordaza" [Gag Law] was implemented. The leadership was severed from its constituency as students were expelled from the university. Official censure was exerted over all meetings, associations, publications, and, naturally, political gatherings.

32. The attraction of the United States that was commonplace among Latin American intellectuals and elites in the early twentieth century was just as strong to Mistral. As early as 1919, she recommended a pragmatic approach to the increasing U.S. control of the technologies of knowledge and to U.S. imperialist, neocolonial policies in Latin America. The ending of "Palabras a la Universidad de Puerto Rico" addresses this concern: "The graduates can also consider this as part of their saga: the University opened the doors of the Southern continent for you. We sent to the unknown island inexperienced technicians and also welcomed your professionals to our countries. You can bring us the experience that we lack, because your University has matured and is capable of teaching us methods, in Spanish, that you have learned from the United States" (*Magisterio y niño,* 270).

33. "Official culture emerges from battles undertaken in several fronts to show its genuine face. The Puerto Rican state will legitimize itself with emblems and rituals of a past, with the House of cultural patrimony, appropriating for itself a lineage to lend prestige to its social function and place. Cultural institutions will henceforth operate under its protection." María Elena Rodríguez Castro, "Foro de 1940: Las pasiones y los intereses se dan la mano" [Forum of 1940: The passions and the interests help each other], in *Del nacionalismo al populismo: Cultura y política en Puerto Rico* [From nationalism to populism: Culture and politics in Puerto Rico], ed. Silvia Álvarez Curbelo and María Elena Rodríguez Castro (San Juan: Editorial Huracán, 1993), 77.

See also Benítez, *La casa de estudios.* Benítez is apparently responding to a letter by Mistral (which was actually dated 30 April 1948), addressed jointly to Inés Mendoza de Muñoz Marín and Jaime Benítez. In this letter, Mistral passes harsh judgment on the student strike at the University of Puerto Rico. She calls the student protest "a communist blowup" and praises Benítez for behaving "like a man": "It's very hard, with our blood, not to lose our character when one is surrounded by those little beasts that we cannot strike because they are children. I'm really, really glad that Jaime has in him that small cold zone that is precious in times like these, and that his pulse did not get the better of him." See Mistral to Inés Mendoza de Muñoz Marín and Jaime Muñoz [*sic:* Benítez], 30 April 1948, Santa Barbara, California?, in *Antología mayor* [Comprehensive anthology], vol. 3, *Cartas* [Letters], ed. Luis Vargas Saavedra (Santiago: Cochrane, 1992), 459.

34. Jaime Benítez to Mistral, Río Piedras, Puerto Rico, 10 May 1948, from the Gabriela Mistral Papers.

35. Ibid.

7. Education and Loss

1. Spanish was barred, intermittently but consistently, during the first decades of the twentieth century.

2. Luis Muñoz Marín was born in 1898 and educated in the United States, where he formed many of his ideas for Puerto Rican social and political enfranchisement. Whether his first nationalist impulses were of the militant variety or he had a cultural and aesthetic sense of nationalism from the beginning, needs to be studied further. After a career as a journalist, Muñoz joined the Liberal Party and was elected to the Senate in 1932. He founded the Popular Democratic Party in 1938 and became pres-

ident of the Senate in 1940. He was the first elected governor in 1948. It seems that his original plans for the Puerto Rican Constitution contained some aspects that were progressive (such as a right-to-work clause), which were later deleted by the U.S. government and don't appear in the final 1952 version. Muñoz, however, soon became a typical example of a populist leader. This populism is increasingly reflected in the letters of Inés Mendoza examined here.

Undeniably, the Popular Democratic Party accomplished real improvement in social conditions in Puerto Rico, where dire poverty and hunger existed. My analysis does not mean to belittle this historical fact. Neither do I have any reason to doubt the sincerity of Inés Mendoza's desire to help the majority with concrete, pragmatic programs to end hunger, enfranchise the *jíbaro,* and modernize the country. However, Puerto Rico's modernizing project depended on narrow, short-term projections that created nearly intractable long-term problems. And these problems became clouded or were made invisible by melancholia, as the analysis will show.

3. For details into the termination of her contract in 1937, see Ricardo E. Alegría, "Inés María Mendoza de Muñoz Marín, insobornable defensora de nuestro idioma materno, el español" [Inés María Mendoza de Muñoz Marín, unbribable defender of our mother tongue, Spanish], *Revista del Centro de Estudios Avanzados y del Caribe* (January–June 1991): 7–17.

4. Inés Mendoza de Muñoz, "La mujer y Gabriela Mistral" [Woman and Gabriela Mistral], photocopy of original newspaper article, Luis Muñoz Marín Foundation, San Juan, Puerto Rico. Unfortunately, I do not have a date or a place of publication for the article, nor the name of the newspaper. Obviously, it was written after Mendoza met Mistral, while Mistral was alive, and, judging by its pronounced populist rhetoric, probably in the 1940s, as Muñoz was orchestrating the Popular Democratic Party's rise to power.

5. Mistral, "La reforma educacional de México" [Mexico's educational reform], in *Magisterio y niño* [Teaching and the child], ed. Roque Esteban Scarpa (Santiago: Andrés Bello, 1979), 151–52.

6. As parts of Rosa del Río's narrative demonstrate, in Beatriz Sarlo's essay "Cabezas rapadas y cintas argentinas" [Shaved heads and Argentine ribbons], in *La máquina cultural: Maestras, traductores, y vanguardistas* [The cultural machine: Female teachers, translators, and vanguardists] (Buenos Aires: Ariel, 1998), schoolbooks were often the only printed material a family had ever seen or would be likely to see. Del Río speaks about not being really sure if she liked to read (25–26). According to Sarlo, schoolbooks often compensated for the lack of a radio, of magazines for mass consumption, of television, and, of course, of the library of high or elite culture. They stood, then, for an enormous sense of melancholia; they were objects that were introjected and made part of the subject's identification with a national idea. National belonging was only possible through this identification, as clearly most nationals would not enjoy those middle-class benefits that the state promised would come to all. Reading, then, meant the minimal competence necessary for industrial society, not the creation of active thinkers or participants in the common political process. The teacher knew that many of her charges would stay in school for only a very brief period of time, not even the whole school year, and wondered how to relate their education to "what they would become in life" (28). So the schoolteacher was straddled with the creation of a national illusion of prosperity and protection for all.

7. Mendoza, "La mujer y Gabriela Mistral." It's important to note here that Mendoza wrote many other such newspaper articles on conventional "feminine" roles.

8. Inés Mendoza de Muñoz, interview by Angela Negrón Muñoz, *El Mundo*, 22 March 1931, 1.

9. I am not certain whether Mistral received letters from Mendoza before this period, while Mendoza was still a schoolteacher. Mistral and Mendoza met in Puerto Rico in the early 1930s. I am also not certain whether they crossed paths in New York; Mistral was a visiting professor at Barnard College, and Mendoza, like so many Latin American schoolteachers at the time, was attending Teachers College of Columbia University. As Isabel Picó notes about the first three decades of the century in Puerto Rico, "In these years the Normal School of the University was subject to the pedagogical principles of the North American Teachers Colleges. Proficiency in English was a legal requirement for certification. Most of the teachers were Americans, and study trips were promoted so that the schoolteachers could familiarize themselves with the lifestyle and the customs of the metropolis." "Los orígenes del movimiento estudiantil universitario, 1903–1930" [The origins of the university student movement, 1903–1930], *Revista de ciencias sociales* 24, no. 2 (January–June 1985): 49. This situation was analogous to that of other Latin American countries at the time. Of course, it was intensified in the colonial case of Puerto Rico. Puerto Rican women, as Picó notes, took advantage of the innovations brought about by the colonial authorities. Picó also notes, importantly, that the University of Puerto Rico was "a breeding-ground for women who wanted to make a living as schoolteachers" (51), suggesting a gendered relationship that was central, not incidental, to the subjective dimension of the university.

10. Inés Mendoza de Muñoz to Mistral, Puerto Rico, 10 March. This letter was written after 1937, probably in 1943. All letters from Mendoza to Mistral that are cited in this chapter are in the Gabriela Mistral Papers, Manuscript Division, Library of Congress, Washington, D.C. The Gabriela Mistral Papers contain ten microfilmed letters, which span from approximately 1943 to 1953. Mendoza did not date most of her letters; I give approximate dates as noted in the Mistral Papers. That the letters date from after 1937 is easy to verify, because Mendoza met her husband, Luis Muñoz Marín, in 1937, and she refers to him constantly. The political context continuously discussed in the letters indicates clearly whether the letters date from immediately before or after her husband's election as governor of Puerto Rico in 1948. After this victory, Mendoza sometimes used letterhead from La Fortaleza, the governor's mansion, which also confirms the approximate dates of the correspondence. All the letters were written in Puerto Rico.

The only letter that I have found from Mistral to Inés Mendoza is a joint letter to Jaime Benítez and Inés Mendoza written in 1948. The letter's content concerns the strike at the University of Puerto Rico, discussed in chapter 6. There is no personal content in this letter. Mistral does make a reference to plans to live in Puerto Rico that had to be canceled; these resonate with Mendoza's repeatedly expressed wish for Mistral to live in Puerto Rico, as explored in this chapter. See Mistral to Inés Mendoza de Muñoz Marín and Jaime Muñoz [*sic:* Benítez], 30 April 1948, Santa Barbara, California?, in *Antología mayor* [Comprehensive anthology], vol. 3, *Cartas* [Letters], ed. Luis Vargas Saavedra (Santiago: Cochrane, 1992), 458–60.

To avoid confusion in what follows, I proceed chronologically. The letters are remarkably homogeneous in subject matter and style: two issues dominate most of their content, so that they may give the impression of one continuous narrative. The reader should think of the correspondence as a story, with two basic plot lines that intersect and eventually mesh together. One is Mendoza's affection for Mistral; the other is her politcal ambition, and the desire to participate in her husband's political program.

11. For a point of entry into the complex matter of the emergence of this figure in Puerto Rico, see Francisco A. Scarano, "The *Jíbaro* Masquerade and the Subaltern Politics of Creole Identity Formation in Puerto Rico, 1745–1823," *American Historical Review* 101, no. 5 (December 1996): 1398–1431.

12. "Muñoz's speeches presage an active participation in the modernizing project, definitively linked to North American capital. An interest which is qualified or, better put, problematized by a great passion; the preservation of a style and cultural behavior, associated just as definitively with a social behavior and style." María Elena Rodríguez Castro, "Foro de 1940: Las pasiones y los intereses se dan la mano" [Forum of 1940: The passions and the interests help each other], in *Del nacionalismo al populismo: Cultura y política en Puerto Rico* [From nationalism to populism: Culture and politics in Puerto Rico], ed. Silvia Álvarez Curbelo and María Elena Rodríguez Castro (San Juan: Editorial Huracán, 1993), 76.

13. See Jean Laplanche and J. B. Pontalis, *The Language of Psychoanalysis* (New York: Norton, 1973), for an introduction to the psychoanalytic concepts of anaclisis (29–32) and identification (205–8). They define *anaclisis* as a "term introduced by Freud to designate the early relationship of the sexual instincts to the self-preservative ones" (29). See also chapter 2.

14. Alternatively, melancholia is also an option, and perhaps a route to a type of pleasure.

15. Marjorie Garber, *Bisexuality and the Eroticism of Everyday Life* (New York: Routledge, 2000), 37–38.

16. Also noteworthy is the fact that Arce never gave up on a political ideal of independence, whereas Mendoza did.

17. Some of the most important artists who were enlisted for this project were trained in the Academia de San Carlos in Mexico City. The Mexican Ministry of Education also sought to deploy radio and cinema to the same effect; Mistral continuously expressed admiration for this development.

18. Ernest Gellner provides an explanation for the importance of national culture to industrial society, stating that education must manufacture a standard idiom in which strangers may communicate. Work is no longer physical or land-oriented; thus, it involves meanings and a standard idiom: "Culture is now the necessary shared medium, the life-blood or perhaps rather the minimal shared atmosphere.... Moreover, it must now be a great or high (literate, training-sustained) culture.... Only the state can do this, and, even in countries in which important parts of the educational machine are in private hands or those of religious organizations, the state does take over quality control in this most important of industries, the manufacture of viable and usable human beings.... State and culture *must* now be linked." *Nations and Nationalism* (Ithaca, N.Y.: Cornell University Press, 1983), 37–38.

19. Armed struggle was part of the Nationalist platform, and the military wing of the party staged an insurrection on 30 October 1950, which Mendoza references in this letter. The specific accusation of a plan to assassinate Muñoz and his family

has not been substantiated. It is widely believed that the Muñoz administration pursued covert operations to assassinate Albizu, in spite of Muñoz's public condemnation of armed confrontations and the use of force. The Nationalists were routinely persecuted and spied on in practically all their daily life activities. The infamous "Ley de la Mordaza" [Gag Law] that the Senate passed on 21 May 1948 corresponds precisely to the time period of the student strike discussed in chapter 6.

20. Albizu was sentenced to prison in 1951. Muñoz pardoned him in 1953, only to jail him again in 1954 after the Nationalist attack on the Congress of the United States by four members of the Nationalist Party (Lolita Lebrón, Rafael Cancel Miranda, Andrés Figueroa Cordero, and Irving Flores). It was then that he was reputedly subjected to inhumane treatment while in prison. Despite the many petitions on behalf of Albizu by distinguished international and national figures, Muñoz did not pardon him until 15 November 1964, when Albizu was so infirm that it was certain he would never recover. Albizu died shortly afterward, on 21 April 1965.

Epilogue

1. Lauren Berlant, *The Queen of America Goes to Washington City: Essays on Sex and Citizenship* (Durham, N.C.: Duke University Press, 1997), 103–4.

2. Mikhail Bakhtin, "The Problem of Speech Genres," in *Speech Genres and Other Late Essays* (Austin: University of Texas Press, 1986), 89. Thanks to George Yúdice for pointing out this connection.

3. José Esteban Muñoz, *Disidentifications: Queers of Color and the Performance of Politics* (Minneapolis: University of Minnesota Press, 1999); David Eng, *Racial Castration: Managing Masculinity in Asian America* (Durham, N.C.: Duke University Press, 2001).

4. Judith Butler, *The Psychic Life of Power: Theories in Subjection* (Stanford, Calif.: Stanford University Press, 1997).

5. Lisa Duggan's work on the "new homonormativity" is relevant here: "The New Homonormativity: The Sexual Politics of Neoliberalism," in *Materializing Democracy*, ed. Dana Nelson and Russ Castronovo (Durham, N.C.: Duke University Press, forthcoming).

Index

abstract vision of children, 98

acculturating project of Vasconcelos, 71, 73, 239n.12

acquiescence to common good, 21–22

"Adiós a Laura" [Goodbye to Laura], 62

adult education: Mendoza on, 209

"A ella, la única" [To her, the only one], 62

"aesthetic eugenics" (aesthetic selection), 12–13, 14, 35

aesthetics, 162; Mistral as purveyor of "aesthetic effect," 201

Aguirre Cerda, Pedro, 6, 8, 9, 10

Agustini, Delmira, 53

"A la mujer mexicana" [To the Mexican woman], 11, 16, 71

Albizu Campos, Pedro, 177–78, 181, 184, 192, 210–11, 212, 255n.19, 255n.20

Alegría, Fernando, xiii, 51–52, 53

Alemán, Miguel, 32, 229n.69

Alone (pseudonym of Hernán Díaz Arrieta), 52

ambiguous sexual discourse in early work, 61–62

Americanism, 180; Mistral as Americanist, 75–76, 78

anaclisis/anaclitic attachment, 194; connection between schooling and, 168; state as source of, 47

"Antillas" [Antilles], 24

Arce (de Vázquez), Margot, 171–72, 181, 202

Argentina, xix; condemnation of racial and cultural intermixture in, 82; as model of racial management, 8; paradigm of white immigration, 15; state program of mothering in, 80, 81–82

Ariel (Rodó), 5, 174

auditory materials: Mendoza's request for Mistral's recorded voice, 208, 210; pedagogy using, 188–89, 209

Baker, Josephine, 17–19, 229n.69

Bakhtin, Mikhail, 215

Barnard College, Mistral at, 253n.9

Barrios, Eduardo, 52

Barthes, Roland, 147

beauty, 162; binary of beauty/ugliness, 11–12; homicidal concept of, 170

Bellessi, Diana, 237n.3

Benítez, Jaime, xxiv, 177–85, 203, 251n.33

Benjamin, Walter, xx

Bergson, Henri, xx

Berlant, Lauren, 84, 91, 213, 215

Bernanos, Georges, 22

Bhabha, Homi, 48, 215

"Biblioteca y escuela" [The library and the school], 168

biological filiation: language of, 138

Licia Fiol-Matta teaches at Barnard College, specializing in Latin American cultural studies, women's studies, critical race studies, and queer theory. She is a member of the editorial collective of *Social Text* and of the board of directors of the Center for Lesbian and Gay Studies (CLAGS).